Military Chaplains and Religious Diversity

Military Chaplains and Religious Diversity

Kim Philip Hansen

palgrave
macmillan

MILITARY CHAPLAINS AND RELIGIOUS DIVERSITY

First published in 2012 by PALGRAVE MACMILLAN® in the United States—a division of St. Martin's Press LLC, 175 Fifth Avenue, New York, NY 10010.

Where this book is distributed in the UK, Europe and the rest of the world, this is by Palgrave Macmillan, a division of Macmillan Publishers Limited, registered in England, company number 785998, of Houndmills, Basingstoke, Hampshire RG21 6XS.

Palgrave Macmillan is the global academic imprint of the above companies and has companies and representatives throughout the world.

Palgrave® and Macmillan® are registered trademarks in the United States, the United Kingdom, Europe and other countries.

ISBN-13: 978-1-137-02515-9

Library of Congress Cataloging-in-Publication Data

Hansen, Kim Philip.
Military chaplains and religious diversity / Kim Philip Hansen.
p. cm.
ISBN 978-1-137-02515-9
1. Military chaplains—United States. 2. Soldiers—Religious life. 3. Religious pluralism–United States. 4. Military chaplain–United States–Interviews. I. Title.

UH23.H28 2012
355.3'470973—dc23 2012011928

A catalogue record of the book is available from the British Library.

Design by Scribe Inc.

First edition: October 2012

10 9 8 7 6 5 4 3 2 1

Printed in the United States of America.

For my wife, Yulia, who believed.

Contents

Chaplain Pseudonyms and Faith Groups

Pseudonym	Self-Identified Faith Group and Abbreviation(s)
Bartley	Church of God in Christ
Beard	Southern Baptist
Bowmaker	Presbyterian Church, USA
Chance	Evangelical Lutheran Church in America (ELCA)
Clement	United Methodist
Cransveld	Foursquare Gospel Churches
Cugrijus	Church of Jesus Christ of Latter Day Saints (Mormon, LDS)
Drozdov	Eastern Orthodox*
Dyren	Catholic
Farrow	Catholic
Feteris	Presbyterian Church, USA
Frantz	Church of Jesus Christ of Latter Day Saints (Mormon, LDS)
Geschka	Catholic
Giraldo	Evangelical Church Alliance
Grams	Presbyterian Church, USA
Gunvant	Catholic
Hamoud	Muslim
Hawthorne	Southern Baptist
Illera	Catholic
Irons	Southern Baptist
Kanaridis	Conservative Baptist

* Ethnicity of church (e.g., whether Greek, Russian, Syrian, or Serbian) withheld.

Koch	United Methodist
Kojic	Lutheran Church, Missouri Synod (LCMS)
Mace	Seventh Day Adventist
Metzger	Chaplaincy of Full Gospel Churches
Michaud	Baptist General Conference
Moore	Church of Jesus Christ of Latter Day Saints (Mormon, LDS)
Oberlin	Evangelical Lutheran Church in America (ELCA)
Squires	Catholic
Street	African Methodist Episcopal
Szmatula	Lutheran Church, Missouri Synod (LCMS)
Timu	Disciples of Christ
Townsend	Reformed Episcopal
Tzilker	Jewish

Rank of Chaplains Interviewed*

Captain	N = 4
Commander	N = 7
Lieutenant Commander	N = 6
Lieutenant	N = 17

* Navy equivalent is given for any non-Navy chaplains.

Note on Quotations

This book relies heavily on quotes from military chaplains on active duty when interviewed. Quotes too long to fit naturally into a paragraph will be presented as block extracts. In transcribing and quoting the chaplains, I adopted the following conventions: A bracketed ellipse means that the chaplain returned to the topic after an interruption or digression. Unbracketed ellipses mean that the chaplain trailed off or made a false start. Where relevant, my own interjections and probes as interviewer are put in brackets, as are descriptions of nonverbal communications by the chaplains, such as sighs, laughs or gestures.

When quoting a chaplain, I provide his or her pseudonym and religious affiliation. No inference should be made between a chaplain's pseudonym and his or her actual ethnicity. For example, "Chaplain O'Rourke" could just as well be of Icelandic or Indonesian heritage as of Irish. Also, to protect the chaplains' anonymity I will refer to all chaplains as male, even though there were women in my sample. I acknowledge that writing about the military chaplaincy as if it were all male is a distortion, albeit a necessary one. On occasion, I have altered or dropped names of ships or bases in the quotes, omitted references to named individuals, and otherwise changed potentially identifying information. Military chaplains take confidentiality seriously, and I have tried my very best to respect that.

Acknowledgments

This book owes much to my teachers and mentors at the University of California, San Diego. Rebecca Klatch gave me the first nudge out the classroom door into the world of research. Michael Schudson validated my initial empirical findings and reassured me that sociologists aren't bound to always bear ill tidings but are allowed to report pleasant results, too. Michael Parrish taught me about the intersection of law and religion in American history. Stanley Chodorow was very generous with his time, offering career guidance, teaching tips, and steady encouragement. Bennetta Jules-Rosette nurtured my confidence as a teacher and scholar by giving me opportunities to talk about the chaplains both formally as a guest speaker in her classes and informally in the group of young academics she gathered around herself. Richard Madsen was and remains my ideal mentor. Kind, insightful, and above all else a wonderful listener, his support for me never wavered, even though I must have tested his patience severely.

Fellow academics and a surprising number of active duty and former chaplains gave helpful feedback at a variety of scholarly conferences. The Military Chaplains Association was extremely gracious with the young sociologist who kept showing up at their meetings, and I fervently hope the endorsing agents and others I met there are content with the result of my labors. I enjoyed informal conversations about chaplaincy and military religion with Michelle Sandhoff from the University of Maryland and with Paul Andrews in Australia via Skype. A 2010 Summer Seminar about "Religion, War and the Meaning of America" hosted by Calvin College and led by Yale's Harry "Skip" Stout introduced me to an exciting and interdisciplinary group of peers. The company of Ben Miller, Trish Tillman, and Matthew Bowman was priceless. As the four of us wandered around campus, a Protestant, a Jew, a Catholic, and a Mormon, I fancied that I finally felt a bit like a chaplain would.

I came to the attention of Burke Gerstenschlager at Palgrave Macmillan thanks to a conference invitation from Matthew Bowman and was thrilled to have found someone who really appreciated "my chaplains." His assistant, Kaylan Connally, and production assistant, Katherine Haigler, navigated a bewildered first-time author through the publishing process with reassuring clarity and confidence. At the proposal stage, the book received valuable and detailed feedback from an anonymous reviewer to whom I am also grateful.

Thanks to the following for reading parts of the manuscript along the way, spotting pointless jargon and embarrassing typos: Virginia McGovern, Don Robson, Josh Corbett, and especially Nathan Kinsey. Because only one of them is a professor, their positive comments give me hope that the book will appeal to audiences outside academia and the military. From the beginning, I have thought that in addition to being fascinating in and of itself, the military chaplaincy can tell us a lot about American society and culture and the life we live together. I made Brittney Todd work harder than any copyeditor should have to. Gracious and sharp, her assistance made the text much clearer. Thanks also to Caroline Eick for solidarity.

The heart of this book is the chaplains themselves. They took time out of their days to share their experiences and thoughts, their struggles and triumphs. I have tried my very best to create a balanced and neutral account of their work. To the extent I succeeded, it's because of their trust and openness. To the extent I failed, it was not for lack of affection.

At home, Yulia Hansen put up with a husband even more distracted and messy than usual. She reminded him to rest, to work, to eat, and to sleep. Most important of all, she taught him the true meaning of the word "moral" in "moral support." Others questioned whether this book should or could be written, but Yulia never did. He couldn't thank her enough.

Introduction

It took me a while to realize the full meaning of what the chaplain had handed me. He was a Christian, and I had asked him about his experience working with Muslims in the military. He didn't stop talking while he made the photocopy, so I just glanced at it and tucked it away; only when I got home did I read it carefully. It was a memo sent to the chiefs of chaplains about the Muslim holiday of *Eid*. The memo explained that *Eid* was a festival of fast-breaking at the end of Ramadan, provided the relevant dates, suggested ways to accommodate Muslims as they prepared to celebrate, and ended, "As in the past, a liberal leave policy is recommended." What struck me wasn't just the matter-of-course attention paid to a religious minority's needs. What really stood out was the header: the memo had been sent from the Office of the Assistant Secretary of Defense at the Pentagon on October 18, 2001.

Fewer than six weeks after terrorists had crashed an airplane into the Pentagon, it was reminding chaplains to take care of their Muslim personnel. While radical Muslims were claiming that America was at war with Islam and right-wing Christians were arguing that we should be, the military chaplaincy was quietly demonstrating the truth of the matter: that the United States is a nation deeply committed to religious freedom for everyone.

This book is about military chaplains and how they handle religious diversity in the US military. Three dilemmas faced by the chaplains will crop up again and again. The first is the *dilemma of diversity*. Not only do they serve a religiously diverse population of sailors, marines, soldiers, and airmen, but they themselves make up a diverse corps within the military institution. Some chaplains relish working in such an environment and thrive both professionally and spiritually; others struggle.

Second is the dilemma of *divided loyalties* or role conflict. Because military chaplains are simultaneously clergy ordained and endorsed by civilian faith groups and commissioned officers in the US armed forces, they face the practical demands of two distinct institutional hierarchies on top of all the day-to-day needs of the military personnel they are endorsed and commissioned to serve. Their two professions, religious and military, often pull in different directions.

The third dilemma they face is the *dilemma of legitimacy.* Because the military chaplains are paid and supplied at taxpayers' expense in a country that separates church and state, constitutional concerns frame everything they do. To deflect challenges on Establishment grounds, the military chaplaincy has staked its legality on the Free Exercise Clause of the First Amendment.

In interviews, I asked the military chaplains about their routine activities and professional relationships, about their successes and failures, and invited them to reflect on their experiences with and feelings about diversity in the military. I aim to let them speak for themselves as much as possible throughout the chapters that follow, because they are both interesting and eloquent. However, I will also try to put their comments into context. It is a sociological axiom that individuals are powerfully shaped by their contexts and react against them. The most salient contexts that frame the chaplains' work are cultural, institutional, and legal.

Culturally, the military chaplaincy raises questions about who we are as Americans and about some of our most cherished values. We think of ourselves as tolerant and inclusive people, committed to freedom and fairness. We don't just take note of religious diversity as a demographic fact; we embrace and celebrate it—in principle. Chaplains are tasked with translating this principle into practice in a very specific institutional context—to take what's written in the constitution and in memoranda from the Pentagon and make it come alive on aircraft carriers, in war zones, and in base chapels.

Even as freedom of religion is central to Americans' national self-understanding, so is Christianity. At the nation's founding, Protestantism was normative. Over time, Americans made room for Catholics, Jews, and maybe Mormons and by the 1950s pragmatically came to think of themselves as a country based on "Judeo-Christian" values. Trends over the past half century have challenged even that forced but familiar construction. Renewed immigration has brought large numbers of adherents of "Eastern" religions such as Islam and Hinduism while more and more Americans are becoming "nones," choosing not to identify with any religious group at all. Is this a Christian country? Should it try to be? Or should we give up thinking of ourselves in religious terms at all? If so, what's left? Are we as committed to religious freedom as we like to think we are? Are our ideals even workable in real life? These kinds of questions are inescapable for military chaplains.

Legally, the dilemma of legitimacy looms large. Imagine being far away from home and invited to church by someone who outranks you in the military. Imagine paying taxes to a government that won't or can't guarantee that those funds won't be used to try to undermine your faith group. Imagine having to attend ceremonies where "we" pray to a different God than you do, which sends the message that you don't belong, even as you're serving your country in uniform. The potentials for abuse are very real. Fortunately, military chaplains are highly cognizant of them, both individually and as a corps, and try to ward them off. Although there's an element of organizational self-defense in this, chaplains are as averse to coercion in matters of faith as anyone else, perhaps even more so. And they're probably more sincerely committed to free exercise of religion than most Americans, who have the luxury of being able to take it for granted. The most salient legal questions raised and confronted by the military chaplaincy are definitional: What counts as coercion? And what counts as religion?

Institutionally, chaplains have to try to reconcile the demands and requirements of both the military and the faith groups that have endorsed them. These two institutions may designate different days for rest, have conflicting guidelines for grooming and attire, endorse different solutions on controversial social issues, and subscribe to radically different systems of ethics, including ethics related to war and peace. Questions of conscience frequently come to the fore. Also, because chaplains are so thoroughly embedded in the military, separated from family and sometimes cut off from coreligionists, maintaining their particular religious identity can be difficult. Integrating the demands of two institutions that both lay claim to their loyalty requires a lot of thought and work.

The chaplains aren't the only ones caught between faith and military service. The enlisted have religious needs, too, and it is the chaplains' job to help make sure these are met. Whether the need is for pastoral counseling, opportunities to worship, the material accoutrements of religious practice, or faith-based exemptions from military demands, chaplains are central in negotiating the outcomes between individuals' rights to free exercise of religion and the military's missions. Many religious needs are met as matters of routine, their provision having been thoroughly institutionalized. But there are frequently requests for new religious accommodations that need to be considered. To what extent can religion be accommodated within the military? What kinds of accommodations cannot be made? Is the military a hospitable environment for all religious groups or just some? What is the proper balance between individual rights and institutional needs?

These are important questions that make the military chaplaincy a rewarding field of study. The issues raised and lessons learned should apply outside its boundaries, too. Readers engaged in other forms of institutional ministry, be it in a prison or a hospital, who have a professional or academic interest in the clergy or the military, or who are concerned with religious diversity "on the ground" should find much with which to relate. Those concerned with the role of faith in American society should read on, as should scholars interested in First Amendment issues. To those interested in the way values are contested and acted out within specific organizational settings, I offer the military chaplaincy as a fascinating case study.

Rather than proposing answers to all the questions raised here, the chapters that follow seek to describe the chaplains and their work as accurately as possible. I will, however, advance a simple sociological argument. It comes in two parts. I aim to persuade the reader that the contexts described really do matter; they shape and channel both thought and behavior, and each creates its own practical challenges. I also want to show what a big difference an individual can make, by highlighting the agency of the chaplains themselves. In the abstract, these are not contentious claims. As it turns out, when people strive to reconcile their noblest aspirations with the complexities of daily life, the Devil really is in the details.

The first chapter provides an overview of military chaplaincy. It covers where chaplains come from and how they fit into the military, as well as how I approached studying them in practical terms. The second chapter is about religious accommodation in the military—about the way chaplains who are deeply dedicated to the free exercise of religion both enable and limit religious expression. The third chapter compares chaplains' experiences with and attitudes toward accommodating two groups that significantly "push the envelope" of diversity, Muslims and Wiccans. The fourth chapter is about the chaplains' own feelings about the diversity they encounter among themselves and in the population they serve. The final chapter discusses a challenge to the Chaplain Corps posed by evangelical Protestants, covering both the evangelicals' own grievances and grievances others hold against them.

CHAPTER 1

MILITARY CHAPLAINS AND THEIR WORK

> There goes many a ship to sea, with many hundred souls in one ship, whose weal and woe is common, and is a true picture of a commonwealth, or a human combination or society. It hath fallen out sometimes that both papists and protestants, Jews and Turks, may be embarked in one ship; upon which supposal I affirm, that all the liberty of conscience, that ever I pleaded for, turns upon these two hinges—that none of the papists, protestants, Jews or Turks be forced to come to the ship's prayers of worship, nor compelled from their own particular prayers or worship, if they practice any.
>
> —Roger Williams, "Roger Williams to the Town of Providence" (1655)[1]

ROGER WILLIAMS WAS AN EARLY CHAMPION OF religious liberty in America.[2] Appropriately, his 350-year-old vision of a religiously diverse ship has become a reality in the modern United States Navy. Before delving into whether the Navy is a "true picture" of society, it is necessary to provide an introduction to those officers most directly tasked with protecting the freedom of religion Williams championed, the military chaplains.

REQUIREMENTS AND ORGANIZATION

Clergy from a variety of religions are recruited by the United States military, given a few months' instruction at a military "chaplain school" in South Carolina, and commissioned as officers. The military does not teach theology but assumes that chaplain candidates already know how to be rabbis, priests, imams, and pastors when they join, so most of the time in chaplain school is spent on learning how to be staff officers.[3] Although some chaplains have military experience from enlisted service before leaving to attend seminary, most need to be taught how to wear a uniform properly and how to work within a chain of command.

Chaplains are required at minimum to have a number of postgraduate credits equivalent to a master's degree. Several of the chaplains in this book had multiple master's degrees, and some had doctorates. Most of their degrees were in the fields of theology and counseling, although many had degrees in social sciences, management, humanities, and music. Chaplains must also meet requirements for age and physical fitness, although these can sometimes be waived.

Most important, chaplains must have the ecclesiastical endorsement of an organized faith group recognized by the Department of Defense. The military tries to recruit a diverse Chaplain Corps that ideally resembles the religious composition of the United States as a whole, in case of a general draft. However, some religious groups fail to supply the military with the number of chaplains they are allowed, whether because of a shortage of clergy or because of ideological opposition, which makes it possible for other groups to increase their representation at their expense In recent decades, conservative Protestant groups have increased their numbers by picking up the slack left by Catholics and mainline Protestants. Although chaplains represent specific faith groups, the military assumes and requires that they help members of all religious persuasions and denominations. For those faith groups that do not have formal clergy the same way the largest Christian groups do, such as Muslims and members of the Church of Jesus Christ of Latter Day Saints (also referred to as "LDS" and "Mormons"), it is up to their ecclesiastical endorsers to certify that their candidates for chaplaincy have the necessary knowledge and are in good standing with their community.

In addition to the military's requirements, the endorsing faith groups may impose their own. Most require that clergy serve three to seven years in civilian parishes before they can become military chaplains. Many interviewees described having to fight denominational superiors for years before being allowed to join the military as chaplains. Some Catholic bishops have needed a lot of "nagging" before letting one of their priests go this way. Among Protestants, many of the more conservative groups have virtual lines of clergy waiting for a slot in the military chaplaincy to open.

There are three military chaplaincies: Army, Navy, and Air Force. The Navy provides chaplain coverage for the Marine Corps, as well as for the Coast Guard and foreign embassies. These three chaplaincies, as well as a chaplaincy for Veterans Affairs, are organized under the Department of Defense. Each chaplaincy is headed by a chief of chaplains, who works out of the Pentagon and reports to the Secretary of Defense. The chaplaincies are coordinated into a joint Armed Forces Chaplains Board, which allows them to support each other operationally and logistically. For example, one of the chaplains in this book had been transferred between service branches.

There are some important differences between the armed forces' chaplaincies. The Army's has generally been the quickest to adapt to increases in diversity, both racial and religious. The Air Force chaplaincy most resembles civilian ministry because chaplains "don't go on airplanes" and are thus more likely to work out of a familiar chapel setting on a base.[4] The Navy's chaplaincy is perhaps the most formal, given its maritime traditions and history of high church dominance. Most chaplains quoted in this book were in the Navy or were Navy chaplains assigned to the Marine Corps, so their rank will be reported in Navy terms.

Chaplains are evaluated for promotion every five years. They come in as lieutenants, then become lieutenant commanders and commanders before achieving the rank of captain. Those passed over for promotion twice are required to leave, which can be experienced as a threat to both personal identity and family financial security. Imagine having to ask yourself what you are if not a chaplain anymore or how you're going to provide for your family. Naturally, the competition for promotions can cause friction among chaplains. Still, the US armed forces operate on the assumption that without rank, chaplains would be viewed as outsiders to the institution and would lack the clout to get necessary things done.[5]

Although chaplains wear the same uniforms and carry the same rank as other officers, there are differences between them. For example, the Geneva Convention defines chaplains as noncombatants, which means they should not carry arms or be held as prisoners of war. More important, in order to make themselves approachable to the enlisted, chaplains deemphasize rank, which other officers rarely do. The correct way to address a chaplain is simply as "Chaplain" regardless of rank—so "Chaplain Smith" and "Chaplain Jones" rather than "Lieutenant Smith" or "Captain Jones." The enlisted are supposed to salute chaplains and call them "Sir" and "Ma'am," but few chaplains would insist on this or reprimand someone who didn't do so properly. Insisting on protocol like that would strike other chaplains as vanity, pride, or having forgotten what they're really supposed to be doing. Among themselves, the chaplains I observed together were on a first-name basis with each other, except when in the presence of the enlisted or when there was a big difference in rank and age between them. They usually refer to each other as "chaplain" to make the point that although the military ranks them, they are all equal as servants of God. They are strangely egalitarian officers.

METHODS, PARTICIPANTS, AND ANALYTICAL STRATEGY

This book is based on semistructured interviews with 34 active-duty chaplains. I chose to conduct interviews for a variety of reasons. First, the kinds of questions I wanted to ask didn't translate well into quantitative measures such as surveys, nor was I trying to test any formal hypotheses that would require me to run advanced statistical analyses. What I was interested in was the chaplains' lived reality. The most straightforward way to get at this was to meet them face to face and ask them. Second, I was interested in meanings, in how the chaplains apprehend and interpret the role they play every day and the interactions they have based on that role. I also wanted to be able to write a report that they would recognize themselves in, rather than one that imposed my own assumptions and priorities on them. In order to be able to probe and ask follow-up questions of the chaplains, and in order for them to be able to question me back and make suggestions, interviews were essential.

One of the things I was interested in was whether chaplains agree among themselves about their mission and various aspects of their roles, so I asked each of them to explain key concepts to me in their own words. I asked them what *cooperation* and *compromise* meant to them and what they thought *facilitation* and *proselytization* were. I also asked them questions about specific religious groups, such as Islam and Wicca, and about some controversies revolving around evangelical Protestantism in the military. To signal a genuine dedication to fair-mindedness on my part, I always asked what they liked about being a chaplain before I asked what they disliked, and for examples of good cooperation before examples of poor cooperation.

As clergy and as counselors, chaplains take confidentiality very seriously. Some of the issues I raised were contentious, and certain questions could conceivably affect the chaplains' chances for promotion; several chaplains thought so. In addition to giving all the chaplains pseudonyms, I am deliberately vague about their rank, age, race, and gender so as not to narrow down their identity too much. All subjects in this study can be presumed to be Navy chaplains, assigned to either the Navy or Marine Corps, except for chaplains from small faith groups. To be able to include those perspectives, I "branched out" to include Army and Air Force chaplains. However, I will describe all participants as if they were in the Navy and carried Navy rank. Rather than giving exact rank, I will tend to refer to chaplains as "junior" or "low rank" for lieutenants and lieutenant commanders and "senior" or "high rank" for commanders and captains. I acknowledge that this is an artificial designation, but I nevertheless find it useful. In terms of age, which with a few exceptions follows rank in my sample, I refer to chaplains as "younger" or "older" with age 45 as the rough cutoff. All subjects, without exception, were on active duty when I interviewed them.

Every chaplain signed an informed consent document after I described my project to him and gave him a chance to ask questions about it. Each chaplain also consented to be tape recorded, although I took handwritten notes as well. I transcribed the interviews myself, without assistive software. It was a time-consuming process but worth it in terms of improving my familiarity with what each chaplain had said. Several chaplains, especially senior ones, stated at the outset that they would be expressing their own personal views and not official positions of the Navy. I reassured them that that was fine, since it was their personal views I was interested in. Some chaplains told me things they wanted "off the record" or elaborated on answers only after I paused the audiotape. I have respected their wishes in all such instances.

Most but not all the interviews were conducted in the Southwest; all were face to face. We met in a variety of settings. Base offices, the chaplains' own or ones they borrowed for the occasion, were most common, but I also interviewed in my own campus office at the University of California, San Diego, at a Subway restaurant, on board a Navy ship, across the aisle in a chapel, in a conference room, and in a cavernous hotel banquet hall during a conference.

To recruit chaplains, I relied on a technique sociologists call "snowball sampling." It is an opportunistic approach that relies on the research project participants themselves for referrals to future candidates for inclusion. I asked each chaplain if they knew anyone else "who might be interested in participating in this study, or that it would be interesting for me to include." All of them did, except for some who were new to their region and didn't know anyone yet. I asked for phone numbers and for permission to cite them as references. After a while, I could call up chaplain "X" and say "chaplains A, B, and C all recommended I talk to you." As word got out about my research, many chaplains expected to hear from me, sometimes joking about how long it had taken me to get to them or about how they'd started thinking they weren't interesting enough to be interviewed.

Although phone calls were the most common recruitment strategy, there were variations. Some chaplains picked up their phone and called colleagues for me at the end of the interview or walked me over to their offices to introduce me. One chaplain at a large base heard about my project and emailed his peers about it, resulting in several chaplains contacting me to volunteer. For example, a Latter Day Saints (Mormon) chaplain volunteered to make sure his faith group was represented. Despite this good rapport, some chaplains did seem to take precautions. One chaplain I called "cold" asked if I would fax him the questions ahead of time, but when I asked for his fax number at the end of the call he admitted that he just wanted to see if I would and then granted the interview. Others asked to call me back, after checking with the chaplains that had referred me to them that I wasn't "some journalist trying to make us look bad." Only four chaplains declined to be interviewed, saying they were about to transfer or were otherwise too busy.

The interviews varied in length from 50 minutes to more than 3 hours, with most lasting about 90 minutes. I let the chaplains talk as much as I could and generally let them exhaust a topic before raising the next question, although I would occasionally try to interrupt tangents about childhood vacations and such. This could often be done nonverbally. One of the most effective ways to signal a desire to move on is simply to stop taking notes, while a desire to hear more about a topic can be communicated by passing on a conversational turn. Some chaplains clearly anticipated my questions, having heard about them from colleagues. I made a point of asking each chaplain if there were questions he or she thought I should raise but didn't, or if there were issues they wanted to discuss that my questions didn't seem to permit. Several chaplains made suggestions, and my interview schedule grew longer and better over the course of the interviews.

One weakness of snowball sampling compared to random sampling is that it may lead a researcher to interview only within a narrow clique of subjects who know each other and tend to agree among themselves. I am confident that this did not happen in my research. I had multiple points of entry, or "seeds," for my chains of referrals, each based on an original cold call or request made to an ecclesiastical endorser. In one case, serendipity struck as a waitress overheard me discussing the project with a friend and referred me to her former boss; she was a veteran and had served as the chaplain's assistant.

More important, the chaplains themselves helped me get a diverse and inclusive sample. When I asked for referrals, they often asked me, "Well, what do you have?" or "What do you need?" They would ask specifically if I had had the chance to interview female chaplains or rabbis. Catholics would make a point of referring me to Protestants and vice versa, with the same being true for "high church" and "low church" denominations among the latter. Versions of "Now, if you want a completely different perspective than what I've given you, you should talk to so-and-so" abounded. Chaplains referred me to colleagues they disapproved of ("he's psycho" and "he's incompetent") as well as to those they admired ("a wonderful man" and "a very interesting background"). In short, the chaplains understood what I was trying to do and conscientiously helped me pursue an inclusive sample. I attribute this goodwill to my openness to including their questions in the project, thus giving them some ownership of it.

The chaplains were wonderful research subjects, and not only because preachers like to talk. Because they all have graduate degrees and many have backgrounds in social science, they were sympathetic to and knowledgeable about the research process and able to make several helpful suggestions. For example, some older chaplains wondered out loud (one bluntly instructing me to go find out) whether younger chaplains had an easier time with diversity. Several chaplains told me they'd enjoyed the interviews and appreciated the chance to express their thoughts. At the end of the interviews, I was often walked to my car and sent on my way with God's blessing and offers of further assistance. One chaplain gave me a hug.

Time and again, the chaplains would express interest in the project, asking me if their answers were typical—"What are the others telling you?" and "What have you found so far?" They also generally approved of my questions. Here are some examples from the end of the interviews when I asked them to suggest additional questions:

> Oh, let's see . . . I think you're covering pretty much all of it. I know, the diversity issue—probably one of the questions is how do you feel about diversity? And sometimes I think you can get a piece of . . . some chaplains honestly are not too wild about it. (Chaplain Dyren, Catholic)

> I thought it was pretty good. It was interesting that you didn't bring up more about the institution itself, in which we work. I'm probably thinking about that because I just came off a conference on institutional ministry and looking at paradigms. (Chaplain Feteris, Presbyterian)

> I think you're doing pretty well. Has anybody talked to you about the chaplains on active duty that are atheists? [. . .] I expect a whole chapter in your book. (Chaplain Cugrijus, LDS)

> I think it was an excellent survey, and if you came up with those questions just based on your experience, I think you've hit on the key issues for chaplains. (Chaplain Irons, Southern Baptist)

These quotes also show how chaplains have their own individual concerns and agendas, and might have asked different questions even though they generally endorsed my approach.

The 34 chaplains interviewed for this project represent 20 different faith groups, including 2 "flavors" of Lutherans and 3 Baptist "flavors."[6] The chaplains' faith groups and the pseudonyms are listed at the front of this book. It is important to note that this sample is not representative of the Chaplain Corps as a whole or of the Navy's alone. For example, Mormons are overrepresented at nearly 10 percent of the sample. The sample is also skewed in terms of rank. It includes 11 commanders and captains for the simple reason that they're easier to interview: lower-ranking chaplains are more likely to be out at sea. Still, exactly half the sample was lieutenants, so I did manage to get a mix of seasoned and novice chaplains. Their years of military experience ranged from 1 to 26 (some counting service as enlisted before becoming chaplains), with a median of 9. Their ages ranged from 32 to 59, with a median of 44. I interviewed white, African American, Hispanic, and Asian American chaplains, both men and women.

This is a work of interpretive, qualitative sociology. When I make claims about "military chaplains" and "the military chaplaincy," I do so for convenience's sake, since "the 34 military chaplains I interviewed" and "the military chaplaincy as described by my 34 subjects" gets cumbersome after a while. Readers should be mindful that my findings may very well be shaped by who was in my sample. Not only was the sample not statistically representative of the chaplaincy as a whole, but it is also possible that my descriptions and analyses are swayed by exceptionally eloquent, insightful, or talkative individuals within it. Some chaplains simply had a lot more to say than others. Rather than argue that the military chaplaincy "really is" one way or another, my goal is to describe some of the kinds of people who are chaplains, the kinds of issues they confront, and the kinds of solutions they find. Hopefully, this will serve as useful guidance for more traditionally positivistic sociological studies in the future.

The Intersections of Military Chaplaincy: Religion, the Military, and the Law

The military is an especially interesting context within which to study religion and religious diversity. First of all, it contradicts one of the main predictions of secularization theory, which is that over time religion becomes relegated to home and church, something compartmentalized, something people keep to themselves.[7] So when religion appears in non-private settings such as prisons, department stores, or aircraft carriers, it catches many people, including many sociologists, off guard.[8] Sociologists of religion, for example, have tended to neglect these areas and focus on congregations, where religion "belongs," with the main exception being studies of the role of religion in politics.[9] The result is a fascinating field of study, which Diana Eck has called "controversies of the public square."[10] I treat the military as one of these public squares.

It makes a big difference what kind of public square religion finds itself in. When someone preaches on a street corner or a college campus, people have the option of listening or walking away. In politics, where controversy and discord is normal, there are debates, elections, and other established ways to adjudicate religion's role, and compromises can be struck. The military, however, throws people together in ways they can't just walk away from and does not have a democratic culture that allows debate and compromise. Like any other institution, it has its own culture. Chaplains have to work with and within it.

The military is bureaucratic, hierarchical, and dominated by instrumental rationality. Unlike public schools or city councils, the military transcends local orientations and brings people together from all over the country and many different backgrounds. But it is not quite a true microcosm of the United States. Despite increasing numbers of women, the military is still a male-dominated arena. It is necessarily also younger and fitter than the nation as a whole. Privacy, highly valued in other institutions, is severely curtailed. According to Jeffrey Weintraub, spatial organization is a key influence on public life.[11] Civilians can, with some effort, largely avoid people with different religious beliefs by choosing their neighborhoods and schools carefully. These are not options in the military. Forcing people to interact with those they would rather avoid is one aspect of what Erving Goffman called a "total" institution. Goffman describes this undesired social interaction as a kind of "contamination" that helps a total institution break down ("mortify" in his terms) the individual's preexisting sense of self so that a new, institutionalized self can be imposed more easily.

This emphasis on the uniqueness of institutions must not obscure an equally important fact: different institutions can nevertheless partake of a shared, overarching culture. For example, all American institutions are in some way permeated by the value of individualism. But they also shape and express this value differently. There's no reason to expect or demand that individualism mean the same thing in the contexts of religion (e.g., the incalculable worth of "thy neighbor"), of economics (e.g., the pursuit of private profit), or of politics (e.g., freedom from communal obligation). Although military individualism sounds anachronistic, consider the ethic of never leaving a man behind. The military doesn't risk a platoon to rescue or recover an individual because it's rational, but because it values the very same individuals. If *individualism* can mean different things depending on the institutional context, then so can *freedom*.

Military chaplains are interesting in part because they have to act out what "freedom of religion" means in the military.[12]

Chaplains also stand at the intersection of competing claims to allegiance. God's demands can clash with those of secular authority, which can cause acute crises of individual conscience, especially since the military's hierarchy makes secular authority very tangible. According to Madsen and his coauthors, "institutions are the settings for moral dramas, in which we act out our understandings of who we are and how we ought to live."[13] This is especially true where institutions intersect.

In addition to the military and religion, a third major social institution is inevitably involved in the chaplains' work, and that is the law. The law doesn't just mediate between the two other institutions; it is itself at stake. As officers, chaplains take an oath to support and defend not the president, the nation, or the people but the Constitution of the United States. Often, chaplains aren't trying to reconcile "God and Country" so much as God and a legal document.

Historical Overview of US Military Chaplaincy

Four recurring themes can be discerned in Dale Herspring's excellent overview of the history of American military chaplaincy. The first is precisely "political socialization," which he claims has been the central focus of American chaplains for over 225 years, along with improving motivation and morale.[14] The second is the military's tendency to pile additional nonreligious tasks onto the chaplains, which chaplains now refer to as "collateral duties." The third theme is how chaplains fit into the military hierarchy, with questions raised about requirements, uniforms, pay, and rank. Finally, and most important for this book's purposes, is increasing religious diversity.

Both the Army and Navy chaplaincies were created in 1775. George Washington wanted chaplains to suppress drunkenness, gambling, and swearing in addition to preaching and also relied on them to convince his soldiers that they were fighting in a just cause. During the first century of chaplaincy, many of these tasks flowed from the fact that chaplains were better educated and often from the middle and upper classes. They were used as secretaries and clerks and especially as teachers. For example, Army chaplains taught English to immigrant soldiers and Navy chaplains taught mathematics and navigation.[15] During the Revolutionary War, there were military chaplains from seven denominations, most appointed by state governors or legislatures rather than the churches themselves. Because most states had an established church, chaplains were almost always the same denomination as their units. The largest group was Congregationalists, followed by Presbyterians, Episcopalians, and Baptists.[16]

Between the Revolution and the Civil War, chaplains were few in number and their role poorly defined. There were many changes in uniform, rank, and pay, matters that say a lot about what a chaplain really is (an outsider or insider to the institution), who really controls him (his church or the military), and what kind of relationship he has with the commanding officer (collegial or adversarial). Many commanders resented chaplains, viewing them as a threat to the harsh discipline of the day or as prudes because of their campaigns against drinking and profanity. A chaplain at odds with his commander had no effective recourse. Still, Navy chaplains were able to help end flogging and daily rations of alcohol ("grog"). The first Catholic chaplains were appointed during the war with Mexico, partly to serve the liturgical needs of Irish troops and partly to show Mexico that the United States wasn't anti-Catholic.[17]

The Civil War required a rapid expansion in the number of chaplains. Concerns about basic competency caused greater attention to requirements and professionalism. The Union Army had more and better-organized chaplains, but on both sides they made themselves useful by visiting and bandaging the wounded, burying the dead and notifying their families, registering graves, and writing letters on behalf of soldiers. According to Herspring, it was during the Civil War that chaplains first fully realized that they had to cooperate across denominational boundaries to meet the needs of the men.[18] The first Jewish chaplain was appointed in 1862.[19] After the Civil War, the number of military chaplains plummeted to around fifty or sixty. Although educational standards were raised, they still had no standardized training or central authority and were heavily burdened with collateral duties.[20]

World War I and its aftermath gave shape to the military chaplaincy we recognize today. When the United States entered the war, the Army chaplaincy expanded from 72 chaplains to 2,217. For the first time, there was a centralized chaplain school. The first Navy chief of chaplains was appointed in 1917 and the first Army chief of chaplains followed in 1920.[21] Ecclesiastical endorsement was required beginning in 1926, the same year that the military started using census data to try to recruit a representative Chaplain Corps. In this era, chaplains continued to work well across denominational boundaries, setting aside theological minutiae for the sake of serving their soldiers and sailors.[22]

Gentlemanly cooperation across denominations continued during World War II, when the chaplaincy expanded once again. By that time, the most pressing questions about their recruitment, rank, promotion, pay, and uniforms had been made and their roles much more clearly defined. With better formal ties to their ecclesiastical endorsers and a hierarchy of their own, chaplains had better recourse if treated unfairly and became harder to push around and overwork. They also proved their worth to commanding officers by engaging in extensive counseling[23] and political socialization. Chaplains helped persuade men that America's cause was just and worth dying for.[24] Because chaplains were expected to be with the men when they were in danger, they suffered high rates of casualties themselves. From December 7, 1941, to the end of the war, 478 Army chaplains were killed in action.

During World War II, 40 different faith groups had chaplains in the Army and 25 had chaplains in the Navy.[25] The best illustration of the chaplains' ecumenical cooperation and sacrifice is the death of the "Four Chaplains." On February 3, 1943, the US Army Transport *Dorchester* was sunk in the Atlantic. The ship was carrying four chaplains—two Protestants, a Catholic, and a Jew—who went down with the ship, arm in arm, after helping organize evacuation on deck and passing out life jackets. The four chaplains were commemorated with a postal stamp in 1948.[26]

During the Cold War conflicts in Korea and Vietnam, chaplains continued to serve as political socialization officers. Religion was believed to strengthen people's resistance to Communism and commitment to the American way of life. Richard Hutcheson lists titles and explanations of some of the lectures chaplains gave during the 1950s: "The You in the USA (why we are here, personal responsibility to country)," "Let's Get it Straight (alcohol education)," and "Made in America (principles and ideal of justice and democracy)."[27] Because the Vietnam War was controversial, criticisms emerged about the chaplains being used this way.[28] Chaplains were also put to work on the new problems of racial strife and drug abuse within the military, and they made important contributions in each of these areas.[29]

The period after the Vietnam War was a period of increasing religious diversity in the United States. By 1987 the Army chaplaincy represented 109 faith groups and the Navy, 90.[30] By 2009, there were chaplains from 175 different religious groups in the military. In the past twenty years, the military has commissioned its first Muslim, Buddhist, and Hindu chaplains. In 2007, a Christian chaplain converted to Wicca and applied to become the first Wiccan chaplain but failed.[31] Diversity will likely continue to increase in the years ahead

There are now about 3,000 active-duty and 2,000 reserve chaplains in the US armed forces. Pauletta Otis estimates that of those on active duty, 1,580 are in the Army, 800 in the Navy, and 549 in the Air Force.[32]

A 2007 Navy document estimates that the Navy had 287 chaplains on active duty in the Marine Corps, 525 in the Navy, and 38 in the Coast Guard.[33] Navy chaplains should expect a tour to consist of three years on shore and two to two-and-a-half years at sea. Chaplains work in a variety of settings, from domestic bases and military hospitals to warships at sea and posts in Iraq and Afghanistan. Some chaplains work alone, supported only by a chaplain's assistant, together constituting what is called a Religious Ministry Team. Other chaplains, on larger ships or bases, work alongside fellow chaplains. For example, a carrier strike group may have as many as twenty chaplains.[34]

The contemporary chaplaincy displays a great deal of continuity with its past. While still providing opportunities for worship, chaplains make themselves useful to the military by participating in political socialization, doing lots of counseling, improving morale, and advising commanders in the field on religious matters relevant to twenty-first-century warfare.

THE CHAPLAINS' WORK AT THE INTERSECTION OF MILITARY AND RELIGION

The military is one of the quintessential "total institutions" in Erving Goffman's analysis. One of the characteristics of a total institution is that it has an "encompassing tendency," trying to become "the whole world" for its members. Ideally, military personnel should conduct their lives only in military places and with other military people, which is why bases are usually in remote areas or cut off from civilian neighborhoods by walls and have their own restaurants, bowling alleys, shops, movie theaters, and chapels. Military personnel should also ideally rely only on information provided by the military itself, which is why the military produces its own radio broadcasts and newspapers. It's not that military personnel aren't allowed outside the metaphorical and physical walls of the institution; except for periods of intense training and indoctrination, they are. The point is that the military tries to be and provide everything for its members so that they don't have much need to go outside. The encapsulating tendency of the military is very functional. It helps socialize new members by reducing the salience of old identities and provides a kind of stable environment for a population that often has to relocate to mention just two advantages. If all military bases are more or less the same, it doesn't matter as much whether you get transferred from Virginia to Guam to Germany and back. The effect is to create and maintain a stable military subculture, which is simultaneously nestled within and separated from the mainstream culture.

The encapsulating tendency complements another characteristic the military has: it is "greedy." Like the family, it makes extreme demands on its members' time, energy, and loyalty. Many of the hardships of military life come from being caught between these two "greedy institutions."[35] Why, then, would military leaders not only permit but actively encourage religion within their institution? Why not leave religion "outside" so that only the most committed sailors, soldiers, airmen, and marines would make the effort to maintain a religious life, having to cross the symbolic boundary between "inside" and "outside" in order to do so? After all, religion also makes demands on its members, so clergy could be viewed as intruders and energy spent on religion considered a loss to the military. What is it chaplains do to make the institution tolerate and even promote them?

Character Guidance as Political Socialization

Chaplains still spend a lot of time doing political socialization, now usually described as "character guidance." Past generations have differed on how much and how urgently the military needs to change the values of its members, but an interesting shift did occur at the end of the twentieth century. After World War II, the military was viewed as a morally perilous environment, because of the drinking, gambling, swearing, and maybe even whoring that happened when young Americans were removed from home. Chaplains were recruited, and character education programs intended to make the military more wholesome. The assumption now is that they have succeeded. The military is now considered more wholesome than the surrounding culture and it is "kids" *outside* the military that are at risk: materialistic, overstimulated, lazy, narcissistic, detached, and almost completely amoral (unless relativism counts as a morality). This sad state of affairs is variously blamed on the consumer culture, the Internet revolution, and family breakdown. At one training facility, Chaplain Gunvant, a senior Catholic chaplain, described the gap he felt between himself and the recruits:

> Secularized society had cut them off from their roots. They probably know less about their faith than a person shopping in a supermarket for some product. I mean, it's that secular . . . The problem with most of the clergy is that we're too well educated. We use words that are much too big. And so our problems are both their complete lack of knowledge of their roots religiously, and our difficulty in speaking to them in a language they can understand, that is engaging and entertaining, I suppose, and captivating.

When I asked chaplain Drozdov, an Orthodox Christian, what was most difficult about working with young people, he answered "probably their apathy." Another Catholic priest, Chaplain Dyren, said, "Mostly, I think, we have a lot of people who are very secular and have maybe just a smattering of a religious sheen over them. And you're called to be with those people. And they don't necessarily care that I'm a Catholic priest, and they don't even know what that is half the time."

Many chaplains described sailors and marines as coming into the military with hardly any sense of morality at all but with plenty of emotional scars and "baggage" from domestic violence, premarital sex, and substance abuse. By contrast, those who have been in the military for a while are assumed to be superior to their civilian counterparts. According to Chaplain Hamoud, "military service members are a cut above the society in terms of their physical training, in terms of their personal conduct, in terms of their social behavior. The military has done sexual harassment training, has conducted drug awareness classes, zero tolerance, suicide awareness, smoking reduction, so all these things help make a better person" (Muslim).

It is often chaplains who conduct training about suicide prevention or raising consciousness about alcoholism. The carrying out of these kinds of efforts, which can also include charitable work such as organizing food drives, is referred to as "running programs." Chaplains report their programs to their churches to show that they are engaged and also count on programs being noticed by commanding officers and entered on their fitness reports, or FitReps, as "bullets" that are taken into consideration when they're up for promotion. On one occasion, a senior chaplain decided to help me recruit more research subjects by walking me over to the base dining hall, where he introduced me to four of the chaplains he supervised. One of them jokingly asked whether letting me interview him would count as bullet for his fitness report, to which his superior quipped, "No, not for you." The encounter illustrates both the casual tone common among chaplains and their mindfulness of hierarchy.

Running programs helps the chaplains perform what they call a "ministry of presence" by putting them in touch with the enlisted. Chaplains do wander and chat with them casually, inquiring about work, family, and weekend plans (just sitting in one's office waiting to be approached is frowned upon), but the programs create occasions for interaction for those who might need an "excuse" to see the chaplain.[36] If nothing else, it allows chaplains to introduce themselves to enlisted personnel, to become a familiar face and known presence. Teaching classes serves the same purpose. Chaplain Bartley, assigned to a training facility where large numbers of recruits turn over every few months, found his educational role very useful: "What we have here, the pastor is the first person that is seen by the recruits and the last person. The chaplain is interspersed throughout the training classes of character development. So they have that interaction with recruits" (Church of God in Christ).

Chaplains are also useful for inculcating basic manners and a professional attitude. Because chaplains wear the same uniform as other officers, people don't always know what kind of officer they are until they're very close. Chaplains like to tell stories about how sailors and marines react when they walk in on profanity-laced or sexually explicit conversations: with shamefaced apologies and sometimes frantic tucking away of pornography or alcohol. Their very presence chills blasphemy and crude speech, which makes for a more inclusive working environment and arguably fosters a more sober work ethic. This is exactly what George Washington had in mind when he described the chaplains as "a gentleman of sober, serious and religious deportment who would improve morale and discourage gambling, swearing and drunkenness."[37] The political socialization role and subordination of religion to military needs are both captured in the current (Fiscal Year 2008–2013) Strategic Plan for the Navy's Chaplain Corps, which describes its own mission as delivering "religious accommodation, care, and advisement, to strengthen faith, values, and virtues, so that Sailors, Marines, and their families may best serve our country."[38]

COUNSELING

As described in the Strategic Plan, the concept of "care" effectively means lots of counseling, which the chaplains themselves recognize: "Counseling is a primary role, or what takes up the majority of our time. We have other tasks and stuff, but counseling is, you know . . ." (Chaplain Irons, Southern Baptist).

The chaplains are expected to deliver "relational counseling" that is "motivated by their proximity and immediate presence, distinguished by confidentiality, and imbued with professional wisdom and a genuine respect for human beings."[39] From the point of view of some chaplains, "professional wisdom" isn't enough, and they feel ill-prepared to do the kinds and variety of counseling the military expects. Some benefit from continuing education programs that help them learn skills needed in marriage counseling or substance abuse counseling, while others bring relevant postgraduate training into the chaplaincy. Yet others are annoyed by how much time counseling takes away from tasks they consider more important. As one chaplain put it, "I'm a Catholic priest. If they wanted a social worker, they should have hired one."[40] Most chaplains, however, take counseling very seriously, came across as genuinely concerned for the well-being of those they serve, and believe that counseling, far from being a collateral duty that ignores or wastes their unique religious training, is a way to emulate Christ's example of serving the suffering. Chaplain Metzger enjoys this role very much:

> I think what we try to convey to them is that we are servants. That even though we wear rank, the servanthood of our call as chaplains, I think nurtures a respect for chaplains and a perception of chaplains as somebody who will assist them. [. . .] It's always very gratifying for me to just be walking around and hear somebody saying, "Hello, chaplain," or smile. And I think that's not because I'm such a great person, but because of the fact that I am a chaplain and chaplains are perceived as friends and as helpers. (Full Gospel Churches)

Confidentiality was almost always mentioned when chaplains spoke of their counseling role. According to Chaplain Gunvant (Catholic), the commanding officer can go to the military's psychiatrists and doctors and demand to see their patient records because he is responsible by law for what happens in his command, but he "may not go to the chaplain and say 'I want you to tell me what this person said.'" Chaplain Irons makes sure everyone knows this: "I tell them, when I do my indoc with new marines, 'I have the luxury of not being in your chain of command. Which means everything you say to me is confidential. My office is a safe place, you don't have to worry about repercussions. I'm not here to make sure your rifle patrols well. I'm here because I care about you" (Southern Baptist). Chaplain Farrow made the same point, offering a dramatic example of how strongly he believes in confidentiality:

> If it's a medical issue, they have to report it. And even the lawyers don't have confidentiality. They don't really have total client privilege in the military. So we are the only ones, the chaplains, that have one hundred per cent total confidentiality. And commanding officers will ask us, we've talked about it as an issue [. . .] And I said, "Well, sir, if I was your chaplain and some sailor told me he's got a gun and he's going to kill the CO, kill you [. . .] I'd probably call you up and say 'Hey, Captain, why don't you take the rest of the day off? I'll explain it to you tomorrow.' And they laugh and think I'm funny. But the fact is, I would." (Catholic)

Lest the reader suspect the priest was guilty of bravado here, Chaplain Farrow was himself a senior officer and not likely to be intimidated by a Navy captain. Along with other senior chaplains, he acknowledged that less experienced chaplains with less institutional clout might have a harder time resisting pressures for information from commanding officers, so they make sure they are available to stand up for the lower-ranking chaplains they supervise and mentor. They believe that without confidentiality, they wouldn't be nearly as effective in serving individuals or the institution. Sometimes, chaplains counsel other officers, even the commanding officer, although most of their work is with the enlisted. Presumably, fellow officers are more mature and better adjusted to the military, which may reduce their need for counseling. Then again, the fact that they know the chaplains better, don't have to overcome the enlisted/officer gap in approaching them, and have greater responsibilities may increase their need. In any case, the enlisted outnumber officers.

Individual members of the military bring all kinds of issues to the chaplains in counseling session: marital crises, domestic violence, and infidelity; workplace conflicts and financial problems; addictions to alcohol or gambling; worries about their children or parents; grief for friends who have died and survivor's guilt; homesickness and loneliness; culture shocks and existential questions. Chaplain Farrow (Catholic) estimated that "99 percent of the time" those who came to the chaplains for help "want something done about what they're telling you." I've personally witnessed a chaplain pick up the phone and make a call requesting that a marine's leave to attend a funeral be extended to allow cheaper return airfare, for example. Chaplains relish sharing examples of how they've "gone to bat" on behalf of "their" sailors and marines, and more than one joked that a good chaplain should be prepared to "lie, cheat, and steal" for those they serve. Part of institutional ministry is to "give them a good, objective opinion of how the system works, how we can best facilitate them with the system, and where we need to go from here [. . .] Get them headed in the right direction. We try to solve their problems" (Chaplain Farrow, Catholic). From the point of view of the enlisted who are new to the organization and lack institutional clout, the chaplains know the ropes better and can maybe even use their rank to work the system for them. One chaplain I interviewed explained that although he was reluctant to pull rank, he had used his authority to get a sailor's paycheck disbursed when a bureaucratic error was causing delays.

The military gains from the chaplains' interventions and counseling sessions on behalf of the enlisted. Two scholars critical of the chaplaincy wrote during the Vietnam era that "what is therapeutically recommended for the individual turns out to be functional for the institution that sponsors the therapist."[41] Chaplain Grams implicitly argued that this is still the case, regardless of what chaplains might intend coming in:

> Many chaplains come in with the idea of "we're going to reform this system." Whatever that means in our mind. It may mean that we heard about the abuses in the military, and we're going to stop that. We're going to make the military nicer, we're gonna make people care about each other. Whatever it is our agenda is. But, what I would tell a young chaplain coming on board is that "your job is to support the chain of command and good order and discipline. That is your job, and you have to help these young men who come in here and are confused and come in here and are just blown away by the rigor of this place, to survive and cultivate within them that sense of humanity that I think is their unique gift in this life." (Presbyterian)

NEW EMPHASIS: OPERATIONAL CHAPLAINS

The chaplains don't just provide the military an important service by helping its members adjust to and cope with its demands. They are also increasingly called upon to reconcile people in other countries to the presence of the US military. One of the "core capabilities" of the Chaplain Corps, as described in the Navy's strategic plan, is to "advise." In an appendix, the document defines *advising* as the "capability by which Chaplains advise COs on issues relating to morals, ethics, spiritual well-being, and morale. Within the boundaries of their noncombatant status, chaplains advise on the impact of religions on operations. They train and educate leaders at all levels in moral decision-making, cultural awareness and cross-cultural communication."[42]

The so-called global war on terror forced the military to recognize religion as relevant not just to the private life of its own personnel but to its "mission and operating areas."[43] Efforts to "win hearts and minds" are not new, however. During nineteenth-century domestic wars against Native Americans, chaplains intervened to decrease tensions both by opposing massacres by the US Army and by trying to convert the "Indians" to Christianity. In the occupied Philippines, a Catholic chaplain repaired schools and persuaded American authorities to make it easier for small farmers to buy enough land to support their families, which made it harder for the insurgent resistance to recruit new members. During the occupation of Japan, chaplains supported missionaries, repaired seminaries, and opposed prostitution in order to try to bridge the gap between occupiers and occupied.[44] Efforts to reduce the suffering of civilians and show the positive side of religion continued through the Korea and Vietnam eras.

What changed after 9/11 was that the attention given to religion by line officers and Pentagon officials ticked sharply upward, in what one scholar described as an "about-face" by a military organization that had been manifestly secular in its orientations and assumptions before that.[45] During the Cold War, most thinking about international relations was framed in terms of a clash between rival political and economic systems. Thus the ethnic and especially religious conflicts that flared up in its aftermath caught much of the national security establishment by surprise.[46] Since then, the operational role of chaplains has been strengthened, generating much interesting commentary, analysis, and reflection.[47]

Some of the operational contributions chaplains can make were described in the 1989 Army field manual: "Liaison with local missionaries and religious leaders, assist in charitable and beneficial endeavors, trains military personnel to respect religious beliefs, promotes peace and harmony." In 1996, Paul Wrigley, a Naval Reserve chaplain, summarized the importance of religion on the battlefield as follows: "An operational commander, however well trained in the military issues, who is ignorant of or discounts the importance of religious belief, can strengthen his enemy, offend his allies, alienate his own forces, and antagonize public opinion."[48] In 2001, the Navy implemented a training program about "religion and statecraft" for all its chaplains, designed to help them take on new roles. At the 2004 annual meeting of the Military Chaplains Association, I listened to Navy Chief of Chaplains Louis Iasiello talk about the need for the chaplaincy to become more "operational." For the Navy, that meant having fewer chaplains on the "green" (land, domestic bases) side and more on the "blue" (at sea, deployed abroad) side.

Several of the chaplains I spoke to had participated in and witnessed activities that promoted a positive image of the United States and its armed forces. A female chaplain I interviewed described her experience while deployed to the Persian Gulf as "wonderful, just wonderful." When I looked puzzled, she explained that she had spent much of her time rocking babies. Her ship, stationed off the coast of a friendly nation, sent a contingent of sailors to an orphanage there. The men repaired the buildings and painted them in bright, fun colors, while the female sailors were permitted into the restricted women's part of the orphanage, where they lavished attention on the infants. The orphanage staff was delighted.

Chaplain Koch was with a group of ships in the western Pacific Ocean, one of them carrying donated items intended for orphanages and charities in East Timor. These included several hundred bicycles, which are the most practical means of transportation given the state of the roads there. According to Chaplain Koch, there was a "reluctance to let the Americans come in there" because of "religious turmoil" and "politics" internal to East Timor. Fortunately,

> it just so happened that the Cardinal, the Catholic cardinal who was there, was one of the players in this whole political spectrum, and the chaplain aboard the ship was a Catholic priest contacted through his sources, contacted the religious organizations who then got ahold of the Cardinal. And through some diplomacy, in dealing with religious leaders, we were able to open that up, in East Timor, for the first time. The chaplain had a major role in this political spectrum, of getting these donated goods in there, and in beginning the diplomatic process. (United Methodist)

This is a good example of chaplains acting as liaisons to local religious leaders. In Afghanistan, chaplains have coordinated with mullahs to get schools built, and in Iraq they have worked with local religious leaders to repair mosques. Sometimes the mere presence of the right kind of chaplain can impress foreign audiences. Normally, chaplains of minority faiths are kept on large bases so that they can "cover" as many coreligionists as possible. For example, putting a rabbi on ship with three Jews on board is less efficient than stationing him near a cluster of large military installations where he can serve hundreds of coreligionists. But one chaplain who had deployed to Egypt right after the 2001 terrorist attacks was able to dislodge an imam:

> I had the honor of having the first Muslim chaplain serving with me, Chaplain Saif ul-Islam. And he's the first Muslim chaplain that was ever assigned to [chaplain's base]. We had to pull some strings to get him assigned to us, because we were a deployable unit. So we made that happen, went there, and he had his work cut out for him when he got in country [Egypt], because people wanted to know more about the Islamic faith. They wanted to know that they actually had a presence in the United States military. That impressed the Egyptians and the other coalition countries.[49]

Sensitive chaplains can reduce tensions even across religious lines. In Iraq, a community was enraged after marines killed two children. Their chaplain was able to explain to them that the deaths had been accidental and that the fault lay with forces loyal to Saddam Hussein, who had used the children as shields. Chaplain Adams went beyond explanation and showed his solidarity with the bereaved Iraqis by helping dig the children's graves and then respectfully observing their burial. In so doing, he reduced tensions that otherwise may have caused more bloodshed.[50]

In order to win hearts and minds in the war on terror, relations with Muslim communities are especially important. Ignorance can easily lead to unnecessary offense and friction, at worst feeding the terrorist narrative that the United States is in a crusade against Islam itself. Carlson suggests that military personnel "may need to become more attuned to their religious lives, desires, beliefs, and pursuits—in other words, to the needs of the soul" and quotes a chaplain who asks, "Do we understand the sacred rituals and rites for dealing with the dead? Do we understand the religious calendar of the area we're operating in and adhere to this?"[51] Among the chaplains I interviewed, it was Chaplain Koch (United Methodist) who seemed most interested in the strategic and tactical dimensions of religion. He referred frequently to Samuel Huntington's influential book about the "clash of civilizations" and offered many examples of how religion could impact warfare. He described how Egypt had tried to gain an advantage in the Six Day War by attacking Israel on the Jewish Day of Atonement, assuming it would give them an element of surprise. According to Chaplin Koch, the stratagem backfired because "it not only caught them off guard, it royally pissed them off . . . It was a very decisive and quick battle." He also claimed that chaplains had advised the Bush administration not to attack Iraq during Ramadan because "we don't want to be perceived by the Arab world as hostile to Islam."

The near consensus that chaplains need to be more involved in operations has not been reached without dissent and controversy, and there are many limitations to what chaplains can do. Some commanding officers might not think of using chaplains this way, line officers may resist chaplains (who are staff officers) expanding their importance within the military, and many chaplains don't have the language or negotiating skills to act as liaisons in any effective way to begin with. Some chaplains come from religious groups that don't permit the kind of interreligious dialogue necessary to impress occupied populations, other chaplains are personally biased against Muslims and only interact with them if ordered to, and those chaplains who do find ways to make themselves useful operationally may burn out or become traumatized by the horrors of war.[52] Another complication is that because chaplains, like other members of the military, rotate into an area and out again relatively quickly, they're not around long enough for lasting relationships to form. At the very least, chaplains playing "operational" roles would have to always be mindful of building on their predecessors' successes or compensating for their mistakes.

As tempting as it is to try to use chaplains to educate line officers about local religious sensibilities and to cultivate trusting or at least respectful relationships with nearby villages, great caution has to be taken so as to avoid serious misunderstandings. If American military chaplains are perceived as "Christian mullahs," locals may have distorted expectations of how much clout they have within the military and what they can deliver. Worse yet, local religious leaders who respond to outreach from American military chaplains may be targeted as collaborators and killed.

Military chaplains themselves may be endangered if they're perceived as spies. According to Hutcheson, "chaplains engaged in humanitarian service among civilians, whether officially or unofficially, often acquire information of value to commanders on connection with military operations."[53] For example, during Operation Desert Storm, chaplains who were distributing food to churches in the Middle East both gained useful knowledge about "expectations Muslims had about Americans, and clarification of the differences between the Islamic and Judeo-Christian manners and customs" and also were given tactically important information, such as the whereabouts of Iraqi secret police.[54] Conducting negotiations or interrogations, gathering intelligence or performing "psychological operations" that deceive or mislead, and playing any role in selecting targets are all activities that violate the chaplains' noncombatant status.[55] If that status loses credibility, chaplains will be both less effective and in greater danger.

MILITARY CEREMONIES AND CIVIL RELIGION

With all these limitations and risks in mind, it is hardly surprising that many chaplains, line officers, and policy makers prefer that chaplains stick to their more obvious and tradition role as religious functionaries. Military personnel who don't actively seek out chaplains in their offices or for worship are most likely to notice them when they officiate at military events and ceremonies. Chaplains will say grace before a banquet, "say a few words" at memorial services, or offer a prayer at command functions such as a graduation ceremony, the commissioning of a new ship, a change of command, or a retirement ceremony. One of the chaplains I interviewed kept checking his watch so as not to be late for an event where he was supposed to pray before a ship was decommissioned and donated to an ally. Another chaplain invited me to a celebration of Martin Luther King Jr. and said a prayer there before a marine with a powerful voice did an excellent job of reading the "I Have a Dream" speech. Yet another mentioned having prayed at the beginning of a Marine Corps formal dance.

Chaplains' praying at such events, specifically the issue of whether the prayers can include the phrase "in Jesus' name," has caused a lot of controversy recently. I will discuss this in the last chapter, in the context of grievances articulated by and against evangelical Protestants. For present purposes, the important thing about the ceremonies is that whatever their individual religious commitment, chaplains act as spokesmen for civil religion in the military.

The concept of a civil religion can be traced back to Rousseau during the Enlightenment,[56] but it is Robert Bellah who has most usefully detailed its American manifestation.[57] Since Christians first arrived in the New World, they have been imagining themselves and their actions in religious terms. The Pilgrims understood their ocean crossing as an "errand into the wilderness" analogous to the Israelites' flight from Egypt, George Washington was described as a Moses-like figure for delivering his nation from tyranny, and Abraham Lincoln towers as a Christ-like figure who laid down his life as part of the nation's punishment for its original sin of slavery.[58] In addition to such analogies, American politicians and clergy have constantly spoken of a covenant between the new nation and God. The covenant is a kind of agreement whereby the United States will be blessed as long as it recognizes its "deep obligation to, both collectively and individually, carry out God's will on earth."[59] Although civil religion resembles Christianity because it borrows symbols from it, Bellah insists that "church religion" and civil religion are distinct because they venerate different things.

Civil religion serves several positive functions for the military. It provides a shared set of symbols and unifying rituals that help integrate men and women separated from their home communities and drawn from many different walks of life. It lends a sacred veneer to American values such as "freedom" and "democracy." Finally, it encourages individuals to set aside selfish pursuits for the sake of something bigger. It equates civic and religious virtue—being a good citizen is the same as being a good Christian. What military chaplains do is throw martial virtues into the mix, so that military virtues also look like good citizenship and good Christianity. Invited to attend a class taught by a chaplain to a group of Marine Corps recruits, I witnessed personally how he explained to them that "taking responsibility" was a way of practicing the Marine Corps value of "honor" and that obeying both parents and drill instructors was a way to demonstrate another Marine Corps value: "commitment." Although the curriculum presented was secular and there's no direct relationship between Christianity and the Marine Corps's motto of "honor, courage, commitment," the fact that it was a chaplain teaching the class meant that both the United States and the Marine Corps were being sacralized.

In Herspring's analysis, religion has historically been a very effective source of motivation in militaries. In ancient times, brute coercion or the promise of plunder sufficed. But in modern societies, ideological by nature and dependent on conscripts, new ways had to be found to motivate citizen soldiers to lay down their lives for a cause, be it democracy, the *Volk*, proletarian internationalism, or freedom.[60] The last term in this list, *freedom*, is crucial. According to Robert Wuthnow, "freedom, rather than religious values, serves as the guiding principle which requires no additional justification or definition" and provides "an excellent value with which to legitimate the American way of life."[61] In character guidance classes and at public ceremonies, military chaplains hold up both freedom and democracy as defining of America and as favored by God.[62] They've been at this for a long time: during the American Revolution, for example, the secretary of war said a chaplain, "besides his religious functions, should impress on the minds of the youth, at stated periods, in concise discourses, the eminent advantages of free governments to the happiness of society."

Conveying that America has God's favor and is worth sacrificing for is something most chaplains, professionally attuned to such questions, do quite consciously and willingly. Chaplain Irons felt it was urgently important, restraining himself from launching a tirade about it:

> There are things worth dying for. OK? Many, even in our House and Senate today, would say there maybe aren't things worth dying for. Because liberalism ultimately leads to that road. But I won't preach that to you here [punctuates with a handclap]. So I think in the military there is that, you know . . . When that's taken away from the Marine Corps, God help us, because if there's anybody who needs to think there's things worth dying for it is marines who will be asked to do that one day. (Southern Baptist)

Wuthnow makes a distinction between liberal and conservative civil religion. The "fracture line" between the two reflects "inherent tensions between symbols expressing the unique identity of a nation and those which associate the nation with a broader vision of humanity," with the conservative version stressing what the United States has to offer the world and the liberal version stressing the United States as an equal and virtuous participant in the world community.[63] In these terms, military chaplains mainly promote conservative civil religion. Their constant identification of the United States with freedom and democracy, the flags on their uniforms, and most of all their dedication to the American Constitution that is acted out in their oath of office illustrate the point. If chaplains didn't celebrate the United States as uniquely important, they would risk undermining the military's demands for extreme sacrifices. In the 1990s under Clinton, it may have been easier to see strands of liberal civil religion in the US military, since it was used for a variety of humanitarian interventions generally accepted by the international community. But during the George W. Bush administration, narrow national self-interest in defiance of world opinion became the norm, making civil religion all the more important. As Coles puts it, "Practical interests, such as securing oil supplies and military bases . . . are often insufficient to arouse public compliance, let alone active support, for a risky military action, but the apparent truths conveyed in the country's civil religion serve to dress those interests up in transcendent clothing."[64]

Silencing the Prophetic Voice

Religious rhetoric and religious leaders also have the potential to strip such sacred cover away. Since the Enlightenment, secular elites have tended to notice and bemoan religion's conservative tendencies. However, the fact that religion can be a powerful source of legitimation shouldn't blind anyone to its radical potential.[65] While it is true that few armies have gone to war without claiming divine approval and that rulers often claim the nation is favored by God, every religion that posits a reality and source of truth located in a distinct and sacred realm is potentially disruptive. This includes civil religion as long as it describes the nation as "under" God and not divine in and of itself. All it takes is for one prophetic voice to point out that in light of sacred, eternal truth a war is fought for "merely worldly" aims and the ruler is a "mere mortal," and legitimacy is threatened.[66] This theological tension between the Kingdom of God and the Kingdom of Man has a sociological corollary, which Robert Bellah has called "the religio-political problem." He argues that the polity "deals obviously with ultimate things" because "with respect to both internal deviants and external enemies, political authority has claimed the right to make life-and-death-decisions." Tension with religion, which also concerns itself with ultimate things, is thus always a possibility.

A few insightful scholars discuss the problem of chaplains' relationships to their churches being strained when the latter tend toward pacifism, but don't consider the problem of chaplains themselves deliberately or inadvertently posing a religious challenge to the very legitimacy of the military.[67] In principle, any chaplain could criticize the military's leadership, methods, or missions as incompatible either with their particular religious tradition or with America's role in God's plan for humanity. In practice, the military's active support for its chaplaincies demonstrates that the religio-political problem isn't believed to be a severe one. Why don't military leaders seem to fear prophetic criticism from their chaplains? How can the military be sure that when push comes to shove and then to war, religion in general and chaplains in particular will benefit the military and its missions?

Even if chaplains have misgivings about what the military does as private citizens or as clergy, as officers they are not in a position to offer criticism. If commanding officers do something wrong that falls within the chaplains' professional area of expertise or concern, for example, something that would hurt their own troops' morale or something that would violate ethical norms in treatment of civilians, a chaplain with the courage of his convictions could privately confront and try to correct them. But a public condemnation would be disloyal and perhaps even criminal within the military. As officers, chaplains are not supposed to comment on national policy. It is axiomatic that a secure democracy must have armed forces subservient to civilian leadership, which makes it wrong for the commissioned military hierarchy to dissent. If chaplains seem to assent to unholy actions, it's not necessarily because they are dependent on the military for their livelihood or compromising to protect their careers. More likely, it is because they understand that the prophetic voice, whether grounded in civil religion or religion proper, is muted by the necessary depoliticization of the professional officer corps. Chaplains may also calculate that in times of controversy and peril, "their" sailors and marines will need them more than ever and that they can do more good devoting their time to serving them than to engaging in politics.

In interviews, most chaplains were careful not to express personal opinions on current events, such as operations in Iraq and Afghanistan. Those who did stray across such topics made their points obliquely with abstraction or historical analogy or by invoking "a friend of mine who might say" something critical. There were also occasions where chaplains signaled their opinion about a policy with facial expressions or hand gestures—that is, without actually saying anything verbally. Keep in mind, though, that this happened in conversation with an outsider. For military insiders, the chaplains' mere presence can be interpreted as a tacit endorsement of the institution: if the chaplain is along for the ride, then the trip must be righteous.

Self-selection likely also makes chaplains safe to have around. Pacifist and antinationalist clergy are less likely to volunteer to become chaplains in the first place. Anne Loveland has documented a decline of mainline chaplains during the unpopular Vietnam War, and there's no reason to think the wars in Iraq and Afghanistan would be lesser deterrents to clergy opposed to war.[68] That doesn't mean that chaplains are glib about war—far from it. Compared to younger enlisted who relish fighting because they want to look tough, chaplains are far more mature and quite often express sentiments to the effect that part of their job is to make sure no one takes killing lightly. If chaplains endorse a mission, it's hardly ever in knee-jerk fashion. Chaplain Mace (Seventh Day Adventist) had thought through the mission in Iraq and decided he was for it. "I'm speaking for myself, but I see the war as a just war" he said, then going on to describe Saddam Hussein as an "evil dictator" and suggesting the possibility that God had used the United States as "His arm of justice."

Anyone applying for conscientious-objector status is required to see his or her chaplain for a formal assessment of whether the application is sincere or whether conscience is being used as an excuse to get out of the military. I asked Chaplain Hamoud if he had met any Muslim personnel who had religious qualms about fighting fellow Muslims in the Middle East. He said he'd had two such incidents in just the past few weeks. One immigrant conscientious-objector applicant, referred to Chaplain Hamoud by another chaplain, seemed set to have his application approved by the command. In Chaplain Hamoud's opinion, however, this individual wasn't really motivated by conscience but was "basically homesick" and "wanted some company":

> I brought him to this area and then to some of the mosques and I introduced him to some [people with the same ethnicity as the applicant], people in the community, and people from his own native country. And then the *Eid* came. We ended Ramadan, the month of Ramadan ended and then *Eid* came, and he spent some time with them. And I explained to him the way I'm explaining to you, about bridging, about America and cultural awareness. And I explained to him, "This is what America has to offer to you also." Over a number of times I gave him the picture that "you are here for a reason, you are not here by an accident. You pick yourself up, you've improved yourself education-wise, you have a solid background in Islam, and your awareness is very solid. Spend some time here, a couple years, and improve yourself, you can be an integral part of our society. And you will be doing what I am doing also, as far as bridging the gap in understanding." So he changed his mind. (Muslim)

What Chaplain Hamoud did here was take the focus off the individual's generalized qualms about war against other Muslims and successfully pitch someone on the verge of leaving the military the idea that he could serve himself and Islam by staying in the military and helping the chaplain build bridges. No one should suspect Chaplain Hamoud of being naively used by the military or of "selling out" to the institution. Time and time again throughout his interview, he expressed his excitement that in the military he could "try to explain to Americans what Islam is about and try to explain to Muslims what America is about." That enlisting a "new" recruit in this idealistic venture meant that the military got to keep one of its warriors was a happy confluence of his and the institution's agendas.

In addition to helping retention, chaplains can boost morale through their counseling sessions. As Hutcheson puts it, "troops who are well-integrated persons, internally at peace (in other words, persons with religious convictions), and with strong core values, are better citizens of the military community and better fighters."[69] It is revealing that Hutcheson assumes religious conviction makes troops internally at peace rather than causing them to struggle with themselves or their profession. Chaplains are unlikely to stir up that kind of trouble as they work to keep troops sober, sane, and ethically alert, promoting troops that the military and civilian worlds alike would prefer to troops who are addicted, suicidal, and vicious. If warriors are to feel good about themselves and if society as a whole is to feel good about its warriors, then the chaplains' work is indispensable. It is, after all, not long ago that American military personnel was held in contempt by civilian elites.

During the Vietnam War, Peter Berger and Daniel Pinard studied the educational materials chaplains used in character guidance classes and concluded that they projected an image of "the morally OK individual" and that chaplains, by promoting "wholesomeness" to military personnel, helped the enlisted to see themselves as precisely that—"morally OK." As Berger and Pinard describe it, "The wholesome soldier is physically and morally healthy. He is clean-cut, dependable, honest. At the same time, he is tough . . . His toughness is never sadism or fanaticism. If he has to kill, he does so reluctantly . . . Also, the wholesome soldier practices the democratic virtues. He votes and takes an interest in the political system, in an attitude of generally positive acceptance of the latter. Very importantly, he is tolerant of other religions and races."[70]

Chaplain Hamoud's agenda and advice is clearly a development and continuation of this "morally OK" theme. In another Vietnam-era study, Arlene Kaplan Daniels coined the term "captive professionals" to describe the Army's psychiatrists. Like chaplains, psychiatrists represent the intrusion of an external, potentially subversive and more humane set of values into the military. The term *captive professionals* applies to experts who are dependent on and constrained by the institutions they work in so that there is uncertainty of whether it is the individual or the organization that is their "true" client. She found that psychiatrists were gradually transformed from "counseling agents" into "controlling agents" and that the military's definition of the situation usually prevailed. This was true even in clinical situations, where the military could override professional diagnoses of anxiety and depression with its own definition, malingering.[71]

My own research suggests that as a group, chaplains are also captive and subservient to the military institution, so that no matter how much they enrich and ennoble the lives of the individuals they meet there, they do so within the constraints set by the Navy, Marine Corps, Army, or Air Force. This finding is not new. As far back as 1957, Waldo Burchard studied chaplains' role tensions, hypothesizing that "the chaplain serves as interpreter of the core values of the organization, helps resolve value-dilemmas of individual service men, and helps promote smooth operation of the military organization." Although he wished he had more data on the subject, he concluded that "such data as are available indicate that the hypothesis is tenable" because "if a service man were in doubt about the morality of military activity, a majority of the respondents would endeavor to assure him that his relationship with God would not suffer thereby." In Burchard's view, character guidance programs are "direct attempt[s] on the part of chaplains to 'sell' military life to service men."[72] On questions of war and peace, faith and violence, chaplains are either unwilling or unable to effectively challenge the military's definitions of the situation.

CIVIL RELIGION AND RELIGIOUS PARTICULARITY

If chaplains subordinate themselves to the military, or are subordinated by it, is there any reason to believe they have been reduced to generic religious practitioners, exploited as symbols to serve a lowest common denominator religiosity? Dressed in officers' uniforms, chaplains advance a civil religion that is inclusive and inoffensive, preaching a spirituality that is bland and generic compared to the particular faith groups they represent and draw on in the worship services they provide. The obvious reason for this is that the military needs to integrate a large number of people who are diverse, not just in terms of race, class, gender, and sexuality, but also in religious affiliation. The institution would be weakened if it wasn't able to get its members to accept a shared ethos.

Contributors to the volume in which Berger and Pinard wrote about the morally OK individual argued that chaplains had gone from representing "religion in the military" to becoming a "military religion." In fact, this was the volume's subtitle. This was an oversimplification at the time and remains so today. Yes, the military prefers civil religion to religious particularity in some matters, such as public prayer, and it was a former soldier, Dwight D. Eisenhower, who most famously expressed Americans' high valuation of "faith in general" (no pun intended) when he said, "Our government makes no sense unless it's founded in a deeply felt religious faith, and I don't care what it is."[73] But chaplains do care and very successfully facilitate the expression of a great range of religious particularity, while sometimes chafing under what they view as "politically correct" concessions to inclusiveness—for example, in public prayer. That, however, is a discussion for later chapters. A more accurate description of what civil religion is and does is captured by Roberta Coles: its "transcendent symbols" allow it to provide "a set of myths that seek consensus, attempts to provide a sacred canopy to a diverse community, and [give] meaning to the community's existence."[74] The diversity is still there, under the canopy, so to speak, and it would be unfair to imply that chaplains have somehow left their churches or "sold out."

Just as the distinction between the interests of the military and the interests of its individual members can be hard to disentangle, so can it be to discern where religion ends and civil religion begins. According to Bellah, American civil religion contains a "dynamic combination of public form and private meaning," which allows chaplains to proclaim its basic tenets while remaining true to their own convictions and denominational teachings. The civil religion, Bellah adds, is not rigidly defined. It has "no orthodox interpreter, no government-supported school of civil theology, no censor with power to forbid what does not conform. The meaning, inner meaning, is left to private interpretation, to the speech of any man—preacher, politician, poet—who has the power to persuade."

Conveniently for the military, civil religion is denominationally and even religiously neutral. A Muslim chaplain presented me with an Islamic basis for it. He explained that the Koran teaches the "unity of humanity," because of common descent from Adam and Eve, and also favors "strength through diversity," because of a verse in which God says he has "scattered you into nations, tribes, and communities, [so] that you recognize each other" and then compete in virtue. He then continued,

> Now, when I look at America, I see that America on a micro level is what the Almighty intended the world to be, based on this verse. America has people from all continents, all across the world, living and working under one human constitution. It's a human constitution, but still the human constitution upholds human values. Just like from my perspective the Koran, the divine constitution, upholds human values also. This is why I said on a micro level, as a microcosm, America is the example of what the Almighty intended the world to be. The unity of humanity—"One nation under God." The strength through diversity—"We the people." (Chaplain Hamoud)

Just as chaplains drawing on Christian and Jewish imagery do, Chaplain Hamoud makes a distinction between the nation and God (two separate constitutions), all the while stressing their compatibility. American civil religion is flexible enough that even religious minorities can exercise their power to persuade in its terms.

The military does act like a denomination in some ways, hiring and paying clergy, purchasing religious supplies, and maintaining buildings dedicated to worship.[75] At least one of the chaplains I interviewed, Chaplain Oberlin, thought there was even more to it: "I'd say the Navy is a religion. I know for certain that the Marine Corps is a religion. He didn't say it to me, but my predecessor told me that he asked the colonel, 'What religion are you?' 'Marine Corps!' was the answer" (Evangelical Lutheran Church in America).

But the armed forces can't ever be denominations in the full sense. If there ever was a danger of a unique "military religion" emerging, it has passed. For starters, if military authorities tried to dictate the content of religion, for example the content of prayers or sermons, the attempt would approach an establishment of religion while simultaneously violating the free exercise rights of those regulated, and these are rights everyone in the military is sworn to defend. Religion in the military cannot be limited to civil religion. Said Chaplain Irons, "You need civil religion. Civil religion is good, as far as the institution goes, but there's gotta be something more than that" (Southern Baptist).

And there is. The "freedom" and Constitution that civil religion celebrates include both the freedom to believe very unique and "granular" things and the freedom from coercion in matters of faith. When pitched in general terms, then, civil religion actually promotes religious particularity. There wouldn't be much point in putting a Muslim chaplain on a ship to impress Egyptians if the chaplain couldn't be authentically Muslim. The close connection between civil religion and the free exercise of religious particularity may have caused this Freudian slip from Chaplain Kojic: "We're here to uphold the First Command . . . uh, the First Amendment of the Constitution. The freedom of religious expression" (Lutheran Church, Missouri Synod). Granted, these are two words easily minced, but Chaplain Kojic wasn't speaking very fast when he confused them. Without reading too much into it, the slip does illustrate that chaplains are aware of the difference between religion and civil religion and of the sanction given the former by the latter. Chaplain Street agreed with a former mentor's assessment that the military is an inherently secular institution and explained, "Now, because it's secular you have an array of faiths and an array of traditions and an array of cultures there. And it just so happens that our Constitution gives this caveat that everyone should worship God as he or she sees fit" (African Methodist Episcopal).

Chaplains don't just view protecting the free exercise of religion as something Americans in general should do or something that officers in general should do because they have sworn to defend the Constitution. Chaplains know that it is their specific responsibility. Chaplain Koch said, "It's important to have a chaplain on active duty [. . .] because we become the advocate for those who want to practice their religious faith. Because it is a clause that's in the First Amendment to the Constitution, a constitutionally guaranteed right. We must provide for it. As well as we can, understanding that we're a military machine, we're trying to win" (United Methodist).

CONCLUSION

The dilemma of divided loyalties looms large on first approach to the military chaplaincy. Understandably, outsiders wonder how two institutions as different in their priorities and values as religion and the military can be reconciled. A closer look reveals that role conflicts generally resolve themselves in favor of the military and that chaplains identify with the institution, care about its members, and usually approve of its missions.

While military personnel surrender some of their basic rights when they enlist, such as the right to trial by jury, the right to free exercise of religion is not one they have to give up. Allowing military personnel to worship as they please, or almost as they please, while in uniform is considered helpful for recruitment and retention, as well as for morale. The question then becomes how much freedom and what kind of exercise can the military permit religiously oriented personnel?

Military chaplains play an important role in determining this, but not just because they have relevant expertise. They are directly involved in helping as many people as possible practice their religion as freely as possible because, like the nation they serve, their own corps is justified by how well it protects religious particularity. How this came about and its implications for the practical accommodation of religion in the military is the subject of the next chapter, in which the dilemmas of legitimacy and diversity come into sharper focus.

CHAPTER 2

ACCOMMODATING AND LIMITING RELIGION IN THE MILITARY

> Congress shall make no law respecting an establishment of religion, or prohibiting the free exercise thereof.
>
> —First Amendment to the United States Constitution[1]

YOU DON'T LOSE YOUR RIGHT TO FREE exercise of religion when you enlist. A Department of Defense directive acknowledges that it "places a high value on the rights of members of the Military Services to observe the tenets of their respective religions" and proposes some guidelines as to how the religious needs of military personnel should be met,[2] and a Navy Instruction recognizes that "religion can be as integral to a person's identity as one's race or sex."[3] Both stipulate that because military commanders operate in such different settings and have such different missions, decisions about accommodating free exercise must be considered individually and made locally. Defense policy assumes that religious particularity can be helpful for the military because it is easier to recruit and retain when individuals' deepest value commitments are acknowledged and respected. Showcasing respect for religious freedom is also considered good public relations, as the military represents the United States internationally.

The best available statistics on the religious affiliation of military personnel are summarized in an issue paper from the Military Leadership Diversity Council, or MLDC. The paper reports findings from two separate sources. One is a survey conducted by the Defense Equal Opportunity Management Institute (DEOMI) and the other from the Defense Manpower Data Center's (DMDC) collected self-reports from new recruits to the military. Both sources agree that Catholics are the largest faith group in the military, at 20.11 percent or 20.22 percent, respectively. This remarkable consistency probably reflects the fact that Catholics tend to know they're Catholic and identify themselves as such. Both also show that Baptists are the second biggest group, at 17.56 percent (DEOMI) or 13.88 percent (DMDC).

Among Protestants, boundaries aren't as clear. Many people may not closely identify with a traditional denomination, preferring nondenominational congregations, or may simply not know what the difference between a Methodist and Episcopalian is. This probably helps explain a big discrepancy between the two data sources in that DMDC reports 19.56 percent of military personnel belonging to the "other Christian" category, while DEOMI only has 3.28 percent "other Christian." Another partial explanation may be that the DEOMI survey was voluntary, so subjects who "know what they are" may have been more likely to respond. In any case, the DEOMI report has consistently higher figures for specific Protestant denominations than the DMDC report. Adding all the individually measured denominations (e.g., Lutheran and Presbyterian) to "other Christian" and "other Protestant" makes the percentage of Christians in the military who are neither Catholic nor Baptist 28.19 (DEOMI) and 35.15 (DMDC). A reasonably accurate gloss would report that the military is 20 percent Catholic, 15 percent Baptist, and 30 percent other Christian. What, then, are the remaining 35 percent?[4]

The fastest growing group, in terms of numbers, is that with "no religious preference," a group that scholars of religion call "nones." Compared to surveys of all Americans' religious preferences, also reported in the MLDC white paper, nones are overrepresented in the military, at 25.5 percent (DEOMI) or 19.55 percent (DMDC), because the Pew Forum on Religion and Public Life estimates that only 12.1 percent of all Americans are nones. This probably reflects the age structure of the military, since young people, and especially unmarried young people, are more likely to be unchurched.[5]

The numbers of military personnel claiming a religious preference that is not Christian is small. Listing the percentages from DEOMI before those from DMDC, the percentage of Jewish personnel is 1.09 and 0.32, Muslims 0.45 and 0.25, Pagan 1.18 and 0.17, Eastern 0.87 and 0.42, and "Less common"—a category that includes Native American, Baha'i, and Scientology—1.19 and 0.62. Excluding nones and self-identified Humanists, the picture of the military that emerges is one where Christians outnumber religious minorities by nearly 14 to 1 according to DEOMI and by more than 35 to 1 according to DMDC.[6] It is worth reiterating that the DMDC figures are based on recruits, who may be under more pressure to conform to Christian norms and less likely to assert membership in a minority faith than the more settled and self-selected respondents to the DEOMI survey.[7] Two more general caveats are that many who state a religious preference may not be very devout at all, and many who don't state a preference may still be very spiritual.

It is a bedrock principle of American jurisprudence that rights attach to individuals regardless of the size of their community. Members of small and unpopular religions have the same rights as those who belong to bigger and popular ones. Fortunately, when the military tries to look after the rights of both religious minorities and the Christian majority, it is aided by Americans' widely shared agreement on and commitment to tolerance.[8] Religious minorities often benefit from the fact that Christianity itself is internally diverse. Some Christian groups, such as Catholics and Mormons, have been persecuted in the past and still feel misunderstood, so that they identify with the plight of other minority groups. Mainstream Protestants can be motivated to speak up for minorities by their commitment to freedom of conscience, whether justified in civic or theological terms. Ideally, the military reflects not just the nation's religious diversity but also the broad-based tolerance that Americans are justifiably proud of.

Alongside American tolerance of religion there is an equally important commitment to the separation of church and state. Not surprisingly, the existence of chaplains as state-funded clergy has been controversial for a long time. In the 1800s, Baptists petitioned Congress in opposition to military chaplaincy without having much impact.[9] The most serious legal challenge was made in the early 1980s by two Harvard law students who sued the US Army over its chaplaincy. Their position was that several practices inherent to military chaplaincy were unconstitutional because they violated the Establishment Clause of the First Amendment. The case lasted several years and ended without "any clear constitutional mandate" for the chaplaincy, because the plaintiffs grew tired and agreed to drop the suit in return for not having to pay any of the mounting legal costs. The preliminary rulings that were made indicated that the chaplaincy would have survived the challenge because of its long historical standing and because of the court's wish to defer to the legislative branch: as evidenced by its consistency in providing funds, Congress has never seriously questioned the legitimacy of military chaplaincy.[10]

The strategy the Army adopted to defend its chaplaincy is nevertheless important. The Army argued that rather than violating the Establishment Clause, military chaplaincy was essential for the sake of protecting the Free Exercise Clause. Specifically, the Army argued that "having uprooted the soldiers from their natural habitats it owes them a duty to satisfy their Free Exercise rights, especially since the failure to do so would diminish morale, thereby weakening our national defense." Israel Drazin and Cecil Currey, who together assisted the Army's defense, write that "the lengthy litigation . . . caused the chaplaincy to focus as never before on its responsibilities to provide for and defend the rights of soldiers to free exercise of their faith." In their analysis the chaplaincies' "purpose became simple and narrowly defined: to secure free exercise rights for military personnel. The chaplaincy has no other legal purpose."[11] Since then, military chaplains who advocate for the free exercise rights of military personnel are doing more than putting an important American ideal into practice. They are defending the existence of their own corps, insulating it from legal challenge. In the Navy chaplaincy's current Strategic Plan, "successful constitutional challenge" is listed as one of nine risks that the corps might face, alongside "increasingly constrained resources" and "lack of training in additional competencies and skill sets."[12]

PROVIDE, FACILITATE, AND CARE

The armed forces are as explicit about their support for free exercise of religion as they are about the risk of being challenged on establishment grounds. The same Strategic Plan describes the Navy Chaplain Corps as having four "validated capabilities" encompassed under the heading of "religious ministry." Two of them, to care and to advise, were discussed in the previous chapter. The caring capacity is expressed in the chaplains' roles as counselors, as well as in their providing combat casualty ministry and offering memorial observances. The advisory capacity refers to their offering professional recommendations to commanding officers about morale and ethics, training leaders at all levels in cultural awareness and conflict resolution, and "within the boundaries of their noncombatant status . . . the impact of religion on military operations."[13]

That leaves facilitating and providing. In this context *providing* means offering worship services, religious education, and other programs to members of the chaplain's own religious group, while *facilitating* means working to accommodate the religious needs of groups other than his own. In interviews, however, chaplains tended to use the term *facilitate* even when discussing providing for their own. Still, the formal distinction is nicely captured in the traditional (but unofficial) motto, "Chaplains provide for their own, facilitate for others, and care for all."[14] This motto captures the chaplains' understanding of their mission very well. The service they render the military in terms of political socialization or as functionaries of civil religion are incidental; ask any chaplain what he does and he is far more likely to describe it in terms of protecting free exercise of religion and taking care of people.

In general, the rights of individuals must always be balanced against their communities' legitimate interests in social order and rule of law. This is true in the particular case of religious rights in the military, too. As discussed in the previous chapter, religion can be used to promote individual well-being (by counseling) and to create a sense of community (with civil religion), but it can also be subversive or disruptive. This latter potential is especially threatening to total institutions such as the military, which strive for uniformity, regularity, and discipline. Where, when, and how individual religious rights can and must be curtailed for the sake of the institution are questions often decided on the basis of chaplains' professional advice.

The courts have upheld that the military may restrict religion for the sake of military necessity but haven't defined what military necessity is.[15] This is something that has to be worked out "on the ground." What chaplains do is negotiate between the religious needs of individuals and the institution's need for conformity and obedience. When religion is limited, it is usually done for the sake of "good order and discipline," which represents the need to maintain a smoothly operating military force. When chaplains help make religion happen, it is usually referred to as "facilitation," which represents respect for individual rights and individual conscience. Both the word *facilitation* and the phrase *good order and discipline* are part of the chaplains' institutional vocabulary, and together they constitute a "symbolic boundary" that is used to organize social life. In specific terms, religion is facilitated up to the point where it threatens good order and discipline, and the question is where and how the boundary between what can and cannot be facilitated runs.[16]

Both terms, facilitation and good order and discipline, require interpretation. A full understanding of the place of religion in the military can't be based simply on noting that chaplains, as members of a professional community, have agreed that facilitation and good order and discipline are valid parameters. It is also necessary to find out what chaplains believe the terms mean. To accomplish this, I asked each chaplain to explain each of the terms to me "as an outsider" and looked for variations in their answers. I also asked the chaplains to give me examples of each term, to get a picture of which religious practices are considered unproblematic, which are agreed to be out of bounds, and which are contested. Finally, I asked each chaplain about his or her own role in mediating between the facilitation of free exercise of religion and maintaining good order and discipline for the military.

Despite the tendency to use the term *facilitation* for both providing and facilitating, chaplains were quick to point out that there were limits on what they could do. Chaplain Hamoud said, "The rabbi, he cannot run Catholic programs. I mean, he cannot preach Catholic Sunday services. I cannot conduct Protestant services" (Muslim). The three obvious constraints at work here are expertise, authority, and conscience. A rabbi wouldn't have the authority to celebrate a Catholic mass even if he somehow knew how, and an imam couldn't conduct a Protestant service without violating the teachings of his own faith. Chaplains cannot be required to compromise themselves this way, even while facilitating for other faiths. The most common example chaplains gave of this tension is that a Baptist chaplain would never have to baptize an infant and could legitimately refuse to do so if told to.

LOGISTICS AND COLLABORATION

The easiest way to meet the needs of a religious group is to have a chaplain from that group provide for them. For many smaller faith groups, however, that's rarely possible, creating practical headaches for high-ranking chaplains such as Chaplain Farrow, who said,

> I think the difficulty comes down to the numbers. And I say that in the sense of, the rabbis would be difficult because only because like I said there's only like ten or eleven of them in the entire Navy. The Muslims are even harder to support because we only have three right now. So they are in huge geographical areas, one on the east coast, one on the west coast, and one overseas. You know, you end up trying to . . . it's the logistical issue of facilitation more than anything else. [. . .] You know, the problem once again is the location of these guys. It's not that there's not a need, but the need is so thin and spread out all over the world that where do you put them? And they can't really travel all the time, I mean that's not practical and so forth. So anyways, it's just trying to use those resources as best you can. And that's where we really resort to the next level of facilitation, which is lay leaders, or readers. (Catholic)

Lay leaders are enlisted personnel who are authorized by their faith groups to conduct limited religious services. They're often called lay readers because the military prefers that "leadership" be reserved for officers. In any case, military chaplains supervise, train, and support lay leaders after screening them to make sure they're responsible and reliable. Chaplain Drozdov described his Jewish, Islamic, and Protestant lay leaders as part of his team because "they're providing the end of ministry that I cannot deliver" (Eastern Orthodox). Chaplain Koch described the lay leader's role more concretely, emphasizing cooperation between the laity and the chaplains: "We have lay Eucharistic ministers for the Catholic personnel to conduct services, lay lead services with consecrated hosts that they receive from a priest prior to deploying. I coordinate that and make sure they have the time and spaces in order to do that, and publicize and work with them to facilitate their ministry" (United Methodist).

Sometimes it's difficult to recruit lay leaders. Chaplain Feteris (Presbyterian) blamed the hectic nature of life at sea, which made enlisted lay people reluctant to volunteer. Not everyone who volunteers is a good choice, either. According to Chaplain Squires, it's important to "make sure they're the right type of sailor. They are a good example of their faith. And that they're qualified. To train them and make sure that they are fully supported in leading these worship services [. . .] And we do ask for letters from the church, faith group that they go to. The synagogue or the mosque. To make sure that this is not some kind of lone wolf or some self-anointed pastor" (Catholic).

Without a designated lay leader, a minority religious community can suffer. One of the larger bases where I conducted interviews used to have a regular meeting of several dozen Wiccans. The group dissolved when their lay leader was transferred across country and no replacement could be found.

When a ship or base has several chaplains, they refer sailors among themselves in order to find the one best equipped to meet his or her denominationally specific needs. Speaking of his colleagues, a young Mormon chaplain said,

> If an LDS serviceman walks into their office, they will try to get him into contact with me [. . .] so if a Catholic comes in and needs some specific Catholic guidance or needs some help with . . . I don't just say, "Hey, you need to talk to a Catholic chaplain." I'll call up and say, "Hey, can you see this guy, make an appointment with him?" [. . .] So I try to facilitate for that instead of just saying, "I can't help you, go talk to a Catholic chaplain." I'll try to call for them or at least give them the phone number and his name, and where they work, so they can get in contact. (Chaplain Moore, LDS)

Chaplain Oberlin, a member of the Evangelical Lutheran Church in America, talked about how he would stay and pray with a very sick Catholic patient while waiting for a priest to arrive and administer sacraments. Generally, he said, when dealing with "things that are specific to Judaism" or "specific to Islam" he would "find a person of that faith."

Cooperation, respect, and communication among chaplains is clearly important if everyone's religious needs are to be met in the military. As one of the senior Catholic priests put it, "We really are a corps. We cannot get on and do our job without the assistance of others. And it makes it a very important fact that we trust in each other. That I can have absolute certitude that if a Baptist goes to an Orthodox Christian priest, he is going to send him, once the problem emerges, to a person who can take care of him" (Chaplain Gunvant).

While conducting the interviews, I witnessed chaplains both receive and make phone calls to refer "cases" among themselves and also to ask advice from chaplains at other bases about how to provide for a specific religious need. On the phone, chaplains would ask their colleagues whether the sailor they "sent your way last week" ever showed up or to jokingly complain that another one of "your kids" stopped by. I was impressed by these examples of informal collegiality and care for the needs of individuals. They are worth keeping in mind when, in a later chapter, I describe conflicts among chaplains, including allegations that some chaplains don't adequately respect religious commitments different from their own. Without being able to quantify the relative prevalence of positive and negative interactions, my impression is that the positive ones are normative. Of course there are occasional frustrations. For example, Chaplain Irons (Southern Baptist) was irritated that he couldn't get hold of the Muslim imam he needed[17] to endorse some lay leaders, because he couldn't "get him on email."

I witnessed expressions of affection, mutual respect, and camaraderie among chaplains frequently, and they struck me as sincere. The chaplains teased each other, shared jokes with religious themes, and laughed together in ways that testified to their *esprit de corps*.[18] On one occasion, a Protestant chaplain picked up the phone to call a Catholic colleague and ask if he wanted to be in my study. Listening for a while, then covering the mouthpiece with his hand, he reported, "He says he'll meet you, but only if he can eat, and he says to tell you that all the Protestants are going to hell." This positive tone surely makes it easier for chaplains to take care of each other's congregants. Chaplain Drozdov, an Eastern Orthodox Christian, was very pleased with how his flock was treated by Protestants: "For five years there was no Orthodox priest here, but we had this chapel that the congregation was meeting in to do lay services. And the Protestant chapel pastors would look in on them just to say, 'You get everything you need? Can we get you anything?'"

Time and Space for Religion

One of the most basic needs religious groups in the military have is a time and space to meet. In civilian life and on many military bases, this is easily arranged, but deployed Navy ships are extremely crowded and the operational tempo in combat areas can be intense. Part of chaplain's facilitation is persuading supervisors to let their Jewish, Seventh Day Adventist, and Muslim workers have their specific day of worship off. In exchange, explained Chaplain Cugrijus, "They may have to work on Sunday when everybody else has Sunday off, but that's not unreasonable to ask for" (Mormon).

On large bases and ships, chaplains help unattached believers find coreligionists by advertising services. Chaplain Clement recalled how he took care of "his" Mormons at sea:

> For me one personal example of facilitating would be my LDS guys. When I was on the ship, I had a group of probably fifteen LDS men on my ship and they wanted to have studies. I made sure that they literally had a place and time in the chapel for doing their services, and we actually typed up a schedule for the chapel that went into what we call the Plan of the Week for the ship. It's basically a newsletter that goes out and lets everybody on the ship know what's going on and when it's going on and where. And they would be right there in the schedule with the Protestant service, the Catholic service, and there's LDS, there's Jewish, and there are Muslim services. So those are ways we facilitate. One is we put the information out there: "Hey, this service is offered." (United Methodist)

On one of the bases where I interviewed chaplains, there were more than a dozen different worship services advertised at the chapel. When stationed on a base or when in port near a major city, chaplains also have the option of referring sailors and marines to the civilian community. Chaplain Clement continued his recollections about helping Mormons: "I send a report out prior to coming into port that requests an LDS pastor if there is one in the city, to come to the ship to do an LDS service. Or to find out where an LDS congregation is meeting. So that I can inform these young men, 'OK, here's an LDS service that's being held at this place and I've already locked down transportation for you if you want to go'" (United Methodist).

Not all chaplains are equally proactive. Many complain of "lazy" colleagues or predecessors who give chaplains a bad name among the enlisted. When asked about practical things they would do or had done for other religious groups, Chaplains Metzger, Cugrijus, and Szmatula illustrated the range of effort they might make. Chaplain Metzger simply said, "I would give them the address of their particular faith group; phone number" (Chaplaincy of Full Gospel Churches). Chaplain Cugrijus (LDS) told me about a time he had checked a "government pickup truck" out to a Jewish sailor so he could travel sixty miles to the nearest city and "worship in the synagogue there." Chaplain Szmatula went further than the other two and actually drove: "I had a Jewish marine. And he had no way of getting to the synagogue, on the other side of the island, so for two Fridays I drove him to the synagogue on the other side of the island. That's facilitating ministry. And then finally a couple from [the base] said, 'Well, we can take him to synagogue with us every Friday night.' So making sure the spiritual needs of your people are met" (Lutheran Church, Missouri Synod). The practicality of these kinds of solutions depends on where you are, of course. Although there are apparently a number of Russian Orthodox congregations to visit in northern Japan, Buddhist temples are probably scarce in Saudi Arabia. When deployed, most religious services have to be provided by the chaplains themselves, with help from lay leaders.

RELIGIOUS MATERIALS AND FOOD

Chaplains help provide the physical objects that religious groups need for their worship. As I raised the issue of facilitation with Chaplain Chance, he paused to write a note to himself before continuing: "We have a couple of Muslim guys, and we give them a place to pray three times a day. And we'll buy them prayer rugs and stuff like that. It's one of the things I've got to do as a matter of fact. I've got to figure out these little woven rugs that they get down and pray on" (Evangelical Lutheran Church in America). Although Chaplain Chance didn't know how to obtain the rugs off the top of his head, the military has made a lot of this kind of practical information available to its chaplains online, which makes their work much easier. If the answers aren't available there, another possibility is to try to call one of the Muslim chaplains and ask their advice.

Deployments and major holidays require advance planning for the needs of his crew. United Methodist chaplain Koch would help his Catholic and Jewish sailors: "If we're going to be out for Passover, I would make sure that I had solo Seder kits, so they could conduct a Passover Seder. I made sure that my wine stock included sacramental wine for them, kosher wine. I also have to have sacramental wine for the Catholics, so that if I were able to get a Catholic priest on board and he was to conduct a mass, he would have the host and the wine to do it."

While the needs of Jews, Catholics, and even Muslims are easy to anticipate, chaplains sometimes encounter requests for accommodation from groups they're not familiar with. Chaplain Cugrijus helped a Native American with a Shoshone ritual: "He wanted his medicine bag. Little buckskin bag, about that big, and it had a small eagle's feather attached to it on a cord, and it was full of cattail pollen. Part of his . . . they do a cleansing ceremony, and it's basically go out and meditate, and you open the bag, you take the feather, dip it in the pollen and you wipe your brows, the bridge of your nose and your eyebrows, Just a couple places on your body. It's a symbolic purification." Unfortunately, this individual was subject to some secular purification as well; he was in the brig. According to Chaplain Cugrijus, the guards "went nuts" because they wouldn't know what was in the bag and worried that it might be used to smuggle drugs in under the cover of religious freedom. So the chaplain had to negotiate: "I said, 'Give me the bag.' I put it in my desk drawer. I said, 'Look, when you need to perform this ritual, come and see me.' So he'd come. He came twice in about eight months. In my office, I just let him in my office and closed the door. He'd be there for about five or ten minutes, he'd come out and say, 'Thank you very much,' and he came to Protestant services every Sunday" (Mormon).

Chaplains can be faced with requests for accommodation that contradict their own deeply held beliefs and morals. Chaplain Clement seemed to have put a lot of thought into what to do about Satanists:

> Currently there are no Satanist priests that are chaplains in the military. However, you can run into young men and women in your unit who will tell you, "Hey, I'm a Satanist and these are the things I need to do a Satanist service." Well, I can facilitate that person, when it fits the operational readiness of the unit, by finding him a place to do his service. If he needs chalices, if he needs wine, if he needs different articles to do his service, I can provide that for him. That's facilitating him with his spiritual needs. Where that would cross a line would be for him to say, "I need you to do prayers at my Satanist service." Then I'm, like, "No, I'm not going to do that." (United Methodist)

This quote pulls together points already made about chaplains not having to violate their own convictions and the importance of physical space, and it also previews the topic of good order and discipline. Notice that Chaplain Clement is only willing to help the Satanist "when it fits the operational readiness of the unit." This is, of course, an extreme example. Most of the time, most chaplains are willing to facilitate for most of the religious needs of their crews. Chaplain Feteris, for example, was carrying a prayer rug for the one Muslim in his battalion with his own equipment because the enlisted are very limited in what they can carry with them. In addition, he said, "I provide some of the religious accoutrements or items of different faith groups. I've got books of Mormon, I've got Jewish prayer books, I've got yarmulkes. [. . .] If a sailor or marine wants to worship green frogs on flat rocks, I'll get him the flat rocks, but I'm not leading the worship service" (Presbyterian). Chaplains also help sailors and marines with specific dietary needs. The military has both kosher and halal Meals Ready to Eat (MREs), wrapped in individual pouches, and it's the chaplain's job to make sure his or her unit deploys with the right kinds and amounts of religiously appropriate MREs.

Sometimes Jewish or Muslim personnel are given extra money, called "com rats" so that they can purchase their own food rather than eating in the common cafeteria. Chaplain Feteris remembered having to go "head to head" with a commanding officer about this, because the CO was reluctant to disburse the funds and questioned the sincerity of the sailor's faith. Chaplain Geschka could recall an incident where he thought that kind of suspicion was valid: "We had a young man that was requesting com rats because he was Muslim . . . and my colonel had sloughed it off as being he was a 'com rat Muslim.' He just wanted, he wanted the bucks, he wanted to eat off base. And I think, after consultation with the Muslim chaplain here, I think we determined that no, this kid was just wanting to get the extra money" (Catholic).

Probably the most creative example of facilitation that I came across was given by Chaplain Szmatula. Four Jewish sailors got caught between the requirements of their faith and their commitment to the military when an important ceremony that required them to wear their white Navy uniforms "fell on the one Jewish holiday where they can't wear leather." By way of background, the Navy's black shoes are made of plastic, while the white shoes worn with the white uniform only come in leather. The chaplain explained,

> I called the endorsing agent for the Jewish faith, and he said, "I will waive that restriction for them that day." But they were so conservative they said, "Well, we don't care what the endorsing agent says, it goes against our faith and we're not going to do it." And so the [military authority] said, "Well, then they're not going to participate in the ceremony." So I said, "What if I painted their plastic shoes white?" I had a picture, but I had to put it away. So I painted their shoes white with spray paint, and they were able to participate. (Lutheran Church, Missouri Synod)

BEING GENERAL IN SERVICE OF PARTICULARITY

To be effective facilitators for other people's religious needs, chaplains have to partially bracket the preferences they have for their own faith group. Chaplain Gunvant, a high ranking chaplain who had both recruited and trained other chaplains, summarized the advice he would give to aspirants: "If you don't like Jewish folk you may want to think of attending synagogue. If you have doubts about Muslims, you may want to attend a mosque. Because if you can't, if you can't understand and support them in the same way that you would support one of your own faith, this is not an organization you want to be in" (Catholic).

Interestingly, the military expects its chaplains to be broad-minded, ecumenical, and general in their approach to ministry so that it can accommodate all the narrow, stubborn, particular needs of the enlisted. This posture comes more easily to some chaplains than to others. In any case, the chaplains do have to be able to justify this to themselves, because in addition to being full-fledged members of the military as officers, they are also representatives of their own particular denominations or faith groups. Some, including Chaplain Michaud, justify facilitating for others by explaining that it's a job requirement and that they don't have to compromise their own beliefs. Michaud explained that letting everyone, including "our own," worship in a similar way to what they were used to was a matter of Navy instructions and that, with regard to others' beliefs, "in no way do we have to officiate, not support what they believe in" (Baptist General Conference). Far more often, though, the chaplains invoked cherished ideals and the Constitution. For Chaplain Giraldo, this was reason enough to help others: "I have come to terms in my own mind that in order to be effective in my own role as a chaplain that I have no problem facilitating for people of other faiths and faith groups. Including the White Wiccan. I have accepted that, I have internalized the principle that we find in the Constitution of the United States. To help people have the right to freedom of religion" (Evangelical Church Alliance).

Chaplain Feteris, a Presbyterian, similarly invoked the Constitution, adding, "I take that very seriously." Chaplain Clement, still worrying about Satanists, explained how the chaplain's role helped him overcome his qualms: "I'm a little uncomfortable with the Satanists. I'm a little uncomfortable doing that. But I do it. Because that's part of what my charge is, and that's what I vowed to do. Because every person, regardless of their faith group, is guaranteed by the Constitution the opportunity to practice their religion. And that's what we do. We're the safe keepers of that within the military" (United Methodist).

Chaplain Koch, also a United Methodist, also mentioned the vow he took "just like every other officer and person that's in the military" to support and defend the Constitution, even when he's "absolutely 180 degrees away from what a person believes that comes to me and asks me to facilitate." He could "freely facilitate" because "that's their constitutionally guaranteed right, OK?" Chaplain Timu, who belongs to the Disciples of Christ, made the same point as Chaplain Koch, while Chaplain Kojic joined Chaplain Michaud in pointing to Navy instructions. Chaplain Street mentioned the Constitution but also seemed to be thinking of what was best for the Chaplain Corps itself: "We know as Christians there's other sheep not of this fold, and that there are people who will not be of your flock. And that to facilitate for their needs, their constitutional rights, is so crucial to the whole command religious program. To the survival of it. Because it is a right. Facilitation is a right" (African Methodist Episcopal). Another way of combining high ideals and self-interest emerged in Chaplain Kanaridis's answer: "Anybody can worship anything they want, you know? I'll give them that freedom. I'll fight for their freedom to do that, because in my fighting for their freedom I'm saving my freedom" (Conservative Baptist).

CHAPLAINS AND COMMANDING OFFICERS

In 1974 the federal courts ruled in a case called *Parker v. Levy* that even though "members of the military are not exempted from the protection granted by the First Amendment, the different character of the military community and of the military mission requires different application of these protections."[19] That ruling, which effectively says "if practical" to the free exercise of religion in the military, serves as background for Department of Defense Directive 1300.17, which says requests for religious accommodation have to be evaluated on a case by case basis. Navy policy puts the responsibility for free exercise of religion on a base or ship with the commanding officer, because it is he or she who can best decide what the needs of the "military mission" are. Secretary of the Navy Instruction 1730.8A said, "Department of the Navy policy is to accommodate the doctrinal or traditional observances of the religious faith practiced by individual members when these doctrines or observances will not have an adverse effect on military readiness, individual or unit readiness, unit cohesion, health, safety, or discipline . . . Accommodation of a member's religious practices cannot be guaranteed at all times but must depend on military necessity. Determination of necessity rests entirely with the commanding officer."[20]

The fact that final authority over free exercise lies with the CO is important to chaplains for two reasons. First of all, it gives them some protection as a corps against charges of establishment or discrimination. Basically, if someone is denied the right to exercise their religion, they won't have chaplains to blame, but the CO. Second, it means that chaplains, in order to be effective advocates for freedom of religion, have to have a good relationship with the CO. Both Chaplains Gunvant and Mace discussed the boundaries of their authority and the commanding officer's. They said, respectively,

> Now, the commander can't make a decision about doctrine, you know, liturgical practice, or the practice of the churches, preaching, all of those things. But the commander can make a decision as to time of day, or day, frequency, place, availability, policy with regard to I don't know . . . Any number of things. [. . .] I do not decide, for example, that divine service will be a ten o'clock on Sunday mornings. I may advise the commander that that would be a good time to have it, but if he decides it's going to be on Saturday at ten then that's when it's going to be. (Catholic)

> Well, it's kind of a subjective thing. If the commanding officer wants to have good order and discipline he can put restrictions on his battalion or unit just to keep cohesion. (Seventh Day Adventist)

As for exactly what "good order and discipline" means, there are several different understandings among the chaplains. One Mormon chaplain, Chaplain Frantz, said good order and discipline was about "the state of affairs of the crew's morale." Another Mormon, Chaplain Cugrijus, explained it as anything that violated the Uniform Code of Military Justice, likening breaches to crimes. Chaplain Clement discussed the matter in broader terms, arguing that perfectly legal religious practices may nevertheless run afoul of good order and discipline, because of the military's manifest functions of preparing for and waging war: "Good order and discipline means that the number one job for the military is defending the country. And whatever leads up to going to war, being a deterrent . . . that's what we're calling good order and discipline" (United Methodist). Chaplain Timu thought good order and discipline meant deference to the military's hierarchy: "It has to do with the outfit we work in. Good order and discipline, respect the rank and structure, the chain of command, chain of influence. Mandates and orders. That's good order and discipline" (Disciples of Christ). There didn't seem to be a single shared definition of good order and discipline, even though all chaplains agreed that religion couldn't be allowed to upset it. Chaplain Tzilker probably hit it on the head when he said, " It's whatever the commanding officer feels, which makes it difficult" (Jewish). Good order and discipline, then, is used to prohibit whatever rubs the commanding officer the wrong way. Chaplain Szmatula sighed with amusement as he explained, "Oh, the Navy uses that for a lot of things. [. . .] That's how we keep some kind of whacko faith groups from having their own services aboard a ship, or a station. And that's basically how that's used" (Lutheran Church, Missouri Synod). Chaplain Farrow, who called good order and discipline "a commanding officer's catchall" for getting things done, talked about how all religious services had to be published ahead of time and supervised by someone responsible, so that a commanding officer can say to anyone wanting to organize a meeting, "'Someone from my command will be there, and if you do anything inappropriate, we will shut you down. And [good order and discipline] will be a standard I set for appropriateness. Not for theology, but for appropriateness within the command.' And he can say, 'Well, I will shut it down for good order and discipline'" (Catholic).

Without the principle of good order and discipline to trump religious claims and compel obedience and conformity, the military wouldn't be able to operate as efficiently as it does. Chaplain Moore thought good order and discipline was "very important, because a lot of times people are told to do what they don't really want to do, from sleeping on the floor to sacrificing their life. And anywhere between there. And so they protect that and they guard that, and that's one of the things, being part of this institution, that I have to guard as well" (Mormon). Chaplain Irons recalled a Supreme Court Justice saying he couldn't define pornography but knew it when he saw it, and said good order and discipline was just the same: you recognize it when you see it.

Despite variations, the recurring themes in chaplains' explanations of good order and discipline were that it referred to the final decision about something, that it rested with the commanding officer because the command religious program was "his" program, and that it was subjective. Assuming the obvious, that commanding officers can't grant every request for religious accommodation, Huerta and Webb list "the requirements of the unit mission, the environment of operations, and public opinion" as factors commanding officers must consider when deciding what to allow and what to prohibit. A clear, unambiguous definition of good order and discipline would defeat its purpose. It's vague because it has to be in order to be flexible enough for commanding officers to use. In the end, it is the commanding officer who decides which religions are "whacko," for example, and which are not. Chaplain Grams pointed out the irony of putting so much power in the hands of one person: "It's an interesting dilemma, because we as Americans hate a tyranny. We hate it! And yet, here it is. Here is a tyranny collective. It's almost a living contradiction. Maybe like Plato's *Republic*, what do they call it? The despot philosopher king? Where you have this guy who is in charge and you hope he's moral?" (Presbyterian).

Over and over again, the chaplains emphasized that while chaplains were instrumental in providing for the free exercise of religion, curtailing it was something the CO did, not them. It was especially senior chaplains who made the point. Chaplain Drozdov (Eastern Orthodox) said that "the chaplain is merely the advisor" in such cases, and Chaplain Gunvant said, "Chaplains are never commanding officers. OK? We don't have to be conflicted with choosing to [facilitate] or not to. That's the commanding officer's role. Our role is to advise the commanding officer on that" (Catholic). In light of its sensitivity to constitutional challenge, it's understandable that the Chaplain Corps would disown its role in deciding which religious practices can't be accommodated and which can. As if being state-paid clergy wasn't bad enough, making final distinctions between whacko religion and nonwhacko religion might really smack of establishment.

However, the influence chaplains have over such decisions should not be minimized. Most commanding officers, in addition to being very busy, have only a lay perspective on their own faith, an outsider's perspective on other major faith groups, and may be completely ignorant about minority religions. As a result, they rely on their chaplains for information and analysis of how a requested religious accommodation would affect their command. They are supposed to weigh how important the request is to the person making it, what the effect would be if the accommodation were made repeatedly, and whether there might be other ways to meet the individual's need. Chaplains Moore and Irons provided good descriptions of how they work with commanding officers. They said, respectively,

> I'm his advisor and say, "Hey, this is what they're going to be doing, this is what it might lead to, the impression that others might get." So I would advise him. He makes the final call. [. . .] And that's our specialty as far as knowing what constitutes the different communities, being familiar with some of their . . . or at least becoming familiar when a situation comes up. We become the subject matter experts on both sides. And so we can be a good liaison in explaining and interpreting for both sides. Explaining, for example, to the service member where the military and where the commanding officer is coming from, and explaining to the commanding officer the religious groups and where they're coming from. So we're kind of an interpreter for the different institutions. (Mormon)

> [I have to] make sure I understand what practice they're talking about, what is the meaning behind it, what is the symbolism behind it, what kind of religious objects will they need, will they be using? That kind of thing. And that may mean visiting and watching and being part of it. So I need to be fully informed. I think 80 percent of the battle, or 80 percent of the problem could be ironed out just by the chaplain understanding what's really being asked or what the issue is. And secondly, it means informing the command, as unbiased as possible, what exactly it is they want. To say, "Hey, this is who is here, this is what they want to do, this is what it will mean." Letting the commander know that. Part of the chaplain's role, however, is not just to inform, but to also kind of give him your gut on "this is how I think it will affect the command." Whether good or bad. OK? (Southern Baptist)

Both Chaplain Moore and Chaplain Irons were relatively early in their careers, so their actual encounters with commanding officers might have more *sir*s and *ma'am*s and less *hey* in them. Even so, chaplains have some characteristics that give them some extra clout vis-à-vis their commanders, so that their "gut" is likely to be taken seriously. In addition to their subject matter expertise, chaplains have a source of authority outside the military, in their endorsing faith groups, many of which are quite well organized. A Catholic chaplain, for example, is seen not just as an expert on his faith and on religion in general but also as a representative of a formidable organization. In addition, clergy of any denomination have high social status in American society. What's more, chaplains tend to be old for their rank. This is because they have to attend seminary or the equivalent, earn a master's degree or equivalent, and often have to put some time into serving their faith group as civilians before being allowed to join the chaplaincy. A commanding officer who is used to having the authority of both rank and age with regard to other officers may find that with chaplains, he or she still has a rank advantage but may be addressing an age peer, or even someone older. As Chaplain Townsend explained, "Good order and discipline, a lot of that is just simple common sense stuff. Now, what's common sense for an eighteen year old and what's common sense for a forty-year-old are not highly related, I understand that. But the commanding officer and I are the same age, we're members of the same generation, we look at things pretty much the same way" (Reformed Episcopalian).

Because final authority rests with the CO, chaplains know they have to cultivate rapport with whichever commander they are assigned to. The CO who won't listen to his chaplains, whether out of pride or prejudice, even when they offer sound counsel, is a recurring villain in the "horror stories" chaplains tell. Often, these stories end with the chaplain "winning" after giving his or her superior a lecture on the First Amendment and warning him or her that intransigence might provoke a career-damaging lawsuit and bad publicity. Another common "horror story" is about chaplains who make commanding officers suspicious of or hostile to chaplains because they go "overboard" on crusades against profanity, gambling, or pornography or because they consistently take the side of the enlisted against the command, even when the enlisted are being unreasonable. Jeopardizing good relationships with commanding officers is bad, thought Chaplain Tzilker, who said,

> The chaplain has to have some kind of credibility with the commanding officer. And once credibility is established the commanding officer is most of the time going to trust the chaplain's judgment. The chaplain at the same time has to look at it from the commanding officer's perspective, you know, he has a mission to get done. So the chaplain is the one that needs to really balance the people's needs and the command needs. It's not the chaplain's job . . . It's to try to make that balance visible to the commanding officer. The commanding officer decides. (Jewish)

NO "WHACKO" RELIGION

When I asked the chaplains to give specific examples of religious accommodations they would advise against and commanding officers would rule out as contrary to good order and discipline, approximately three quarters of them spontaneously mentioned Wicca. Even those chaplains who didn't personally object to Wicca knew it had a "whacko" reputation. The chaplains saw many problem areas in facilitating for Wicca. Some believed Wiccans sacrifice animals and explained that you couldn't have live chickens and blood all over a ship. Another problem raised by the chaplains with regards to Wicca was nudity. Chaplain Kanaridis described an event that happened when he was stationed in Europe and a female officer had wanted to start a Wiccan service: "When the guys on the base heard that there was a Wicca, they thought it was something different than what it is. That there's going to be nudity there and all this other stuff, and so they're thinking, 'Boy, this is going to be great! Got a woman running it and she's probably going to get stripped down and we're going to have a great time!' Well, she can't do that. It's not within the regulations. You can't run around nude" (Conservative Baptist).

There are limitations on sexual expression in the military, and any ritual that required it would violate good order and discipline. Chaplain Clement, still worrying about Satanism, also worried about sexual rituals but took solace in the regulations that Chaplain Kanaridis referred to, concluding, "We would not be able to facilitate that" (United Methodist). Chaplain Townsend, who was working in an all-male environment, speculated what might happen in a mixed gender crew if the enlisted got creative: "There may very well be some constraint out there that I would accidentally stumble over at some point if we had females. 'Cause who knows what some enterprising sailor would come up with as their personal religion if they had the opportunity" (Reformed Episcopalian).

Most Americans, as heirs to the Puritans, probably associate religion with restrictions on sexuality. These chaplains seemed to agree that this is what religion was supposed to do. The idea that copulation, perhaps as a celebration of fertility, might be permitted under the guise of religious freedom was anathema. Interestingly, Chaplain Clement argued that the Army would be more lenient on matters of nudity and sexuality than the Navy could afford to be, because Army bases are big and more likely to have secluded areas where "deviant" religious groups could dance nude away from prying eyes.

A few chaplains mentioned Shi'a Islam as a religion that would be difficult to facilitate, given the rhetoric of Iranian leaders. Other chaplains mentioned white supremacist churches or anyone who wanted to do human sacrifice. Chaplain Hamoud, the Muslim chaplain, thought the Nation of Islam would probably cause too much trouble because it would stir up racial tensions. He also thought certain political points of view had to be suppressed: "If someone is at the base and he is appointed as a lay leader, and he is giving a Friday sermon, and he starts talking about that America is an evil empire. OK, that's against good order and discipline." Most reasons to restrict religious expression fell into two broad categories: not antagonizing other religious groups and safety.

DON'T ANTAGONIZE OTHER RELIGIOUS GROUPS

Wiccans should not take it for granted that they'll be allowed to use the same spaces as Christians. When a solo practitioner[21] of Wicca asked Chaplain Koch for a space to worship, the chaplain lent him his own office:

> Now, had this young man wanted to start a coven aboard the ship, and started recruiting people, and wanted to have it published in the plan of the day, and it upset all the evangelical Christians on board, and the Jews were outraged because Wiccan [. . .] it's a pagan religion, it's exactly what the Canaanites were practicing before the Jews went into that part of the world. So everything they've existed for the last four thousand years is contrary to that, the Jews might be a little upset over that. So instead of

> inciting everybody, I kept it low key. So it would not impact good order and discipline. (United Methodist)

Other chaplains mentioned giving smaller religious groups space in ships' libraries and base conference rooms. Although base chapels are supposed to be multifaith, there are limits, according to Chaplain Kojic, who said there were Wiccans on one of his ships "wanting to use the chapel where you have the mass for the Catholic community or you have the Eucharist for the Episcopal community, and then the Wiccan community comes and says, 'Well, we want to sacrifice a chicken on your altar.' Obviously, you're not going to let that happen" (Lutheran Church, Missouri Synod).

Both Chaplain Kanaridis (Conservative Baptist) and Chaplain Illera (Catholic) feared the commotion that would result if pagans or Satanists were allowed to use the same altar as Christian denominations. For Chaplain Kanaridis, this was also a personal issue. He seemed to have a strong commitment to keeping certain things ritually separate, saying, "If I have a space here that I do Sunday service in, I'm not going to let them come into His place." Despite space being at a premium in the crowded conditions of life at sea, to Chaplain Kanaridis, some spaces belonged to the Christian God as much as to the secular Navy.

In general, it was symbols and practices that might be labeled "occult" that were unwelcome among the Navy chaplains. Chaplains Gunvant and Illera, both Catholic priests, made the point explicitly. The former argued that "the dark side of animism" or "symbols that generally are viewed sociologically to be diabolical in nature" could not be promoted among officers or the enlisted. The latter said curses "would definitely be against good order and discipline because people get very nervous, they get very superstitious." The two priests differed on whether Wicca was inherently diabolical or "dark," with Chaplain Illera believing it was and Chaplain Gunvant stressing that it might or might not be.

The issue of proselytization, of trying to convert someone else to your faith, is contentious among chaplains, who often call attempts to raid other shepherds' flocks "sheep stealing." Obviously, proselytization can cause a lot of resentment among chaplains, undermining collegiality, trust, and effective cooperation, and every individual I interviewed agreed that they aren't supposed to do it. The biggest umbrella organization for faith group endorsers that send clergy into the military is the National Conference on Ministry to the Armed Forces (NCMAF). At the time of the interviews, its Covenant and Code of Ethics for Chaplains of the Armed Forces included the statement, "I will not proselytize from other religious bodies, but I retain the right to evangelize those who are non-affiliated."

This specific wording, from 1990, is not in the most recent version of NCMAF's Covenant, adopted in 2011. Although the new one doesn't use the word *proselytize* the emphasis on respecting others' beliefs is unmistakable throughout.[22] More important, not proselytizing is part of Chaplain Corps culture and has been for a long a time. According to Hutcheson's book from 1975, "a 'no proselytizing' ground rule is generally recognized by chaplains."[23] The difficulty with the self-imposed prohibition against proselytization isn't so much whether there should be one but the fact that chaplains don't agree on what *proselytization* means. Chapter 5 will discuss this lack of consensus in more detail. This lack of clarity creates situations in which some chaplains, in the eyes of others, proselytize even as they themselves believe they're doing no such thing. For the present purpose of describing accommodations and limitations of religion in the military, the relevant question is what role religion should play in chaplains' counseling.

Many chaplains have some training in behavioral science or counseling before they join the military, and it's natural that they would draw on that expertise. However, they also know that their faith groups, the military, and some of those who come to them for help, expect them to be "clergy first." Religion, however, does not necessarily come up at all in counseling sessions. When I asked Chaplain Irons if he worked mostly with fellow Baptists, he answered, "There are a lot of Baptists in the battalion, but to say that I work more with Baptists? No. I spend a lot of my time counseling, and often that issue isn't even broached. But I don't see any kind of known distinction that I make or put on myself working with marines and sailors" (Southern Baptist).

Chaplain Illera seemed more motivated by patriotism than denominationalism, and his voice swelled with emotion as he said, "I'm not out to make a whole bunch of Catholics. I'm not out to make a whole bunch of anything, except to help them be the best men and women they can be. And to do the best job that they can do. To be the best husbands, to be the best wives, i.e., to make America a much better place. That's my approach" (Catholic).

Both Chaplain Hamoud and Chaplain Giraldo agreed that most of the concerns brought to them were secular. Chaplain Hamoud admitted being confused by all the varieties of Protestantism but didn't believe they mattered that much, either: "There are differences in theology that don't affect how I approach them or how I counsel them. That's not an issue. They need help, as far as family or finance, or marital, or anything . . . So yes, we help them" (Muslim). As part of his explanation of proselytization, Chaplain Giraldo said, "I'm not able to minister to them religiously.

The way I minister to them is morally and just as a leader, as I am as an officer. If there are any personnel issues that need to be addressed, any stresses in the work place, any discrimination that may take place, that's where I step in and facilitate for them as a chaplain" (Evangelical Church Alliance).

One of the reasons proselytization is considered inappropriate in counseling sessions has to do with the chaplains being officers. One of the Presbyterian chaplains cut to the chase: "For example, I'm a lieutenant, so if I were to have a young seaman check on board and I were to ask him, 'Are you a Christian, son?' and he . . . 'Well, no, sir.' 'Well, I'm giving you a direct order, you're going to get on your knees and you're going to do the Jesus prayer'" (Chaplain Grams). I laughed at this, but the chaplain was serious. Another reason proselytization is inappropriate was described by Chaplain Oberlin: "When someone is in a very vulnerable situation, you tell them, 'You gotta go my way.' I mean, think of a hospital setting. We have persons who are sick and could be near death, and you come along and say, 'You're going to hell if you believe like that.' That's unacceptable" (Evangelical Lutheran Church in America).

Chaplain Gunvant, responsible for supervising several other chaplains, agreed because the military gave him

> a captive audience that does not have any alternative but to listen and attend to what I'm saying. Now, *captive* can also be defined in many different ways. Chaplains see people at the most vulnerable moments of their lives. And that person in a certain sense is at least emotionally captive for that moment. So I think in the privacy of counseling it becomes also very important that those moments not be violated by the intrusion of a faith requirement which this person may not have. Now, admittedly death is one of those moments and I think lots of chaplains are hard pressed in their counseling if they don't know what the faith group is or the person has no particular faith. (Catholic)

Importantly, Chaplain Gunvant does suggest that religion can be appropriate if it is what the person in question needs, and some people do want the chaplains to include matters of faith. Chaplain Street had counseled a young man who didn't have any religious affiliation earlier the same day that I interviewed him: "He came in the office, ironically, seeking a chaplain's point of view. Not at one time was I dogmatic about my counsel. But I think without even saying a word I was demonstrating the unconditional love of God" (African Methodist Episcopal).

When chaplains put virtues such as charity and compassion into practice through counseling, they may pique their clients' interest in religion.

Chaplain Bowmaker admitted to being very up front about encouraging religiosity: "And then in the process of counseling sometimes people will say, 'I'm really confused, where should I start?' And I'll say, "Go find a church that's comfortable for you. Like-minded people. Try to find a community of faithful individuals and go from there'" (Presbyterian). While Chaplain Bowmaker didn't perceive any problem with including religion in counseling, he also tried to respect whatever religious beliefs people brought to him, worrying that he might not know Mormon scriptures well enough to counsel them very effectively. Even so, the kind of approach to counseling Chaplain Bowmaker represents might trouble strict separationists, who want a high wall between church and state. Even if counseling by military chaplains doesn't promote any one religious tradition over others, it still uses a public office (the chaplain's commission as an officer) and public resources (his office space, paid time, and access to military personnel) to promote religion over "no religion."

Chaplains unsurprisingly take a different view, with several arguing that the inclusion of religion was necessary to get to the bottom of what was troubling a person and to make sure "all bases" were covered. Chaplain Koch, who had taught classes on how to respect religious diversity, outlined his strategy to counseling:

> People come to me that have no religious preference, for counseling. But their life's a shambles. What do you think one of the first things I'm going to tell them to do is? I'm going to give them good advice on, you know, communication skills and debt management. All the things that you have to give that address problems. But ultimately I'm going to address the spiritual sickness in their lives. Because of my religious perspective, I believe that we're physical beings, we're emotional beings, we're spiritual beings. I think all of us have a soul. So I'm going to address the nurture of the soul. We take care of ourselves physically, we get the sleep that we need, we eat what we need to eat in order to stay healthy. We take care of ourselves. We do that for ourselves physically. Why shouldn't we do that for ourselves spiritually? So if they're not taking care of themselves spiritually, that's where I'm going to direct them. So is that proselytizing? No. I think that's just the whole person concept to . . . to care and nurturing. (United Methodist)

The imam agreed. He too invoked the need to be holistic, spoke in terms of an innate and pure soul, which he called *ruh*, and asserted the need to be respectful: "Somehow, there is some kind of gulf between our physical self and our spiritual self later on. A human being tries to fill that void with many different things. My goal is to fill that void by bringing them . . . trying to make them complete as a holistic view. In so doing, I don't think I am stepping on anyone's religious beliefs. I don't think I'm stepping on anyone's faith traditions. So I am helping a person, in my way, to realize his own utmost potential" (Chaplain Hamoud, Muslim).

The boundary between church and state is not the only one implicated in the question about religion's role in counseling; the boundary between professions is as well. In counseling, chaplains need to make sound judgments about which problems fall outside the boundaries of their expertise and might better be referred to psychiatrists or law enforcement. One experienced Catholic priest grew visibly upset as he complained about evangelical Protestants who tried to use religion as a substitute for clinical therapy rather than a supplement to it:

> They get a person in a moment when they're down, or they're in the pits, or alcohol has claimed them. And what they do is they say, "Come this way and I know the truth and I know the way and you need to follow my way." As opposed to saying, "Let's get him to alcohol rehab," which is probably where he needs to go first. Now, if they choose to believe in a higher power, or they choose to follow a certain faith tradition . . . Hey, great! [claps his hands] Amen! Wonderful! But if [the chaplains] instead, seeing them in their plight are saying, "Well, you need to get to Jesus" and we're going to cover up this alcohol problem and they want you to keep coming [to church] . . . Then what happens one day down the road when the enthusiasm isn't there any longer and they start drinking again? All we've done is covered it up, and that's inappropriate proselytizing. (Chaplain Dyren)

The belief that "giving your life to Jesus Christ" is a solution to all of life's problems is common among evangelicals; President George W. Bush's personal narrative included it, the arguments for faith-based social services assume it, and many chaplains subscribe to it. Evangelicals are not alone, however, in their desire to bring a more faith-based approach to their counseling. The rabbi I interviewed, who deeply resented and repeatedly complained about evangelicals proselytizing "his" sailors and marines, also strained in the same direction:

> We [the Chaplain Corps] are about taking care of people. And we're all about helping people grow spiritually. And helping people deal with life's challenges, you know, with the answers that religion gives. We've kind of [sighs heavily] . . . been thrust into other areas as social workers and this and that, and that's not what we're all about. [Interviewer: "The counseling takes a lot of time?"] It does. ["You don't see that as sort of inherent in the job?"] It . . . it would be if they would let us counsel, allowing us to use more of our own faith perspective on it. As opposed to . . . They want everything to be more and more neutral. That's not who we are. (Chaplain Tzilker, Jewish)

While chaplains understand that like it or not, there are limitations on religious proselytizing, not all the enlisted do. Overzealous enlisted personnel may cause resentment among their peers by proselytizing in aggressive or insensitive ways. In such cases, chaplains have to "rein them in," which means that chaplains might actually have to encourage members of their faith groups to calm down about their religion. Chaplain Grams described his approach to eager enlisted personnel:

> "You are bound by the rules of good order and discipline, which bind even me. And what this is, this is when the Navy rules come over the religious rules. We all take an oath, whether we come from Haiti or Zaire or the Philippines or New York City or Los Angeles, whether we come from a strict Baptist background or Jewish or Muslim or whatever, we all put on the uniform and take the oath." So beginning there and saying, "If you were just a citizen you would have the right to go out there and share your religion with anybody, and if you want to yell at them, if you want to condemn them because they're not . . . That's your prerogative. They punch you in the nose, that's what happens. On the ship, you are bound by good order and discipline." (Presbyterian)

It was especially chaplains representing minority groups who worried about proselytizing. The rabbi, Chaplain Tzilker, and the three Mormon chaplains I interviewed, all brought it up. That the Mormons were worried about "their" sailors and marines being proselytized is somewhat ironic given their own reputation as persistent, door-to-door proselytizers. Mindful of this reputation, the Church of Jesus Christ of Latter Day Saints has instructed its chaplains not to proselytize—period. Even if a sailor or marine approaches a Mormon chaplain and specifically asks for information about the LDS church, the chaplain is supposed to refer him or her to a civilian counterpart in a nearby community. Finally, in addition to problems caused by interpersonal proselytizing, some of the Catholic priests were bothered by anti-Catholic tracts that sailors would hand out or leave lying around in common areas.

FOR THE SAKE OF SAFETY

Safety was the other big category of restrictions put on free exercise of religion. Fire, for example, can be very dangerous on warships despite its religious significance. Chaplain Oberlin pointed out in a deadpan way, "You don't light candles when they're loading ordinance. That's not good" (Evangelical Lutheran Church in America). Chaplain Drozdov discussed also discussed the sacred use of fire: "For instance, I use incense.

We light candles in our worship. Well, if I'm visiting a hospital where there's patients on oxygen, it wouldn't be wise for me to walk in there with an open, exposed flame. So I dispense with the candles. If I'm in a closed space with a fire alarm that's going to, you know, maybe pour sheets of water on me to put out that fire, I don't want to use incense right underneath that" (Eastern Orthodox). Less likely to be needed, but also off limits on Navy ships, are animals. Chaplain Illera speculated on what might go wrong if they weren't: "Perhaps we're sacrificing a bunch of goats, or a bunch of sheep, or are dancing around with poisonous snakes, rattlesnakes get dropped in a church and they get away . . . Not too good" (Catholic).

Recall the Presbyterian chaplain quoted earlier on the hypothetical case of a sailor wanting to worship green frogs on flat rocks? He said he'd get provide the rocks, but didn't say anything about the frogs. Although the idea of live animals on Navy ships seems absurd, Chaplain Irons was very sensitive to those who might need them, although he did chuckle affectionately as he explained, "There are Pentecostals in the mountains of east Tennessee who I know love the Lord with all their heart but would have no problem having an open service in tongues, and some of them might even handle snakes, OK? Do I question their faith in the Lord? No. I'm sure they're very genuine and sincere about their faith and it may very well benefit and prosper their lives, here and hereafter. But we can't have snakes on aircraft carriers. You understand?" (Southern Baptist).

I did. Without explicitly mentioning glossolalia, the speaking in tongues, Chaplain Gunvant told me that religious services couldn't be permitted to get so exuberant or spontaneous that people got carried away. Any religious service in the military, he said, had to be public, held at a designated time, and held "with an order of some kind, with permission of the commander and so forth" (Catholic). Secret meetings are out of the question, since every commanding officer needs to know what's going on in their command. Surveillance, as Goffman points out, is an important mechanism for control in total institutions, and on this the military doesn't make any exceptions for religion.[24]

Sometimes, religions require that leaders or lay people wear special clothing or groom themselves a certain way. This, too, can be limited on the grounds of preserving good order and discipline, and for the sake of safety. Chaplain Drozdov provided functional context for the issue, which affected him personally in that the Navy made him shave:

> Uniformity. We wear a uniform. We're not supposed to be individuals. We're supposed to be identified with the organization and the uniform makes us that way. Therefore, wearing religious apparel that's visible is

> inappropriate, except where it's allowed in uniform regulations. [. . .] [Turbans] are not allowed yet. There are Muslim headscarves for women that they can wear when they attend Muslim prayer, but it's not something that they can permanently wear while they're in uniform. In fact, the yarmulke right now is the only external religious symbol or piece of apparel that can be worn while in uniform at all times. Now, good order and discipline says there might be reason why you have to take that off. For instance, if you're wearing protective equipment, and it poses a hazard . . . Well, beards would probably be the one that would be more appropriate or less desirable for someone wearing firefighting gear or gas masks, because it will break the seal. I mean, I should have a beard. (Eastern Orthodox)

The legal basis for the current policies governing religious apparel was laid in a case from the 1980s, regarding an Air Force psychologist who had been wearing his yarmulke to work for several years when a new commanding officer decided that it violated a regulation prohibiting the wearing of "headgear" indoors and ordered him to take it off while in uniform.[25] The Navy also has this prohibition, which created one of the few situations in which I ever witnessed a chaplain "disciplining" a subordinate. An enlisted sailor passed us in a corridor, still wearing his hat (cover), prompting the chaplain to sarcastically comment, "Nice cover." The sailor instantly removed his headgear and the chaplain explained to me that if a supervisor had seen the sailor first, there might have been trouble. Although the sailor looked embarrassed by the incident, he was probably grateful that he'd been corrected by a chaplain and not another kind of officer.

To return to the Goldman case, the psychologist's position was that his yarmulke should not be lumped in with all other "headgear" because it had religious significance. He had been allowed to wear as an exception from the rules already, and his wasn't the only kind of headgear to be permitted indoors, since military police were allowed to wear helmets inside for protection. In addition to that, all the armed services had rules that allowed individual variations from the uniform such as watches, sunglasses, and wedding rings. Why no flexibility for the yarmulke? Refusing to take it off, Goldman sued and his case made it to the Supreme Court.[26] The court was sympathetic to Goldman, writing that his wearing the yarmulke while in uniform was "an eloquent rebuke to the ugliness of anti-Semitism" but still ruled against him by a 5–4 vote. The majority decided that the military's need for discipline and "instinctive obedience, unity and esprit de corps" trumped individual preferences, because being in the military is all about "the subordination of desires and interests of the individual to the needs of the service."[27]

The following year, Congress passed legislation that would let military personnel wear "unobtrusive religious headgear," including yarmulkes, while in uniform, maintaining that "our citizens in uniform should not be deprived of their basic constitutional rights, such as the free exercise of religion, the minute they enter the military." The law still allowed the military to regulate the size and appearance of religious apparel, again including yarmulkes, to prevent religious accommodation from becoming an operational liability.[28] Congress reaffirmed its support for wearing religious apparel in the military in 1996, as long as it doesn't jeopardize military duties and the apparel is "neat and conservative."[29] A shiny red yarmulke would draw too much attention to the person wearing it, both as a unique individual standing out from a uniformed crowd and as a target for enemy snipers. In the Navy, regulations require that yarmulkes all look more or less alike and spell out what "neat and conservative" means in practice.

The Goldman case is sociologically significant for a couple of reasons. One is that it captures the tension between individual and institution very well. The Air Force's position had been that "the traditional outfitting of personnel in standardized uniforms encourages the subordination of personal preferences and identities" that is functionally necessary for the military.[30] When all individuals are (literally) of one cloth, they identify with each other more easily, and when the cloth worn is issued by a powerful authority their dependence on that authority is reenacted every time they get dressed. In Goffman's analysis of total institutions, the clothes and other articles individuals use to "present their self" to the world is called an "identity kit." Controlling the identity kit yields control over individual selves, an insight shared and practiced by monasteries and prisons in addition to militaries. The second profound sociological significance of the Goldman case is that it shows just how seriously Americans take religious liberty. A case that, in historical or international perspective might seem trivial, was weighed by the very highest reaches of two branches of the US government.

The yarmulke is easier to accommodate than other religious headgear because it can be worn under helmets and other protective gear. Larger and more complex garments, such as turbans, make for more difficult negotiations. Sikhs lost their permission to wear turbans in the Army in 1984, for example, only to regain it in 2010. If they need to wear helmets, they have to change to "mini-turbans."[31] Uniform regulations can raise safety issues for others than religious minorities, although they may be less urgent. Chaplain Oberlin mused, "Although technically I suppose I could walk around the ship at sea wearing a clerical collar and a robe, I probably couldn't do that. One thing, wearing a robe, it's dangerous enough just going from the state room to the shower . . . You have to climb ladders and work around machinery" (Evangelical Lutheran Church in America).

The sacramental use of drugs is also regulated in the military. Obviously, chemically altered states of consciousness are not conducive to good order and discipline. Standing guard, operating heavy machinery, and handling weapons need to be done without hallucination. In light of such obvious safety concerns, it's a bit surprising that Native Americans actually are allowed to use peyote, although only under certain conditions, as explained by another ELCA chaplain, Chaplain Chance: "If they're not operational and they can be in a safe place, there was a document printed by the Navy saying they could use peyote in religious rituals. But obviously, on a ship, when you're out at sea, you don't want people stoned out of their gourd on peyote."

Chaplain Farrow provides the best summary of the discussion thus far: "You can't take away the free exercise of religion, but you can control it. And what I mean by control is keep it within the framework of good order and discipline" (Catholic).

CONCLUSION

The examples provided in this chapter show that chaplains do much to accommodate free exercise of religion in the military but also help to limit and control it so that it doesn't become disruptive. When individual religious needs and institutional goals collide, the institution wins. In cases where no compromise can be found between individual conscience and military demands, the only mutually satisfactory solutions are administrative reassignment or discharge from the military.

When the chaplains negotiate the tension between facilitation and good order and discipline, they are negotiating the extent to which and the ways in which values such as piety, individual rights, tolerance, freedom, and the rule of law can be expressed in the military. As clergy, as officers who have sworn to defend the Constitution, and as members of a corps that has tied its legitimacy to the Free Exercise Clause, military chaplains are acutely conscious of religious freedom. They are also unavoidably and constantly aware of the institution they work in. The issues and their context cannot be separated. As Madsen et al. point out, "ultimate meanings and values are embedded in social institutions."[32]

The particularities of the military institution matter. Hierarchy matters. The fact that the military approaches Goffman's ideal typical total institution matters. The way the military intersects with the churches, the law as interpreted by the courts, and politics as practiced in Congress also matter in shaping freedom of religion. Values don't just play out according to their own logic. Perhaps the best statement of this point was made by Robert Wuthnow: "Culture always exists in a social environment. It draws resources from that environment, reflects the categories and distinctions built into that environment, and is influenced by that environment in the very act of trying to influence it. The institutional resources of religious groups and the manner in which changes in the larger society have affected these resources, therefore, play a critical role in the discussion."[33]

This is an important insight, especially when it is combined with the evidence here provided of how decisive individual agency is. Commanding officers have great discretion in matters of religious freedom. They may be more or less positively inclined toward religion in general, or toward specific faith groups. They vary among themselves in how much disorder they're willing to risk accommodating and how seriously they take their chaplains' advice. Religious believers, in turn, can be more or less insistent on having their spiritual needs met. The chaplains, as demonstrated, can vary in the degree of effort they make and enthusiasm they show for facilitating sailors' and marines' religious needs. They can be very creative in negotiating tensions between individual and institution, or fall back on regulations and hierarchy.

Chaplains also vary in how much they're willing to set aside their own religious particularity for the sake of others' particular religious needs. Before analyzing the chaplains' own experiences with this tension, it will be useful to look more closely at just how sharp it can be. The next chapter therefore describes chaplains' efforts to facilitate for two minority faith groups that really test their commitment to freedom of religion, Islam and Wicca.

Chapter 3

Muslims, Witches, and Chaplains

No, no! You don't understand! I'm not approving, I'm just helping you.
—Southern Baptist chaplain to a group of Wiccans

Just a little more than a generation ago, "religious diversity" in the military referred only to variation within Christianity, plus Judaism. The norms that guide chaplains' behavior and the principles those norms rest on didn't necessarily anticipate just how diverse the American religious landscape, and thus its armed forces, would become. It's useful, then, to see how military chaplains respond to the presence of minority religions relatively new to the institution.

I chose Islam and Wicca because each has received increased attention, within and outside the military, in recent decades. Islam, of course, is a major world religion and implicated in some of the most urgent contemporary controversies: the rights of women, the nexus of faith and violence, the Arab-Israeli conflict, and the much debated "clash of civilizations."[1] Wicca, although newer and with fewer adherents, can serve as an example of so-called New Age religion, loosely described as antiauthoritarian "self-spirituality."[2] Although some New Age groups are much more materialistic than Wicca and few follow the cycles of nature as closely or with as much reverence as they do, Wicca is a valid representative of the larger New Age movement.[3] This movement embodies many of the cultural traits Bellah et al. identified as characteristic of the late twentieth century, such as expressive individualism and a "therapeutic" mentality.[4] A close look at Islam and Wicca makes it possible to see how chaplains respond both to a monotheistic religion rich in history and to an innovative, polytheistic or pantheistic religion that may be too internally diverse and incoherent to define authoritatively. The chaplains' responses will in turn say something about the place of minority religions and the terms of their acceptance in the United States.

Members of minority religions are at greater risk than others of being discriminated against, ignored, or completely overlooked. That Americans are more likely to like a religion if they know someone who is part of it has been established empirically and called the "My Aunt Susan" principle. One explanation of Americans' religious tolerance is that almost everyone has an "Aunt Susan" or "pal Al," a relative, friend, coworker, or neighbor of undeniable character and piety who belongs to a different faith group. These kinds of bridging relationships make it harder to believe that one's own faith is the only true one.[5] Muslims and Wiccans in the military are therefore more likely to suffer hostility simply because they are few and most likely to remedy that exact problem by letting others get to know them. This of course requires that Muslims and Wiccans are comfortable identifying themselves as such, which is not always the case. Young recruits may be especially cautious when asked to volunteer a religious preference, which limits the reliability of manpower data collected by the DMDC.

An issue paper produced by the Military Leadership Diversity Commission asks whether too much pressure is put on commanding officers who may not know enough about religion and therefore "may approve religious-accommodation requests with which they are reasonably comfortable or familiar, but may not approve of those with which they are uncomfortable or unfamiliar," even to the point where they reject almost all requests in order to avoid playing favorites.[6] Because it is chaplains who familiarize commanders with religion and make them comfortable with an accommodation (or not), the chaplains' views of religious minorities are important.

ISLAM IN AMERICA

Islam has a long history in North America. Half the slaves brought to America in chains came from societies familiar with Islam, and about 15 to 20 percent of them were Muslims.[7] Scattered, mixed, and submerged in a Christian society where literacy had to be hidden, most slaves gradually assimilated, losing their native languages and faiths.[8] Some nevertheless managed to continue practicing Islam. The evidence includes slave owners' accounts that comment on Muslim practices with a mixture of admiration and condescension and elderly African Americans recalling their grandparents praying on mats facing east.[9]

After emancipation and especially after the Great Migration to the northern cities, Islam experienced a kind of revival. Looking for a more authentic and less oppressive alternative to Christianity, African Americans looked to Africa for religious inspiration. Enigmatic and charismatic leaders, including Father Divine, Noble Drew Ali, and W. D. Fard emerged in the 1920s and 1930s claiming to be Muslims. Some of this movement's teachings departed sharply from traditional Islam, in that African American leaders would claim the mantle of prophethood and produce updated scriptures, contradicting the teaching that Muhammad was the "seal" of the prophets and the Koran God's completed revelation to humanity. In the context and aftermath of the civil rights movement, African American Islam produced well-known leaders such as Malcolm X and Louis Farrakhan and in many ways began to conform more closely to Islam as practiced elsewhere in the world.[10]

African Americans account for a sizable percentage of Muslims in the United States, with immigration rather than conversion accounting for most of the rest.[11] In 2005 the nation had "approximately 3,000 Islamic centers, mosques and prayer locations" in addition to "approximately 200 Muslim schools, 500 Islamic Sunday schools, and six schools of Islamic higher education," with most of the mosques built since 1970 and about two thirds of their members either first- or second-generation immigrants.[12] Although post-1965 immigration is driving the growth of Islam in America, there are older communities. North Dakota, Iowa, and Maine have Muslim populations that can be traced back to the arrival of Syrian, Lebanese, Jordanian, and Albanian immigrants before 1920. Despite what the Christian majority assumes, most Muslims in America today are not from the Middle East or North Africa; only 41 percent of foreign-born Muslims are. The rest come from farther east (e.g., Indonesia, Pakistan, and Bangladesh) and farther south (e.g., Nigeria, Ghana, and Senegal) than that.[13] According to the Pew Research Center, "more than a third of Muslim American adults (37%) were born in the United States," but "more than three-quarters are either first-generation immigrants (63%) or second-generation immigrants (15%)" with the remaining 22 percent being third generation or later.[14] In 2010, the United States' 2.6 million Muslims made it the country with the fifty-fifth largest Muslim population in the world. By 2030, this population is projected to be 6.2 million strong.[15]

WICCA IN AMERICA

In the late nineteenth century, middle- and upper-class Europeans were inspired by knowledge they were gaining of "other religions," especially from Asia, to take an interest in spiritualism and the occult. Helena Blavatsky and Henry Olcott founded the Theosophical Society in 1875, Sufism was brought to Paris by a Russian-born man named Gurdjieff, and the famous psychoanalyst Carl Jung wrote about symbols, archetypes, and myth. Many 1960s "New Age" leaders found their approaches, principles, and concepts by looking back to this earlier era of experimentation.[16]

The modern origin of Wicca is attributed to an English civil servant named Gerald Gardner who was interested in folklore and archaeology and had worked in Southeast Asia. Gardner claimed to have been initiated into witchcraft by a woman he called "Old Dorothy" in 1939, although he probably invented Wicca himself. His most important influences included Aleister Crowley, who systematized European and American occult practices in 1929, and Margaret Murray, who had produced an influential history of European witchcraft in 1921.[17] Murray believed witchcraft was an ancient, organized, "pre-Christian fertility cult" whose teachings were distorted by the Inquisition and whose practitioners were scattered and driven into underground secret societies during "the burning times."[18] When Gerald Gardner published on witchcraft in the 1950s, he claimed to stand in an ancient and unbroken line of witches. His teachings and organizational principles, described by Partridge as "an eclectic mix of occult, Eastern and indigenous beliefs and practices," were brought to the United States by one of his students, Raymond Buckland.[19]

As with other imported religious traditions, Wicca was shaped by its American context and departed from European witchcraft in significant ways. According to Helen Berger, American witches place greater emphasis on "mysticism, ecological concerns, women's rights and antiauthoritarianism," while Luhrmann contrasts the Americans' general acceptance of homosexuality with the more heteronormative views of Europeans witches who are more ritually concerned with fertility and balancing male and female essences. On both sides of the Atlantic, witches initiate each other into covens that meet regularly and congregate at festivals. They exchange information on the Internet and advertise seminars and lectures on bulletin boards at New Age book stores. Many are self-taught and "work" magic alone, as solo practitioners.[20]

Despite the stature of founding figures such as Gardner and the popularity of contemporary authors such as Starhawk, Wicca has no official hierarchy, no definitive scripture, and no formal creed.[21] The whole point of Wicca is to start with the self and its innate freedom and then let individuals "discover their own path." Many covens founded by young adults in the 1960s and 1970s have flourished and now have to decide how and whether to own property together, choose leaders, make a list of members (which requires making boundaries), and agree on and maybe write down shared beliefs. These challenges of what Max Weber called "routinization" hold out the promise or threat of covens beginning to resemble Protestant denominations.[22] There is no unifying response to these challenges among Wiccans, who often disagree on what it means to be Wiccan at all (another trait they share with Protestant denominations). Even if they collectively imagine themselves as a modern resurrection of an ancient fertility cult, individual Wiccans are Wiccan if and when they say so, and there's no one to validate or negate such a claim.

This lack of definition makes Wiccans very hard to count. Montgomery cites different estimates ranging from about 1,500 to as many as 134,000.[23] Terminological confusion only complicates matters further, as the categories "Wiccan" and "Neo-Pagan" are sometimes treated as equivalent and sometimes not. A quantitative study of the Neo-Pagan movement counts Wicca as one of many spiritual paths within it, the others including Druids, Shamans, Pagans, Unitarian Universalist Neo-Pagans, Goddess Worshipers, and Odinists.[24] Partridge breaks Wicca itself down into five subgroups: Gardnerian Wicca, Alexandrian Wicca, Hereditary Craft, Traditional Craft, and Feminist Craft, with Dianic and Hedge witchcraft as possible sixth and seventh subgroups. Some military personnel may identify as both Unitarian Universalists and as witches, some with Neo-Paganism but not Wicca, and some may not even make the distinction.

Compared to all Americans, Neo-Pagans are younger, more urban, more highly educated, more liberal, and more likely to report having had a mystical experience. Although most are middle class, Neo-Pagans aren't as affluent as their level of education would suggest. This is probably because two thirds of Neo-Pagans are women, disadvantaged by the wage gap between the genders. The typical Wiccan is a young, educated, politically liberal, white woman.[25]

ISLAM AND WICCA AS MINORITY RELIGIONS

Although very different theologically, Islam and Wicca are both minority religions subject to prejudice and misunderstanding by the much larger Christian majority. However, they face very different prejudices and misunderstandings. Muslims are more likely to be victims of racial prejudice and profiling because many are immigrants and because there are styles of grooming and dress associated with being Muslim. This forces Muslims in America, especially second-generation Muslim Americans, to make choices about how they present themselves.[26]

Americans have become more interested in Islam since the 9/11 terrorist attacks and the American invasions of Iraq and Afghanistan, which has led to the dissemination of both accurate and inaccurate descriptions of what Muslims believe and want. Federal law enforcement has documented an increase in anti-Muslim hate crimes since 2001.[27] Across the nation, communities have used zoning laws to prevent the building of non-Christian houses of worship, the Republican Party has cynically exploited hatred of Islam, and the "clash of civilizations" thesis has been given new and often distorted life.[28] Misunderstanding and hatred of Islam is nothing new, of course. The ethnic stereotype that Muslims are all Arabs, the ubiquitous depiction of Muslims as "bad guys" in television and movies, and the erroneous belief that they "worship Muhammad" can be seen as extensions of the old Christian prejudices that cast Islam as inherently fanatical and violent, a "religion of the sword."[29]

On the other hand, many Americans have gained knowledge and respect for Islam, having their stereotypes dispelled. Symbolic gestures visible to the whole nation, such as having a Muslim cleric offer prayer at the memorial service after 9/11 and the US Postal Service issuing stamps to commemorate the Muslim *Eid* holiday, are encouraging. While 51 percent of Americans "would welcome Muslims becoming a stronger presence in the United States," 27 percent of American Muslims have experienced discrimination or know someone who has,[30] and Islam is the least popular religious group in America.[31] The big picture is decidedly mixed, so Muslim parents have legitimate concerns about their children being teased and bullied at school.[32] Both they and their children may also be subjected to proselytization by zealous Christians convinced that theirs is the only true religion.

Wiccans experience many of the same problems. They too worry about their children, including losing custody of them in divorce proceedings if their faith is made an issue. Many Americans associate Paganism with drug use, blood sacrifice, sexual excesses, and Satanism.[33] Although Wiccans go to great lengths to disassociate themselves from Satanism, they are contending with deeply ingrained prejudices going back to medieval Europe, just as the Muslims are. However, because Wiccans are mostly white, they don't have to contend with racism the way many Muslims do.

Wicca emerged in the United States at roughly the same time that mass immigration of Muslims began, and both groups face uncertainties about transmitting their religious beliefs and values to their children. They are not the exact same uncertainties. For Muslims, as with other immigrant groups, assimilation causes friction between the first and second generations. The status of women is an especially thorny issue, since questions about arranged marriages, access to education, modest dress, and female circumcision can bring Muslim communities into conflict with American law.

Wiccan parents worry not just about how to raise their children as good Wiccans in a Christian context but also about whether to do so at all. Because Wiccans focus on the self, as all New Age movements do, and are committed to each individual finding their own path, it's not self-evidently right for Wiccan parents to "impose" their beliefs on their children.[34] While sociologically naïve in that it ignores the social reality of religion, the value of everyone finding their own path intersects with other core values of Wicca, including freedom and creativity. Most Neo-Pagan parents do raise their children to be the same,[35] but the potential for intergenerational conflict is clear: what, after all, is a Wiccan parent to do if their adolescent starts dabbling in Roman Catholicism or, even worse, decides that their spiritual path is to join the Southern Baptist Convention?

This radical individualism also undermines the stability of Wiccan covens, which are especially likely to splinter when they grow large enough to require organization and leadership. While festival rituals and Internet discussion boards provide some integration, they don't seem to provide shared standards and practices strong enough to unite Wiccans. Even though many Wiccans do want to become more organized and more "mainstream," their groups "tend to be too small and too unstable to transform themselves into a congregation."[36] On this point there is a stark contrast with Islam, because Muslims have a concept of *umma*, a single authoritative text, and a tradition of scholarship that together legitimate homogenization, community, and leadership.

Both Wiccans and Muslims want and need to educate the Christian majority about their beliefs and practices. Islam has clear advantages over Wicca in the United States because it is far more comprehensible to Christians. It is a monotheistic, Abrahamic religion that claims to complete a revelation that incorporates Christianity, making Jesus a revered prophet. It is not hard to find Islamic analogies to Protestant cultural traits, such as Biblicism, individualism, moralism, activism, and millennial optimism.[37] Like Protestants, Muslims have a sacred text, believe each responsible individual must submit to God's will, lift up the destitute and oppressed, and try to persuade others to convert before linear time ends with God's judgment. Even those Christians who view Islam as rank falsehood will still recognize much of it and are unlikely to dismiss it as "whacko." Despite resentments and competition, there is enough that is respectable in Islam as a monotheistic, patriarchal religion to provide some common ground for meaningful, mutually respectful exchange. The empirical part of this chapter will amplify this point.

Wiccans, on the other hand, have no sacred book, abhor passing judgment on others, have a tradition of keeping secrets and worshipping in seclusion, are more likely to approach the sacred with a mind to manipulate it with magic than submit to its revealed commands, and have a perennial rather than linear view of history. Wicca emphatically rejects both monotheism and patriarchy, and many elements of Wiccan worship (e.g., nudity) would scandalize Christians and Muslims alike. So in addition to being far fewer than Muslims, Wiccans should have a harder time gaining Christians' understanding and approval because they have greater theological distance to overcome. But there are cross-pressures on Islam that Wiccans simply don't have to contend with. No one imagines Wicca to be a demographic or military threat to "the West," there have been no Wiccan terrorists or insurgents, and there are no Wiccan nations with strategic oil reserves. In other words, although Wicca may seem to pose the greatest challenge to the Protestant moral order, it has not been assimilated into the image of the United States' enemy. Islam has.[38]

Based on these reflections, I asked the chaplains I interviewed about Islam and Wicca with certain expectations. I expected that there would be great ambivalence about Islam because all my subjects were committed to an Abrahamic religion and served in a hierarchical and highly ordered institution waging war against Muslims, if not Islam. I was prepared to hear expressions of respect and concern, hostility and understanding. I expected mostly negative attitudes toward Wicca. I also expected the chaplains to be willing to facilitate for both, within the boundaries of good order and discipline as laid out in the preceding chapter.

There are many reasons why Navy chaplains would do their best to respect and accommodate Islam and Wicca. Pride in America's history of toleration, professional commitment after swearing an oath to defend a Constitution that guarantees freedom of religion, and organizational incentives that reward ecumenism in order to deflect legal challenges are all relevant factors. Add to this a genuine concern for the sailors and marines they serve, and for Islam, an awareness that there are geopolitical and strategic advantages to disproving the "crusader" rhetoric used by terrorists, and it makes sense to expect an accommodating chaplaincy.

ISLAM AND WICCA IN THE MILITARY

Islam and Wicca are both small groups scattered throughout the armed forces. Islam's presence is in many ways more firmly established and routinized. From 1996 to 2001, the official seal of the Navy Chaplain Corps included a crescent moon alongside a Christian cross and tablets to represent Judaism. That seal was replaced in 2001 with the current one, which doesn't have any specific religious symbols in it at all, the reason being that the military didn't want to constantly have to redesign an increasingly cluttered seal as new groups joined the chaplaincy.

Neither Islam nor Wicca have clergy in the same sense that mainstream Protestants and Catholics do, complicating the matter of ecclesiastical endorsement. The military has relied on two organizations, the Graduate

Schools for Islamic Social Sciences and the American Muslim Armed Forces and Veterans Affairs Council (AMAFVAC) to provide endorsement to imams. These two groups check character references, make sure candidates have enough postgraduate education, and provide additional training. Lay leaders are also trained by AMAFVAC, which provides a course covering topics such as "Working with Your Unit Chaplain" and "Understanding Other Faith Groups."[39] The Navy's first Muslim chaplain was Malak Ibn Noel, who came on active duty in 1996. At a conference of military chaplains, I heard him speak about his experiences working with Kurdish refugees and also about the consternation he initially caused in the Navy because many sailors didn't understand the crescent moon he wore on his lapel in place of the cross Christian chaplains wear. To break the ice, he would joke that he was in the "astronaut corps."[40] The number of Muslim military chaplains has varied over the past decade but has generally been between ten and fifteen, with most in the Army.

There are as yet no Wiccan chaplains in the US military. In 2006, a Christian Army chaplain named Don Larsen had a crisis of faith after witnessing religious violence while deployed to Iraq. He decided to convert to Wicca and contacted the Sacred Well Congregation, a Wiccan organization that was already trying to get the Department of Defense to recognize them as an endorsing agent for Wiccan chaplains. Having been told by the Army chaplaincy that they had met all requirements of an endorsing agency except putting forth a viable candidate, they thought Larsen would be ideal, given that he already was an Army chaplain. Unfortunately for Larsen, his original endorsing agency, the Chaplaincy of Full Gospel Churches, found out from the Army that he was planning to convert. They immediately rescinded his ecclesiastical endorsement, which made it impossible for him to continue serving as a chaplain. He was quickly pulled out of Iraq by the Pentagon. In a classic catch-22, the Sacred Well Congregation could not renew his ecclesiastical endorsement, because they were not yet recognized as an endorser by the Department of Defense.[41] These events unfolded in the summer of 2006 and are as close as Wiccans have come to having a chaplain in the military.

Practical Accommodation for Muslims and Wiccans

The first question I asked the chaplains was an open-ended one about whether they had "had any experience working with" these two groups, which elicited many spontaneous anecdotes. I probed, asking what they thought the specific needs or concerns of these two groups were, partly to test their knowledge and partly to find out what they perceived the problem areas to be. Writing in defense of the Army chaplaincy, Drazin and

Currey concede that "on occasion soldiers' religious rights are trampled upon by the ignorance of chaplains themselves." Chaplain Drozdov also raised this point, saying "when the institution doesn't bother to understand the needs of a particular faith, then the institution isn't making ministry to that group one of its programs" (Eastern Orthodox). If chaplains are not educated, or haven't bothered to educate themselves, about minority religious needs, these needs may go unmet.

I also asked the chaplains what they could do to facilitate for Muslims and Wiccans and whether there was anything they could not do for them. Some gave examples of things they had already done by way of facilitation, while others answered in hypotheticals about what they'd do if approached. I asked them what challenges Islam and Wicca posed to them as chaplains and what challenges, if any, they thought the military posed to Muslims and Wiccans. Finally, I asked them whether they thought Muslims had been adversely affected by the terrorist attacks in 2001. My overall goal was to find out whether Muslim and Wiccan requests for religious accommodation would be met as routinely and effortlessly as those of larger groups.

The incident involving Chaplain Larsen was not the first to draw national attention to Wicca in the military. In 1999, ABC News, *The Washington Post*, and *Time Magazine* all ran stories about a Wiccan community meeting at Fort Hood, located in a conservative Protestant part of Texas. The Army had been letting the group use a remote campsite on base for gatherings. There were protests outside the gates and criticism from Republican legislators, including Strom Thurmond and Bob Barr. The latter complained, "What's next? Will armored divisions be forced to travel with sacrificial animals for satanic rituals? Will Rastafarians demand the inclusion of ritualistic marijuana cigarettes in their rations?" Referring to another Texas base, the state's governor, future president George W. Bush, weighed in on the controversy saying, "I don't think witchcraft is a religion, and I wish the military would take another look at this and decide against it." The commander at Fort Hood, encouraged by Christian chaplains and supported by the Department of Defense, decided to continue letting the Wiccans meet on base.[42]

Finding space to worship is also a concern for Muslims. On some of the larger bases where I conducted interviews, the chaplains proudly showed me rooms set aside for Muslim worship. Chaplain Drozdov, for example, was able to show me a carpeted room where the Muslims could meet. Chaplain Metzger knew of another space set aside for Muslims that he wished was used more, because it was so nice. Remembering a previous assignment, Chaplain Metzger said, "We had an Islamic service there. We had an imam in town that would come to us. But that ended about halfway through my tour because I talked with the imam and he said, 'We're just not getting people coming to service. And he said, "So I'm just going to stop coming" (Chaplaincy of Full Gospel Churches).

Almost all chaplains I interviewed said they'd had some experience working with Muslims. Chaplain Hawthorne, a Southern Baptist, said matter-of-factly, "Sure, we have a Muslim lay leader. And we have about half a dozen, probably, Muslims who identify themselves on board." Chaplain Townsend said, "Wherever I've been, there's at least been a handful of Muslims. So that's my experience." Chaplain Szmatula had worked as an instructor:

> The only problem we had, in facilitating some ministry, was when I had my first three Muslim students one summer. And they wanted to observe the six prayer times during the day. [Interviewer: Six?] I don't know. Five? Whatever it is. But it would mean them missing class. To go and put their prayer rugs down and say their prayer. So I called the endorsing agent for the Muslim faith and I said, "Good order and discipline demands that they attend these classes." And he says, "Absolutely! I will give them permission not to have to do that." (Missouri Synod Lutheran)

Although Chaplain Szmatula was uncertain about how often Muslims pray, he knew it was done on rugs and didn't hesitate to talk to their endorsing agent before making them stay in class. Another Lutheran chaplain, this time Chaplain Chance from the ELCA, mentioned Muslims doing three prayers a day. When I asked if it wasn't five he said, "It's supposed to be, but in the military, it's just kinda hard to make happen. So they do it in the morning when they first get here, at lunch, and then right before they go home. Something like that." When I asked what problems Muslims faced in the military, Chaplain Michaud thought of prayer right away but didn't think it posed any insurmountable challenges because he too had noticed that the Muslims seemed to have a "close enough" attitude: "The troubles that they often have in the military setting is having the opportunity to pray all through the day as they do. Getting off work to be able to do that. But they're . . . Islam makes means for them, provisions for them to be able to . . . If they can't pray five times a day, they can pray three times a day" (Baptist General Conference).

Other chaplains emphasized Islam's simplicity and egalitarianism, rather than its flexibility. According to Chaplain Farrow, "the Muslim sailors and Muslim marines usually don't need a lot of care and feeding. Theologically. Because the fact is it's an autonomous-in-and-of-itself type of religion. Because, they have imams and sure do they have communal gatherings if they want to go to one, yeah. But they can do everything in and of themselves. They do their days and their prayers and so forth" (Catholic).

Having listed all the things he needed to do a Christian service, including "unleavened bread, wine, candles," Chaplain Oberlin said he was "impressed" with Islam because "it's a very down to earth, basic . . . You don't need a lot. For the Muslim, doesn't even need a prayer rug. The idea is to be clean. Some understanding of which direction points toward Mecca, which I tell you is very confusing on a ship, because the ship is constantly changing directions" (ELCA).

Just because Islam is a simple religion and Muslims are flexible, doesn't mean it's always easy for Muslims to pray as much as they want or need. A Muslim interviewed by another scholar was denied accommodation by his commander: "I continued praying but I had to hide it. I pray whenever he goes somewhere, I pray when he's not around. I felt like I'm not even a human being if you can prevent me from praying, and I had to hide myself behind the curtains just to do the prayer."[43] Chaplain Moore ran into a similar problem. He was approached at sea by a sailor who was having a problem because his supervisors weren't giving him time off to pray during the day: "So I talked with some of his supervisors and said, 'Let him do it, they're not long prayers.' I appealed to them to let him go. 'He doesn't smoke, you give everybody else a smoke break. Can't you give this guy a prayer break for ten minutes? And the line to pray is much shorter than the line for the smoking spots! He can probably get in and out a lot faster'" (Mormon).

The main communal prayer for Muslims is supposed to be on Friday. Muslims often work Sundays in return for accommodation on Friday, just as Seventh Day Adventists and Jews do in order to get Saturday off. Sometimes, a few hours off would be enough, since Friday prayers don't last all day. Chaplain Hamoud's Friday services would last about an hour and a half, followed by an hour of "fellowship and question and answer." He was fine with adjusting his schedule to the military's needs: "I am very comfortable in making at least my sermon, or my worship schedule or my Friday *khutbah*, that's a speech, just enough so that service members who are coming from the ship, where Friday is a work day . . . so that they participate in good order and discipline, they're not gone for long" (Muslim).

As I was waiting to interview Chaplain Gunvant, I saw a bulletin board announcing Muslim prayer services on Sundays. When I asked him why it wasn't Fridays, he said it was a matter of getting the best leadership possible:

> Well, in fact in this particular instance, Sunday is the only day we can get the imam. So we have to decide. Shall we observe with a lay reader the day typical of that faith group? Or, considering that in so many instances in America today people come in and say, "Yeah, I'm Protestant," but they don't have the slightest notion of what it means, is it more valuable to these young men who are perhaps in the process of reviewing their traditional religious roots, to have someone who really knows what this faith group is about? So we came down [on Sunday]. Well, we had to because we couldn't find an imam to help us, and no sailor was really ready to lead the others in Islam. (Catholic)

Just a week before I interviewed him, Baptist Chaplain Michaud had had two Muslim sailors in his office, asking to get out of training sessions in order to attend Friday prayers. He gave them a list of mosques in the area, and they were able to find one that had prayers on Saturday for Muslims who couldn't come on Fridays because of work or school.

Chaplain Clement helped bring an imam from the community to one of the facilities he had worked at for the sake of the "decent-sized Muslim population" he had there and organized some meals where Muslims and non-Muslims could meet. He was very impressed: "That was the most incredible experience that we've ever had. Just the sharing and the learning. Talking about diversity! I mean, that was the epitome of it. And what this man was able to do in the short time I was there was to make more visible the Muslim community, and because that was more visible, I believe there was a better attitude of cooperation among people that weren't in the vocation of being clergy" (United Methodist).

As useful as visiting imams and civilian mosques can be, the easiest way to accommodate Muslim religious needs is to have Muslim chaplains and lay leaders available. Having Muslim chaplains is also the best way to make available marital or pastoral counseling consistent with Muslim beliefs or to offer insight on questions about identity and assimilation. Chaplain Townsend thought the general spiritual malaise he saw among young Christians affected Muslims, too.

> Even the Muslims who come to you for counseling, yes I have had that, to deal with their various and sundry issues . . . They're not there being an Osama bin Laden type. What they're saying [is], "I'm a Muslim, I'm in America, you're my chaplain, my life is screwed up, can you help me?" And sometimes the answer is, "Yes, I can help you. Here is the phone number for the Muslim base chaplain. Here's what time services go for you on Friday. Furthermore, here's the instruction to show your boss saying that you can go." And sometimes their response is, "Oh. I didn't know that." (Reformed Episcopalian)

On smaller bases, where a chaplain may be the only one around, lay leaders become especially important, said Chaplain Farrow: "[If] you're the only chaplain there, then your obligation, let's say you're Protestant, is to make sure you have plenty of Catholic lay leaders, a well-trained Jewish lay leader, a well-trained Muslim lay leader. And if even necessary, a well-trained Wiccan" (Catholic).

Because there are no Wiccan chaplains, the task of recruiting, screening, and supervising Wiccan lay leaders and making sure they get the right training falls to chaplains of other faiths. Chaplain Beard had met a "contingent" of Wiccans on one of his ships, describing them first as a "very strong group" before qualifying, "Well, at least a strong leader. And I worked with him. And he would give me regular updates on what they were doing. I also helped secure holidays for them. To make sure they were given the holidays they needed" (Southern Baptist). Chaplain Bartley had received similar help from a Wiccan who wasn't a lay leader, but a line officer on a ship. "He provided a lot of information, and he was a resource person. We listed him as a resource person. And he provided that kind of leadership for the Wicca services here at [our base]. Unfortunately, he left" (Church of God in Christ).

The qualities chaplains say they look for in Wiccan leaders reveal something about their attitudes toward Wiccans. The following quotes make the point:

> What we're looking for is a resource person, a point of contact. An adult person! [laughs] A person that we can consider a resource person, that we can tap into and get information. Other than a recruit. (Chaplain Bartley, Church of God in Christ)

> We interview them and find who is a mature solid individual and understand what a Wiccan is and how to practice it in a mature, level, command . . . good order and discipline context. (Chaplain Farrow, Catholic).

> I try to make sure there is a strong leader for them. What I find is there are some guys who are power grabbers and you've got to sort of get a stable, sensible guy, who has some rank, who will be their sort of . . . who will pull them together. If they get somebody good like that, like any group, they tend to toe the line. (Chaplain Dyren, Catholic).

I did not ask these chaplains what qualities they looked for in Wiccan lay leaders. So when they volunteer that what they're looking for is maturity, stability, sensibility, and willingness to compromise, it suggests that they view Wiccans as at least potentially immature, unstable, silly, and recalcitrant. Chaplain Squires agreed the military had to make sure a Wiccan lay leader was "a good character, or a good representative of their faith group." In addition, it had to be someone willing to accept these conditions: "These are the dos, these are what you are authorized to do: You're under the authority of your captain, commanding officer, and supervision of the chaplain. These are the things you don't do: You don't preach, you don't counsel people, you do not as a rule administer the sacraments or ordinances of your faith group. That's for clergy" (Catholic). Chaplain Squires stressed that these requirements applied to Jewish, Mormon, and other lay leaders as well. However, he also pointed out that unlike Wicca, these groups have their own certifying process, guidelines and requirements for lay leaders, and provide "standard letters [a prospective lay leader] has to have filled out and endorsed by their pastor, rabbi, imam, priest, whoever they'll be worshipping with." The Wiccans, he concluded, could not do that.

Chaplain Bartley agreed that "Wicca had been a challenge." When the resource person he mentioned earlier was transferred out of the region, he and his fellow chaplains couldn't find anyone suitable to replace him. He had to keep in mind that on his base "there are recruits who are seventeen, eighteen, nineteen, twenty years old and each of the other groups had a leader" and had to make decision about the Wiccans:

> The conflict was not so much whether or not Wicca is a good religion or not, for me. The conflict was in an environment of good order and discipline, do I allow recruits ranging from twenty to forty recruits, to sit out without a leader, without a resource person? We could have the group conduct services without a [lay] leader, but there was no resource person or point of contact. So my big conflict was to decide "what do I do?" And so ultimately what I had to do was to cancel that service until we can find an identified resource person. I have asked recruits if they know of someone. But what we're struggling with in this environment is that there are some who are just curious. The curious come out and they may want to gather in a particular place, but there's no leadership. And this is not the right environment for that lack of leadership. (Church of God in Christ)

This was a clear case of military necessity, training recruits, trumping religious freedom—of good order and discipline limiting facilitation. The improvised, egalitarian nature of Wiccan worship contradicted the military's need for accountability, which is especially urgent in a basic training setting where radical resocialization is an explicit goal. Because "we have a shortage of rabbis in this area, and we have a shortage of imams," Chaplain Bartley continued, Jewish recruits were bused from that base to another one nearby for their high holidays, but this was only possible because it didn't "restrict the mission" of training recruits.

Even Wiccan groups with proper leadership may not be trusted. According to Chaplain Farrow, the commanding officer would tell Wiccans, "Someone from my command will be there, and if you do anything inappropriate, we will shut it down . . . I will shut it down for good order and discipline." Another Catholic priest, Chaplain Illera, was obviously suspicious of Wiccans when they met. He said, "I had someone standing watch all the time. 'Cause I would have to answer for their problems if they made a big mess. So there would be someone monitoring from a distance, someone watching. [. . .] If they just come in for ladies' Bible study or ladies' meeting, you won't have too many crazy things happen. That's not exactly a fringe group. That's pretty mainline."

The "someone" set to watch the Wiccans wouldn't necessarily have to be in the same room, he added, and could make themselves useful by answering the phone, making photocopies, or providing refreshments for the Wiccans while there, but "you just don't turn over the facility to them." Since there was almost always someone around to do these things anyway, other groups might end up being "watched," too. But Chaplain Illera clearly thought the Wiccans needed closer surveillance than others.

Some chaplains were happy not to have had much experience working with Wiccans. Chaplain Szmatula, a Missouri Synod Lutheran, said, "Thank God we haven't had the kind of Wicca problems the Army has had." When I asked Chaplain Tzilker, the rabbi, if he had encountered Wiccans he answered, "I really haven't, thank God." The Wiccans at a base where Chaplain Feteris had worked would meet at a nearby Air Force base so that he "didn't have to deal with that," punctuating his statement with a comical facial expression of relief, as if he had dodged a projectile. He thought he hadn't had much to do with them because he hadn't been assigned to any bases large enough to have "a real issue" with Wiccans, although he was aware his installation had a married couple practicing witchcraft together.

Most chaplains, however, had interacted with Wiccans. Chaplains Geschka and Gunvant, both Catholic priests, had both worked on bases where there were several dozen Wiccans. Chaplain Gunvant listed "Buddhist, Muslim, probably Seventh Day Adventist," and "probably Jewish folk" as groups that were "smaller demographically," so that in terms of numbers "the Wiccans are right up there." Chaplain Clement thought Wiccans were "a growing group," although he didn't have exact numbers. Unsure of what Wiccans actually do other than "that one nature ritual thing in the woods," he thought the problem was that they liked to keep to themselves:

> One thing about Wiccans is you don't normally hear them talking about, "Hey, I'm a Wiccan." You know? They're pretty close to the cuff on that. They tend to . . . They don't proselytize, really. So when they're there, they sort of sneak up on you. If you're not looking for them you can go from "Man, there's no Wiccans in this unit" to "Man, I found out last night there are 25 Wiccans." And the reason why you found out was because maybe the commander said, "Everybody, go and get new dog tags!" And while they're getting them you start hearing, "He's a Wiccan and he's a Wiccan and . . ." (United Methodist)

Consistent with the scholarship on Wicca, many are solo practitioners who are happy to go it alone spiritually.[44] One of the Mormon chaplains I interviewed had been assigned to a ship that had "both a large group that held weekly meetings, and then also individual sailors on smaller ships" (Chaplain Frantz). Some of the solo practitioners were new to Wicca, however, and wanted to get in touch with others for guidance and support. Chaplain Frantz helped them get in touch with each other, although he thought they more often than not found each other without his help. When they did use him, he thought "their bigger issue was feeling legitimate, or gaining legitimacy, and then also having a meeting place" (Mormon). When I probed him on the matter of legitimacy, he explained it in terms of being a group "that deserves to have a time and space set aside for them, so that they could meet." In other words, practical accommodation and facilitation on the same basis as other groups is important in making religious minorities feel welcome and accepted.

Does accommodation in the military and facilitation by chaplains do more than just include Wiccans? Is it possible that the military actually promotes the Wiccan faith? A few of my subjects seemed to think so. Chaplains Gunvant and Bartley had both worked at a large facility with high turnover. The latter explained, "Because the Wicca service already existed. So . . . every time a new company comes, we would have power point presentations of groups and various services that are here. Wicca was on one of the power point presentations. So the curious came out, in addition to maybe those who are faithful Wiccans. Now we don't get as much interest because it's not on the power point presentation any more" (Church of God in Christ).

Chaplain Chance argued that because the Chaplain Corps exists "primarily, and it's been taken to the Supreme Court, to provide for the religious freedom of others," it is actually easier to explore new religions in the military than it is in civilian life:

> It gives people more opportunity to . . . I don't know. Investigate this kind of stuff. Because they say, "We want this," and I go, "Well, I'll see what I can do." You know? Whereas if you're in Grand Forks, North Dakota, and you want to become a Wiccan, and you tell your boss at Safeway, he'll look at you like "Are you nuts?" You know what I mean? It's just a . . . We almost have a state-sponsored religion in the military in the sense that we have an office, and officers, whose job it is to make sure this stuff happens. (ELCA)

Wicca may not just be something individuals bring into the military and then ask to have facilitated; it might be discovered in and even because of the military, as happened to Don Larsen, the would-be first Wiccan chaplain who converted from Pentecostal Christianity. Chaplain Bartley thought Wicca was especially strong on Army bases in Germany, because they were so big. I don't know what he, or the Catholic Church, would make of Chaplain Dyren, who actively encouraged Wicca by reaching out to them and instructing them in their own religion. Admitting to a "fascination" with "the occult," Chaplain Dyren described his Wiccans as follows:

> Some of them are young guys who are out of what I call . . . the Dungeons and Dragons, where you play those video games, or the computer games, and those young people are a little bit different. They don't quite fit in with the average sailor. Or marine. And so what you do is you find with them, you sit them down and talk to them because sometimes their understanding of the history of the Wiccans and which way certain groups and certain orientations moved . . . they don't quite have it all together. So I try to . . . give them a little information, saying, "Well, actually, it works sort of like this." And give them a little edge. So I've gone to their little meetings or their covens and watched and I just, if they want any ideas or suggestions, I'll help them out. (Catholic)

While Chaplain Dyren's account of Wiccans as somewhat confused misfits who "play games" was shared by many of the other chaplains I interviewed, his willingness to encourage them and facilitate was less so. In general, the chaplains' assessments of Wicca were much more negative than those they had of Islam. Where Islam is simple and Muslims flexible, chaplains find Wicca confusing and its practitioners often antagonistic.

According to two Southern Baptist chaplains I interviewed, "Wiccan is a broad, general term that has many different sects, just like a Baptist has five and a half thousand different kinds of Baptists" (Chaplain Beard), and "part of the problem with trying to define the Wiccans is even they would define it differently among themselves" (Chaplain Irons). Chaplain Frantz had found that "you can't just say they have specific needs because every group of Wiccans can be slightly different. You know that some practice Norse mythology, some are Celtic, others are . . . Egyptian. So it's very hard to know what one group is going to want" (Mormon).

Like Chaplain Frantz, Presbyterian Chaplain Bowmaker wanted to help the Wiccans but had difficulty doing it: "On deployment on a ship . . . I got them all together and said, 'Anyone you know thinks they're a Wiccan, let's all get together at this time.' And they sat down and they couldn't agree what they wanted to do. [chuckles] There were, like, seven of them and they had twelve opinions."

The two Wiccans Chaplain Kojic had on his ship weren't interested in communicating with each other at all. "They just didn't get along," which the chaplain thought "was kind of a weird thing," even though he belonged to a Lutheran denomination, the Missouri Synod, that has a reputation for not getting along even with other Lutherans.[45] Chaplain Gunvant gave the best explanation of why Wicca caused the military and many chaplains some grief:

> Our problem with the Wiccan service and the Wiccans in specific is not with their religious faith. Well, there are some folks who do have obviously a lot of problems with the Wiccans' faith. [. . .] But our specific problem with them is they are not organized. They do not have as yet representatives to whom one could refer. When you try to find out how to support them, it becomes very difficult. They are not nationalized, if you will. They are not institutionalized as other organizations might be. So our problem institutionally has not been "Are we going to support the Wiccans?" Our problem institutionally has been "How are we going to support them? What is the requirement?" [. . .] As a theology, that hasn't been the problem, even for the commanders. The problem is "What do I do with this?" (Catholic)

Without a familiar and recognized denominational structure to represent them, Wiccans are at a disadvantage. This is exactly the problem the Sacred Well Congregation has been trying to remedy. Although there are chaplains who dislike Wicca, even if they do manage to bracket their theological aversion to witchcraft, they may simply be frustrated by the practicalities of facilitation.

With no central authority, be it an organization or a scripture, it's not surprising that some chaplains find Wiccans unable or unwilling to cooperate with each other. In addition, some chaplains believe Wiccans have a problem with *them*. Chaplain Michaud described a Wiccan who came to his office as "very antagonistic," asking theological questions in a way he found "belligerent" and "almost to the point of being rude and disrespectful." He found out why: "And at the end of our talk, I could tell something obviously was going on, and he said, 'Well, part of my initiation was to come and challenge the chaplain.' It was part of his initiation as a Wiccan. So that's what that was . . . He was right on the edge of being disrespectful. That's what he had to do. The group told him he had to do that" (Baptist General Conference).

Remember that even though chaplains de-emphasize their rank, they are still officers. They wear officers' uniforms and are used to being addressed in a deferential and polite way. Chaplain Geschka also had an experience with a confrontational Wiccan. Waiting in line to eat and exhausted after a day of military exercises, he encountered a man who commented on the cross he wore to identify himself as a Christian chaplain. He said, "I think I was getting a soda or something and he was standing there waiting for his food, and then, 'I am not put off by your cross.' I go, 'What?' and he goes, 'I'm Wiccan.' I says, 'Great, go away, leave me alone, I'm tired. If you want to have an intelligent conversation about this, track me down tomorrow. I'm the guy with the red bottle. Go away.' Commenting on criticism from other chaplains about having dismissed a marine like that, even though he was tired and the marine had an attitude, Chaplain Geschka continued, "I'm sorry. He's an idiot. I had no time for him. Well, after further pondering, twenty-twenty hindsight, I probably should have said something like, 'Yeah, and wait until Jesus comes off his cross and comes to kick you in the butt,' but I didn't say that" (Catholic). He never saw that Wiccan again, but a week later he had the chance to help another marine find fellow Wiccans to worship with. This encounter was different because he was dealing with "a young man who was truly interested in something, as opposed to the idiot I had met at the snack bar."

Chaplain Kanaridis, a Conservative Baptist, made no effort to hide his contempt as he told me about a female officer who claimed to speak for Wicca. Pointing out that she was subordinate to him in rank, he described the situation:

> She came in, and she was looking for a fight. I wasn't the senior chaplain then, thank the Lord. But the senior chaplain was the one that they went to. And he was a Lutheran, and he was just bent out of shape: "What am I going to do? What am I going to do?" But this woman was a militant, which a lot of those are, and so she wanted to fight. And so she came in here demanding that we facilitate her needs, to start a Wicca service.

It was hard to tell whether Chaplain Kanaridis meant Wiccans or women when he said "those" are "militant." His was one of the longest interviews I conducted, and it was clear to me that he had little use for either group in the military. His portrayal of the mainline chaplain as indecisive was also in character. In the end, the Wiccan was told to try to get accreditation from "the organization of the Wicca" so she could become a lay reader "like anybody else."

Chaplain Chance (ELCA) did not think Wiccans were militant. Rather, he found them reluctant to talk about their beliefs. "The Wiccan guy on our ship felt persecuted," he said, because others would "start giving him crap about it" if they knew he was a witch. Chaplain Townsend also thought Wiccans were skittish, attributing it to unpleasant interactions and the Wiccans' world view:

> No evidence of Wiccans in this command. There may be some, but if so, they're hiding pretty deep underground. [. . .] Sometimes they just don't want to reveal themselves. Some have had bad experiences with chaplains or have had bad experiences with the command. [. . .] If you look at Wiccan websites . . . what they say is "We are the old religion. And we were here before you were. And that all we are is trying to practice that which you forcibly obliterated and we're afraid of you because you're violent and you're mean" and that kind of thing. (Reformed Episcopalian)

As a result of this attitude, the chaplain felt he had to "really go the second mile, a lot of times, with a Wiccan. To let them know that you care about them and you care about whatever their particular needs are. Because they come into the situation, they come into the situation with a sense of being persecuted before you ever open your mouth."

Chaplain Townsend remembered a sailor he worked with who was unusually reluctant to talk about spiritual matters. Only after six months did he reveal that he was a Wiccan, "prepared for some mountain of vituperation to fall on his head, and when it didn't he was very surprised and I think very happy." Chaplain Feteris had asked a woman identifying herself as Pagan if she needed anything. She said no because she was a solo practitioner, but "was kind of shocked that I would offer" (Presbyterian).

Even when chaplains and Wiccans are inclined to get along and help each other, there's a possibility of prejudice and misunderstanding disrupting things. Chaplain Beard, a Southern Baptist, knew the Wiccans on his base were avoiding him. When a new chaplain arrived, they went to her for facilitation. At the time, he thought it was because she was younger or female, or because his own "Christian witness was pretty strong." But after she left, he found out from the Wiccans that they had assumed he wouldn't approve of them or help them. "They made a judgment, not I. That I wouldn't have helped them. But I did facilitate for them. I wrote the instruction and I made sure they had a place to worship and so forth. But then they misunderstood, because then they started sending me, like, Wiccan jokes and stuff on my email. And I said, 'No, no! You don't understand! I'm not approving, I'm just helping you'" (Southern Baptist).

Once the ice is broken and misunderstandings cleared up, collaborative relationships between chaplains and Wiccans can happen and often do. Chaplain Cugrijus, a Mormon chaplain who said, "I have a bunch of Wiccans in this regiment" had good relations with them. He continued, "I talk to them. They talk to me. And you know, they don't run away when I come up to them. One of them wanted to work for me! As a matter of fact, I wouldn't have had any trouble having him work for me." Chaplain Metzger, from the same group that revoked Chaplain Larsen's ecclesiastical endorsement when he converted to Wicca, was friendly with "his" Wiccans, who met for a Wiccan discussion group every Saturday: "They even invited me to attend. I never did, but . . . I ate with them once and just talked with them so I was able to establish some identification with them" (Chaplaincy of Full Gospel Churches).

As discussed briefly in the previous chapter, Wiccans can't realistically expect to be allowed to use the chapel for their meetings or services, even though the chapels are intended to be multifaith. Chaplain Frantz (Mormon) said, "The chapel is not going to be generally allowed to be used by Wiccans," and the "militant" woman Chaplain Kanaridis described demanded "that she was going to use the chapel" until the senior Lutheran chaplain, apparently having regained his composure, denied her on the grounds of good order and discipline. Chaplain Kanaridis agreed with that decision, saying, "She just really wanted to do some weird stuff . . . I mean, you think about it, as a Christian and as a . . . You've got the fundamentalists, you've got the charismatics, you've got all these other Christian groups meeting in this place, and on Tuesday night they have Wicca in there? I don't think so!" (Conservative Baptist).

Chaplain Farrow violated this norm at least once, offering the chapel to a solo practitioner. Out on a bitterly cold and "miserable" desert on Halloween, he suggested the Wiccan use the chapel so he could stay warm. He knew the Wiccan Halloween observance was supposed to take place outdoors and was surprised when the young man took him up on the offer: "I said, 'Son, you're welcome to use the chapel here' and so forth, 'but don't you want to go out and do it outside?' He said, 'No, sir. It's cold outside.' 'But where is your faith and commitment?' 'But sir, it's cold outside.' Well, it once again reinforces to me that it's kinda like a novelty, as long as it's convenient" (Catholic). Apparently realizing that he'd questioned the sincerity of an entire religious group, Chaplain Farrow quickly added, "And that's understandable, and I'd probably be the same way. I don't want to be cold, either." Not all of his colleagues were as generous.

OTHER MUSLIM NEEDS

Since Wicca has few specific requirements, a scheduled time and place to meet and proper lay leadership is usually all Wiccans need from the military. Islam, on the other hand, requires accommodation for prayer, which has already been discussed, and also for dietary restrictions and fasting. Many chaplains spoke in detail about food. "Military chow is not very conducive to either Buddhism, Hinduism, Islam, or Judaism," said Chaplain Townsend (Reformed Episcopalian), and Chaplain Geschka said the military uses an "inordinate amount of pork in the chow halls" (Catholic). Pork is hard to avoid, according to Chaplain Metzger, who said, "Often times when we're served green beans on board the ship, there would be pieces of pork in with the beans. So in many ways the Navy menus almost promote the use of pork, as a sort of flavor enhancer in many of the dishes, including the vegetable dishes" (Chaplaincy of Full Gospel Churches).

As mentioned in the previous chapter, military personnel can get funds to purchase more appropriate food for themselves, so called "com rats." The chaplains I interviewed were often involved in approving that for Muslims, Chaplain Tzilker among them: "Dietary is one of the big ones that I get involved in. Because we have similar dietary restrictions. So I get involved a lot. From my experience. To enable that" (Jewish). Chaplain Drozdov (Eastern Orthodox) had helped a sailor who was, ironically, working as a cook making food he couldn't eat himself, to get separate rations. On one occasion, another sailor saw this Muslim cook eating pizza and jealously complained to Chaplain Drozdov that pizza wasn't "Muslim food." Sometimes, it is chaplains themselves who say and do thoughtless things. Chaplain Drozdov attended a meeting of chaplains and found that the others had ordered nothing but pepperoni pizza even though that was inappropriate both for him, since he was fasting, and for a Muslim chaplain in attendance. Chaplain Drozdov said he could have just picked the meat off his slices, "but in solidarity with my colleague, I didn't want to." The two men left the meeting for a while and bought tuna sandwiches. The thoughtlessness of the majority had created an opportunity for them to bond.

Leaving to get separate rations isn't as feasible when in the field or at sea. Fortunately, Chaplain Clement (United Methodist) could report that the military had gotten very good at providing religiously appropriate MREs, or Meals Ready to Eat. In fact, his division was stockpiling special MREs for Muslims, Jews, and vegetarians. This kind of foresight and preparation was only possible because the needs of Muslims and Jews are predictable. Wiccans were generally viewed as unpredictable. It was hard to anticipate what a Wiccan might claim to need, or when.

In addition to finding appropriate food, going without food because of religious fasting is a recurring issue. When I asked Chaplain Koch about his experiences with Muslims, he observed that "Ramadan begins today" and explained that this was an area where military needs might have to supersede individual preferences:

> From sunup to sundown, Muslims fast. They don't eat, they don't drink . . . If it's going to be a ten-mile hike with a full pack on that weighs 75 pounds, and they're going to wear MOPP gear, which is very hot and causes people to sweat, you're going to have heat casualties if it's really hot in the summer. You know, if the Muslim guy is not eating or drinking, to expect the person to do that would be to try and kill them. So exceptions have to be made. Now, we try to accommodate, during the month of Ramadan, but if this is an absolutely mission-critical, essential thing, the Muslim is going to have to acquiesce. But we try to accommodate. OK? (United Methodist)

Chaplain Gunvant's base was dedicated to physically rigorous training, which put fasting out of the question. "There is no fasting here," he said. While he would arrange alternate meals for Muslims and other groups, he said, "as for not eating or drinking or restricting a diet in a training environment, we can't do that" (Catholic). When he brought the point up again later, he added, "and Muslims have accepted that." Having felt the summer heat reflect off the asphalt parade grounds myself, I'm sure that any Muslim who attempted to run around on it for hours in heavy gear without drinking would have suffered a rather pointless martyrdom.

In other settings, however, accommodation was possible. Chaplain Feteris (Presbyterian) and Chaplain Cugrijus (Mormon) had made arrangements for Muslim personnel to eat between sunset and sunrise. Chaplain Feteris made sure the mess hall saved some food so his Muslims could eat after dark and had them eat breakfast with the cooks since they ate before sunrise anyway. When the commanding officer questioned Chaplain Cugrijus making a similar arrangement for a Muslim individual, he said, "Well, then he has a reasonable complaint." The commander allowed the accommodation.

The chaplains didn't mention Muslims having very many needs beyond prayer and dietary accommodation. What material objects

Muslims required were supplied to them without apparent difficulty. For example, Chaplain Feteris carried a prayer rug with him for his Muslim marines to use, since they were so restricted in what they could carry on their own persons, noting that "they'll basically have their weapon, a pack, and a sea bag, and that's got to hold a lot of stuff" (Presbyterian). Similarly, Chaplain Irons traveled with a small library: "They need to be provided with the use of their own scriptures, so I have probably about twenty in my own mount out box. I have New Testaments, I have Bibles, I have Korans as well for them" (Southern Baptist).

By way of summary, chaplains report few serious problems accommodating the practical needs of Muslim military personnel. They give some of the credit for that to Islam. "It's a very flexible religion," said Chaplain Michaud from the Baptist General Conference. His Evangelical Lutheran colleague, Chaplain Oberlin, mused, "It wouldn't surprise me if it was a Muslim who invented the asterisk." Because Islam was so simple, another Lutheran chaplain, Chaplain Szmatula, claimed, "We have more trouble with Seventh Day Adventists than we do with Muslims," and Chaplain Hawthorne said the Muslims he had met "seemed to not really need anything the whole deployment" (Southern Baptist).

In addition to Islam's simplicity and flexibility, chaplains give the military's Muslim personnel get credit for being easy to facilitate for. Chaplain Bartley said, "Many of them have prior service and they know the system well enough to be able to work within it" (Church of God in Christ). Chaplain Frantz, who is Mormon, thought "Muslims have done a good job of fitting in," and Chaplain Clement wasn't surprised by their willingness to take the "nice to haves" of their faith when they can and settle for the "bare bones" when they have to: "I would suspect that in the Arab nations, too, they don't stop fighting and go, 'Oh, it's time to pray.' They realize that, you know, we're in this fight, we have this operation, and we just can't stop the fight five times a day" (United Methodist).

A few chaplains noticed Muslim military personnel struggling with their conscience after the United States invaded Afghanistan and attacked Iraq. Chaplain Michaud didn't think they were all sincere. He said there were "quite a few folks . . . turning to Islam during that time, for various reasons." There were actually many cases to deal with. He said, "We saw them coming out of the woodworks. And there was controversy there because not many of them, but a certain percentage of the people were, it appeared, using their religion to try to get out of an armed conflict, saying, 'How can I fight against my brother?'" (Baptist General Conference). Chaplain Michaud didn't think that even those whose qualms were sincere had a good case for conscientious objection, laughing hard as he continued: "You think that through and it doesn't take very long to figure out that Muslims have been fighting Muslims for a long time! You know? And I have this regularly." I didn't ask whether he would apply the fact that Christians have fought each other to individual cases in the same way.

Chaplain Townsend had also met a Muslim sailor who "brought religious issues up" and "wanted out of the Navy in the worst way." He felt he was falling behind friends from high school who had gone on to college and found girlfriends, and the chaplain also thought "there was probably some family pressure that he had made a mistake" (Reformed Episcopalian). It was Chaplain Irons, a Southern Baptist, who described the most sincerely conflicted Muslims. He'd met with "a couple of Muslim marines" who were uncertain about fighting in Afghanistan. They had not headed straight for the conscientious objector path, but talked to their superiors who then referred them to the chaplain.

> So I talked. In one case I talked to the guy. I listened to him, really, is what I did. Where he was coming from. And I did a couple of things. I did remind him, obviously, as a US Marine that this is not so much about religion at all but it's about our national interests, and maybe we're looking at two different planes here . . . But I also did suggest to him and to his command that if this really becomes an issue that we might consider [making] sure that this guy is not necessarily put in a position to fire. (Southern Baptist)

Initially failing to get this marine to set aside his religious perspective on the conflict, the chaplain suggested a noncombat role "because he didn't not want to be a marine; he just didn't want to go over there and fight other Muslims." Both of them knew it was a partial solution, given the nature of insurgency, which blurs the boundaries of combat and noncombat roles, and the Marine Corps's slogan that "every marine is a rifleman" who might have to fight. However, the case resolved itself: "Basically, what happened was after a few weeks of him thinking, he said, 'I'm fine where I am, no big deal.' But I was willing to go where he wanted to go with it."

Islam is an easy religion for chaplains to facilitate. There are established lines of communication, knowledgeable Muslim chaplains to consult, and recognized ecclesiastical endorsers who help train lay leaders. Chaplains are also simply getting used to Muslims' requests. They know what kinds of needs to expect and have accumulated experience in meeting them as a Chaplain Corps.

Wicca is different. Some chaplains have read or written instructions within their commands about how to meet some Wiccan needs, and some chaplains have worked in areas where there are established Wiccan communities that don't cause any problems. Both Chaplain Irons and Chaplain Beard could refer to specific Wiccans who "completely understood" (Beard) that they had to restrain themselves within the military for the sake of safety and to avoid "chaos" (Irons). These two chaplains, both Southern Baptists, were not worried by Wicca—or at least not by "their" Wiccans. Another Southern Baptist, Chaplain Hawthorne, felt lucky that "ours are pretty, pretty tame so to speak," which suggests a potential wildness in Wicca. Chaplains Geschka (Catholic) and Drozdov (Eastern Orthodox) thought good order and discipline restrictions were more likely to be placed on Wiccans than on any other group, Drozdov explaining that it was because in Wicca there are no specific faith requirements, so that "everybody is free to do what they feel is right." With no recognized agency to tell the military what is and what isn't a legitimate Wiccan religious need, chaplains are left nervous, never knowing if someone claiming to be Wiccan will want to "dance naked in the moonlight" (Chaplain Chance) or ask for "a dead cat or something like that" (Chaplain Michaud).

AFFECTION AND PREJUDICE: ATTITUDES TOWARD ISLAM AND WICCA

Thus far, I have considered the organizational, structural, and theological factors that separate Wiccans and Muslims in the chaplains' eyes. Naturally, culture and politics matter as well, especially in wartime. Is the chaplains' professional and generally positive attitude toward Muslims an expression of genuine respect and goodwill? Are their anxieties about Wicca merely based on frustration about practical challenges, or is there an element of prejudice? The face-to-face encounters, between chaplains and religious minorities and between chaplains and commanding officers, that determine whether religious accommodation is made or not are encounters between human beings with their own private attitudes. They also take place in an institutional and political climate that has been very highly charged. Considering how important one person's decisions can be in matters of facilitating free exercise of religion, it's necessary to both describe the cultural climate they work in and assess their individual feelings about Islam and Wicca.

In the aftermath of the terrorist attacks in 2001, politicians and other influential people made statements that were hostile to Islam. Although George W. Bush carefully argued that his quarrel was with Saddam Hussein and terrorists, not Islam, he occasionally used terms like "crusade" and frequently relied on absolutist distinctions between "good" and "evil" that made it easy for both domestic and foreign audiences to hear religious undertones. His first attorney general, John Ashcroft, was highly visible in the media as the nation debated means of defending itself against future attacks. Ashcroft, an unabashed right-wing Christian, told a reporter in 2002 that "Islam is a religion in which God requires you to send your son to die for him" whereas "Christianity is a faith in which God sends his son to die for you." This statement convinced many that he was prejudiced against Islam.[46]

Less prominent politicians and media celebrities have continued to exploit public fears and hatreds of Islam. In the weeks leading up to the midterm elections in 2010, long-standing plans to build an Islamic community center in lower Manhattan were turned into a "Ground Zero Mosque controversy." Also in 2010, the state of Oklahoma passed a law prohibiting its courts from applying Islamic sharia law. That politicians and television personalities resort to hyperbole is nothing new, but anti-Islamic rhetoric, including the persistent rumors that President Obama is a "secret" Muslim, could not be as widespread as it has become if there wasn't an audience for it. One survey of Americans found that 23 percent favored "making it illegal for Muslim groups to meet in the United States" and 60 percent supported "the US government collecting information about Muslim religious groups." These statistics reveal a gap between America's legal system, which compared to other countries has a good record of protecting minorities' formal civil rights, and the attitudes prevalent at the grassroots level.[47]

Bias against Islam has been expressed in and about the military as well. A general named William Boykin made derogatory remarks against Islam while speaking to evangelical congregations in uniform. Boykin claimed America was at war with Satan and said, "I knew that my God was a real God and his was an idol" when he recounted a confrontation with a Somali warlord. Although he drew criticism for his remarks, he was also promoted to Deputy Undersecretary of Defense for Intelligence after apologizing for them. On Veteran's Day in 2011, a Tennessee congressman addressed a conference saying, "Personally, I don't trust one Muslim in our military," adding, "My solution is, and I guarantee you this will work, you don't let any Muslims serve in the military."[48]

Acts of insensitivity, prejudice, and cruelty against Muslims by the military and its members have been varied and well publicized, hurting the nation's reputation and possibly helping insurgents recruit activists to kill Americans. Some incidents have been quite subtle. A company manufacturing high-powered rifle scopes engraved references to Bible verses on them, so that American soldiers and marines had weapons in Iraq and Afghanistan that said "2COR4:6" for Second Corinthians chapter four, verse six, and "JN8:12" for the eighth chapter and twelfth verse of the Gospel of John.[49] Far less subtle was what members of the 109th National Guard Infantry did in Iraq in the Spring of 2004, when they "commissioned the Special Forces interpreter, an Iraqi from Texas, to paint a legend across their Bradley's armor, in giant red Arabic script" that said, "Jesus killed Mohammed." They drove the tank-looking vehicle out into the streets of Samara, a city considered holy by many Muslims, interrupting the evening call to prayer with chants of "Jesus killed Mohammed" in English and Arabic from the vehicle's bullhorn. Their taunts drew fire, which they returned.[50] In May 2008, an American sniper was caught using a Koran for target practice in Iraq, forcing the US Army to apologize.[51] In February 2012, deadly riots broke out in Afghanistan after a number of Korans were accidentally burned as trash.[52]

Such reports, whether explained as accidents or as isolated instances of rank stupidity, have forced military officials and civilian leadership to apologize over and over again in order to salvage efforts to "win hearts and minds" around the world. However, some abuses of Muslims and Islam in the military have seemed intentional. Although much of the blame for the torture of prisoners at Abu Ghraib in Iraq and at Guantanamo Bay on Cuba can be laid at the feet of the CIA and the civilian leaders in the Rumsfeld-era Department of Defense, the participation and compliance of military personnel is undeniable in light of published photographs and exposés.

The military chaplaincy has not escaped controversy either. For example, conservatives have asked that the agencies that provide ecclesiastical endorsement to Muslim chaplains be investigated for ties to terrorist groups such as Hamas.[53] The best known and most dramatic incident, however, involved a US Army chaplain named James Yee, who later wrote a book about his experiences. He believed he was sent to Guantanamo Bay to bolster the government's claims that detainees were having all their need met, even spiritual ones, but once there he witnessed "a very strong anti-Muslim hostility that was directed not just to the prisoners, but also at the Muslim soldiers, the U.S. Muslim soldiers" who served there, which the command encouraged by showing videos of 9/11 and other terrorist attacks to new personnel as they arrived.[54]

He also saw Islam used as a "secret weapon" against the prisoners. In interrogation sessions, they were forced to watch a woman simulate masturbation, to endure her sexually inappropriate touches, and had their hands forced onto her (covered) breasts and genitals. They were also forced to bow before Satanic symbols by guards who yelled, "Satan is your God, not Allah! Repeat that after me!" In the detention areas, there were other abuses. There were cross-gender searches where women would pat down prisoners' genital areas and buttocks and guards mocked the prisoners while they prayed, rattled their cages, threw gravel, and played rock music to disturb them. They also provoked confrontations by disrespecting Korans, handling them roughly, tossing them, and dropping them on the ground. Chaplain Yee tried to end some of these abuses for the sake of creating a less volatile atmosphere, only to become a victim of anti-Muslim prejudice himself.[55]

A third-generation Chinese American convert to Islam, Chaplain Yee started out as the Army's "poster boy" for religious tolerance. At Guantanamo Bay, his advocacy on behalf of religious sensitivity and military professionalism made him enemies. In the fall of 2003, he was arrested at a Florida airport on his way home to Tacoma, Washington, for leave. He was charged with dozens of crimes, running the gamut from giving a pastry to a detainee without authorization, viewing pornography on a government computer, and adultery to espionage, mutiny, and sedition. The core of the accusations against him had to do with whether or not he was allowed to travel with certain documents that he was using to write a research paper. Yee himself believed he was targeted because he and other Arabic-speaking Americans at the base were mistrusted because they were Muslim and believed to be getting too close to the detainees.[56]

Imprisoned for two and a half months and threatened with the death penalty, the Muslim chaplain was denied his own free exercise rights. He was given food containing pork and was denied a rug on which to pray. At first, the only religious book available to him was a Bible, until he was visited by another chaplain who gave him his own English translation of the Koran.[57] He was released after pressure was put on the military by his attorney, his family, and Washington state officials.[58] A 2007 Inspector General's report within the Department of Defense later concluded that the Army had acted correctly in detaining him and initiating an investigation, because he "possessed suspected classified information," and that he was not the victim of religious bias, although the Army prosecution was unable to prove in court that the documents he had actually were classified.[59] In the end, all charges against him were dropped.

Some of the chaplains I spoke to reported witnessing hostility toward Muslims. Asked about 9/11, Chaplain Szmatula thought anti-Muslim feelings in the military actually began in 1991. He had met pilots, who flew in that war on an aircraft carrier he visited, who "were very much against bringing ragheads, that's exactly what they call them, ragheads into the military" (Missouri Synod Lutheran). Chaplain Szmatula seemed to make excuses for the pilots when he added, "because they had fellow pilots who were shot down." His ELCA colleague, Chaplain Oberlin, said he was having trouble getting Muslims in touch with each other because "these days it's not the most popular thing to say you're Muslim," so that many Muslims never chose to identify as such in their paperwork and on their dog tags. Chaplain Geschka compared Muslims to the Japanese-American *Nisei* who had to "prove themselves" as loyal citizens during World War II and told me about one Iranian American Muslim who had put an end to verbal abuse from other sailors by "pouncing on one young man" and daring him to repeat the taunts. "There would have been blood on the wall" if he had, Chaplain Geschka thought. When I asked him whether taunts like "raghead" were mainly racial or religious, he answered that "your average jarhead" was unlikely to even make the distinction. Chaplain Drozdov went so far as to suggest that because of tensions between Arabs and Israelis and with Saddam Hussein in the 1990s, "it was almost like the military was predisposed to be, I would say, hateful" toward Islam before 9/11. Like Chaplain Geschka, Chaplain Drozdov saw an element of racism as well: "Well, first of all, there was a lot of bias or prejudice, which I believe is probably directed more to their ethnicity. When you hear some of the things that are said, and I'm not going to repeat any of them because they're not worth repeating, but they're obviously stereotyping based on being Arabs, which not all Muslims are" (Eastern Orthodox).

Despite working in this political, cultural, and institutional climate, the chaplains themselves had very little to say about Muslims or Islam that was negative. Chaplain Farrow (Catholic) believed Islam was "so self-contained" that Muslims should be able to take care of their own needs, so that those who "played the religion card" asking for accommodation were "probably very weak in their religion," possibly implying that a good Muslim is one that keeps quiet about it. Chaplain Townsend (Reformed Episcopalian) had a bad experience with an imam he heard speak while in seminary, saying this imam seemed more interested in trying to convert his audience to Islam than speaking on the topic he'd been invited to address.

Only one chaplain I spoke to was clearly prejudiced against Muslims, and that was Chaplain Mace (Seventh Day Adventist). He didn't even like talking about them. Having spoken at great length on every question, he suddenly challenged me when I asked about his experience working with Muslims, demanding to know why I was asking about that. When

I explained it was because Islam had been in the news so much lately, he answered,

> I would assume that the only friction is they come from countries where terrorists are threatening us. And so, for them to come into our country and try to be brothers and to, you know, claim that . . . [they] have their own freedom and all that, and at the same time be at war with us, that's kind of a problem. So, my take on it is that, like among sailors on a ship, other sailors, the shipmates, are going to think, "What's this guy doing here?" You know? So they're going to be kind of suspect by coming here. (Seventh Day Adventist)

In Chaplain Mace's view, then, Muslims are all immigrants, all from "terrorist" countries, and apparently "at war with us" rather than included among us. None of the other 33 chaplains I interviewed said anything even close to this level of hostility. Quite the contrary! With Muslims' religious needs easy to anticipate, flexibility in the religion itself, and helpful Muslim chaplains to get advice from, several chaplains had very nice things to say about Muslims. Many seemed proud that there were Muslim imams in their corps and were eager to help get me in touch with one to interview. Chaplain Metzger, who had told me sadly about personal and religious conflicts with other chaplains, said by way of contrast that "I've enjoyed seeing Muslim chaplains come on active duty" (Chaplaincy of Full Gospel Churches). The same Chaplain Townsend who disliked the imam he heard speak in seminary made several phone calls trying to track down a Muslim chaplain he mistakenly thought was in the area for me. In between calls, he offered this: "Wonderful man. He's really taught me a lot. It's not like we go over to each other's house and have dinner, but we certainly smile at each other and that kind of thing." To me, it sounded like he was trying not to boast about being friends with him. Chaplain Clement had also learned a lot from a Muslim chaplain: "As a clergyman to work alongside an imam and to understand their training process, to understand their understanding of the Koran and their understanding of the Bible, was just eye-opening for me. It was just a wonderful exchange" (United Methodist). Chaplain Clement had also been touched by how closely the imam worked with a rabbi assigned to the same area, which he thought was "awesome." Granted, Chaplain Clement was a joyful man who tended toward exuberance in all of his answers, but he really did seem to have enjoyed the diversity he was exposed to during that specific assignment a lot. He kept bringing it up.

It wasn't just Muslim chaplains who impressed their non-Muslim peers. Many were impressed by enlisted Muslim sailors and marines. Chaplain

Street, who described his encounter with Islam as "a learning process, to be blunt with you," told me about an immigrant in his battalion:

> He is very devoted to his faith. And I sit there and watch him. In fact, during Ramadan, he's doing his fasting and all. He's very disciplined. Categorically, we disagree on theology, but I do admire his . . . tenacity and his love and his discipline for God. And I regress and I think, well God, if we get Christians that act like that sometimes they'd be very, you know, gung ho about our faith. So there's no static. There's no issues. Of course, we take little stabs now and then, but that's all in the form of brotherhood. (African Methodist Episcopal)

My interviews suggest but don't prove that African American chaplains had a different attitude toward Islam than the others. It wasn't that they knew more about Islam or liked it better, but they seemed more likely to have gotten to know Muslims personally, to have debated Muslims theologically, and to hold Islam up as equal to Christianity in dignity, if not in truth, as Chaplain Street did. This may be a fruitful area for future scholars to explore. White chaplains also found things to admire in Islam. Chaplain Cugrijus compared Islam favorably to Christianity, too: "Allah is very kind. And understanding. More so than many Christians would allow God to be" (Mormon). Chaplain Chance, from the Evangelical Lutheran Church in America, said that "all the Muslims in the Navy that I've met were nice guys and gals" and that Islam is "actually a religion of grace." Grace is a core concept in Lutheran theology, so to recognize it in Islam is to acknowledge an important similarity.

In addition to learning about Islam, the chaplains frequently had opportunities to educate others about it. According to a senior Catholic chaplain, the Chaplain Corps acted fast and tried to "make a strong effort" to do "quick education about the Muslim faith" after 9/11:

> Helping people to understand what a Muslim is. And what's the difference between a Muslim and a jihad, and an Arab, and all these other things. Is it a faith issue? Or is it an intellectual, political issue? And what is the difference and so forth? And once we're able to separate those for people, they become more and more comfortable with [it] and understanding. It's more, "This person can be a good Muslim or believe in what he believes, and not be a terrorist." We had to show them that. And reaffirm that. And make sure of that. (Chaplain Farrow)

The chaplains also reached out to Muslim sailors and marines. Chaplain Drozdov said, "Right after 9/11, a lot of us made a point to attend the Muslim service just for a show of solidarity." Even though they didn't participate in the Muslim prayers, they "wanted to be there" (Eastern Orthodox). Chaplain Grams, who is Presbyterian, enlisted a young Muslim petty officer and asked him to offer a prayer at a memorial service he and other chaplains organized. According to Chaplain Grams, the petty officer was "very touched" to be asked and helped him develop a class about Arab culture and the predominantly Muslim region they were deployed to. They were able to invite Muslim guests from the armed forces of a US ally to the class, which helped combat "this enormous prejudice that sprung up against Arabs and Muslims" in the time after 9/11. The class made a difference; he said, "It was very enlightening for the crew to realize that the enemy is not the Muslim or the Arab, that these are men, just like us. In fact I had some very interesting conversations that arose out of the ability to create that dialogue. I'd like to believe that part of the chaplains' job is to facilitate that sort of courage and vulnerability among lay people."

In Chaplain Tzilker's experience, Muslims had received "tremendous support" from the military (Jewish). Chaplain Oberlin thought that "most Muslims in the military are discovering far more hospitality, understanding, and compassion in this setting than outside of the military" (ELCA). Findings from another study show that civility can be coerced as well, with one Muslim saying, "I met some people [in the military] that I knew thought of me as some evil terrorist or something, [but] because [the military] is an equal opportunity organization you can't openly go out there and make accusations or make fun of somebody because the repercussions are pretty severe."[60]

Chaplain Hamoud confirmed his colleagues' impressions. He spoke at length about how touched he was by a farewell party he had been given at a previous command, and when called on to educate other chaplains about Islam he said he found them "very eager to learn and know how best they can help." I asked all the chaplains if there were any faith groups they had trouble getting along with and will report their answers in the next chapter. But when I asked this of Chaplain Hamoud, he seemed baffled: "No! I mean . . . [thinks hard] No, none whatsoever!" Then he laughed in disbelief that I would ask such a silly question. Luckily, he liked the rest of my questions: "the reason I'm excited is because I think this study is great. It's going to help create more awareness" (Muslim).

"Awareness" was Chaplain Hamoud's favorite phrase, which he used 22 times during the interview. He also spoke of "building bridges" a lot. Bridging the gap between Muslims and other Americans was his personal motivation for being a chaplain, it was exactly what he found himself doing every day, and he was unwaveringly optimistic about the future.

If the United States lagged behind other nations, for example ones in Southeast Asia, in terms of Christian-Muslim understanding, that was only because the United States was a young country and "the process of getting to know each other has just begun, in my opinion." He looked forward to the day when Muslims would be as accepted in America as Jews are, explaining the difference in terms of Jews having had a head start in the inexorable trend toward interreligious harmony. This observation was ironic in light of the interview I had with Chaplain Tzilker, who was quite frustrated and disillusioned about how he and other Jews were treated in the military. Making a show of taking a conspiratorial look down the corridor outside the office we met in, he told me his supervising chaplain was indifferent to the needs of Jewish personnel and that in general the military wasn't a good place to be a practicing Jew.

Chaplain Hamoud did concede there was occasionally "friction" that took the shapes of ignorance and prejudice, but he reassured me this was a temporary and normal part of the process toward tolerance. He listed specific accommodations the military had made for Muslims already and concluded that there had been "great progress. Oh absolutely! They have gone out of their way, everyone." As for the Chaplain Corps, it was "moving in the right direction," specifically "in the direction of pluralism, multireligious, multicultural, and this is what I like about America also." When I pressed him on whether there had been hostility to Muslims because of 9/11, he immediately stressed the positive and then returned to his favorite theme:

> Um yes. And at the same time there has been a tremendous amount of support also. Outpouring of love and affection. So both extremes. They're both extremes. I have received tremendous email from many people, making sure that if there is anything I need, they're available. Or email for kindness, for making . . . outpouring of their own feelings, wishing that they could do something to help, in any way or form. At the same time, yes, there have been cases where, not myself, but I'm worried about someone who is E1, E-2, E-3, enlisted. As education level rises, awareness level increases with that also. So out of ignorance, out of emotion, people may have said something or . . . I haven't heard of any physical harm, but verbal, yes. (Muslim)

Was Chaplain Hamoud's optimism sincere? Was he simply doing a really good job of putting the military and the Chaplain Corps in a positive light? He had had many occasions before to do presentations on these issues. However, in the interview, we were working off my script, not his. My questions set the agenda, and although he clearly anticipated some, he was just as clearly surprised by others. Nothing in his body language or emotional reactions of mirth, puzzlement, annoyance, and excitement made me think it was an act. We also met off base, at his suggestion, which wouldn't have been necessary if he was just planning to give me the "party line." To me, Chaplain Hamoud came across as an idealist fully aware of how lucky he was to have the chance to make a real difference. His officer's rank may have protected him from hostility he might otherwise have had to endure, as most military enlisted know not to insult officers to their face. Obviously, Chaplain Hamoud was having a much happier career than Chaplain Yee had. Maybe he was smarter or more careful about making enemies. Maybe he was better connected to and protected by other chaplains. He might also have been luckier.

The chaplains were very aware of and concerned about the public relations implications of Muslims' experience in the United States and its armed forces. Talking about the war in Iraq, Chaplain Irons said, "If you listen to Islamic clerics and you start to buy into what they're saying, then this is all about religion." "Obviously," he argued, that is an "absurdity" to anyone familiar with America's religious landscape. He counted "probably thirty or forty" different faith groups in his battalion, and the idea that the United States would decide to go to war against one of them was preposterous to him. "This is about another issue," he concluded (Southern Baptist). Chaplains minded their own manners, aware of being representatives of the United States. Chaplain Bowmaker, for example, was careful not to drink alcohol in the Middle East, "out of respect for the host country" (Presbyterian).

In addition to educating Americans about Islam, the chaplains also had chances to educate Muslims about America. Chaplain Oberlin told me about an Arab American sailor who called his family back in Egypt to tell them how well Muslims were treated in the United States, even after 9/11, and to reassure them that they need not worry about him. He had also witnessed a Muslim sailor go ashore while in a Muslim country's port to tell locals about halal MREs and other accommodations and to "make some connections with the culture" so he could get them to "understand that it [Islam] is one of America's religions" (ELCA). Chaplain Drozdov had also seen the military send forth Muslim personnel to make the point that Muslims "actually had a presence in the United States military." In so doing, he thought the Muslims had "been relegated to what I like to call mascot status," which any religious minority might have to put up with: "We see that a lot. And it's not something that's unique to them. Because sometimes Catholic chaplains become a mascot, to even their non-Catholic commanding officers or the staff. Certainly I've been treated that way in certain contexts. You know, we have contact with Greeks or

Serbs or something like that. So they're kind of brought out when it's useful and put away when they're no longer useful" (Eastern Orthodox).

Being a mascot can have its rewards, both gastronomically and adventure-wise. One of the Presbyterian chaplains I interviewed had fun describing how an African American Muslim who wasn't very important on his ship was trotted out as a kind of goodwill ambassador in both Kuwait and India, getting all kinds of fancy meals and attention for his efforts. Sometimes, local leaders would be uncomfortable talking to a Christian, especially a stranger, so this enlisted man was useful as a bridge builder, as someone who could demonstrate that "our ship hasn't got issues with Muslims, and not only that, but we can facilitate on behalf of Muslims." Of course, mascot status can be demeaning and burdensome. But any exploitation of Muslims in this role comes with a big dose of protection, which simply isn't available to Wiccans. There are no known geopolitical or operational advantages to being nice to witches.

Despite the perception among chaplains that Wiccans are disorganized and potentially both confrontational and disruptive, a few of them did have nice things to say about Wiccans and their beliefs. Here is Chaplain Farrow's explanation of Wicca: "They're not Satanist worshippers, they're actually tree huggers is what they are. They're environmentalists. They're about one grade above Greenpeace in that sense of loving nature" (Catholic). While the terms "tree hugger" might be a bit dismissive, Chaplain Farrow's point was that Wiccans weren't dangerous and that they were dedicated to at least one worthwhile cause. Chaplain Geschka, the same Catholic priest who had dismissed the irritating Wiccan while waiting in line for food after maneuvers, had also had "two positive encounters" with Wiccans he thought were "just good, intelligent people" who "weren't idiots or airheads, that was just the path they were on." Like Chaplain Farrow, he made sure I knew they weren't necessarily Satanists: "The Wiccan, God bless them, you know, they range from 'I love trees' to 'I love the devil.' And anything in between . . . It's more of a 'I love nature, I love trees, I love the earth.' So it's not going to have an adverse effect, I think, in people" (Catholic).

Not surprisingly, Chaplain Mace, who liked Islam the least, also didn't like Wicca. He put them in some very unflattering company and grew visibly angry as he blamed the media:

> I think more attention is going to be given to these way-out religions, like Wiccan or Satanist. I mean, the ones that are sensational. You've always got some liberal reporter who is going to write some front-page article over one incident, so the visibility for the one is going to be more than the 99 percent that do nothing. That kind of ticks me off. [. . .] It's sad that

> national policy is written for some jerk who just wants to push the limit. That's the way I look at it. [. . .] It's like the white supremacists. We don't hear anything about those any more, but when I was in parish ministry that was the hot topic because they were the ones that were pushing the envelope. Now it's the Wiccans or the Satanists. The people who like to push the envelope are the ones that the reporters like to give high visibility to. Sell the newspaper and give the shock therapy. [. . .] All I can see is more promoting of the weird, just to try to keep things neutral. (Seventh Day Adventist)

Chaplain Mace was isolated in my sample of chaplains in his distrust of Islam, but in good company when it came to disliking Wicca. Chaplain Farrow (Catholic) thought that while sailors might be able to take Wiccans in stride, many marines would "want to take them out and frag them, get rid of them, you know" and that most commanding officers would "just cringe" when they heard of Wiccans in their commands because they associated it with Satanism. Chaplain Dyren had known other chaplains who "didn't even want to deal with them; they'd just go into a rage about it." Maybe he had met Chaplain Mace? He said these chaplains who have "a sort of morbid fear of the Wiccans" probably thought "Catholics are on the verge of being pagans," too.

Chaplain Cugrijus vacillated on whether Wiccans actually were devil worshippers or not. Conceding that they claimed not to be and that Christians had done "some pretty satanic things," he still thought the nature of Wiccan worship might be one of the devil's "guises." He hadn't fully made his mind up and said, "Now, philosophically, do I believe that they're probably following Satan? Possible. I'm not sure whether to say yes or no [laughs]. God said, 'If you're not for me, you're against me.' I absolutely believe in the reality and divinity of Jesus Christ. Anything besides that then would be a false God, OK?" (Mormon).

Another Mormon, Chaplain Moore, told me he was very "disappointed" and "discouraged" by how other chaplains spoke about Wiccans, joking about them behind closed doors and making "not positive" comments about them behind their backs. Both of these chaplains from the Church of Jesus Christ of Latter Day Saints looked at Wicca through the lens of their own minority status. Chaplain Cugrijus hesitated to give a definitive answer about whether they were devil worshippers because he hated it when others presumed to define and categorize his religious beliefs, and the younger Chaplain Moore said, "Maybe I am sensitive to it [the jokes] because comments are made about my denomination, too, that I don't think are appropriate."

While the Mormons found common ground with the Wiccans as outsiders, the Catholics seemed to appreciate the Wiccans because of their shared emphasis on ritual, content notwithstanding. In my interviews, it really did seem to be the more liturgical chaplains, the Catholics, Eastern Orthodox, and "high church" Protestants, who were most likely to say nice things about Wiccans.[61] Chaplain Dyren, who reached out to the "Dungeons and Dragons" generation and helped Wiccans develop rituals, was the most enthusiastic. Acknowledging that many other chaplains "get real up and irate about the Wiccans," he said, "I really like the people who are in the Wiccans" because they are trying to "reclaim something that's been lost" in the world of globalization, science, and technology. What had been lost was "the more primitive" and "archetypal inside all of us," which is "primitive or wild, more basic" and more reverent toward nature.

Chaplain Drozdov had had a very positive encounter with a Wiccan. At an earlier assignment, he had been frustrated by how badly the people who came to his weekly worship service behaved, dressing inappropriately, bringing food, slurping their drinks, and swirling ice cubes around their paper cups loudly. By contrast, a sailor who didn't attend the service was helpful because he would use the public address system to remind everyone to "maintain silence about the deck" before turning his own radio music down. When Chaplain Drozdov sought him out to thank him, he learned that this sailor was a Wiccan, and the chaplain "thought it was very profound that he had a greater sense of awe and comportment toward the sacred than some of the people who professed to be Christian coming in" (Eastern Orthodox).

It was mostly Protestants, especially the more conservative ones, who weren't fond of Wicca. Their dislike was more than professional exasperation with a group that's hard to facilitate for or with annoying individuals. They disliked the belief system itself. Sometimes this attitude would be attributed to them by other chaplains; sometimes they'd express it themselves, both intentionally and in slips. Chaplain Cransveld, from the Foursquare Gospel Churches, referred to Wicca as "that Satanic cult, or whatever" and to a Wiccan as someone he "would have to" facilitate for even though he clearly didn't want to. Chaplain Cugrijus had been sent "inflammatory" material about Wiccans by a Navy chaplain, which alleged sexual perversions ranging from homosexuality to bestiality. Chaplain Bowmaker acknowledged the prevalence of the myth that Wiccans "want to play with knives and blood and draw things on the floor and do hocus pocus black magic stuff" (Presbyterian). Both United Methodist Chaplain Koch and Eastern Orthodox Chaplain Drozdov knew which faith groups were most likely to hold anti-Wiccan prejudices, Koch indicating that "people from conservative traditions will automatically associate them with something demonic" and Drozdov saying, "Conservative Christians—I mean that in the sort of fundamentalist sense—they equate them with being Satanists." When I asked Chaplain Drozdov if that included chaplains as well, he answered, "Sometimes. I mean, people draw the line at all kinds of places. You asked me, and I said I wouldn't minister to somebody or facilitate someone who is a Satanist or a member of the Unification Church. There are people who would draw the line before Wicca."

According to Chaplain Chance, a determined commanding officer can simply deny the free exercise rights of Wiccans, no matter what the individual does or the chaplain advises: "If you have a conservative evangelical captain, and there's a Wiccan on board, he might just say, 'You can't practice that on my ship.' And he can write his congressman and everything, and basically [. . .] you can advise him, but it's his ship. You know?" (ELCA)

The enlisted can react negatively, too, not only with the (hopefully exaggerated) threats of bodily harm mentioned by Chaplain Farrow, but also by trying to disrupt Wiccan gatherings. Chaplain Dyren once had to go between two groups to prevent a clear breakdown of "good order and discipline" from getting worse:

> I had to separate some of the African American brothers, who are more fundamental; they were always over there pounding on the wall or something like that, you know, praying that their souls would be saved or trying to place the healing power there, and say to them that wasn't necessary. So what we did was we just separated the two groups a little more so that, heh . . . Because the Wiccans, you know . . . because these guys stand inside the passage way and say, "You're a heathen and you're going to hell." (Catholic)

Among chaplains who disapproved of Wicca, the most common response was to question either whether it was a "real religion" or whether its practitioners were sincere or serious about their faith. These issues came up over and over again in the interviews. Even the most positively inclined chaplain, Chaplain Dyren, implied Wiccans were immature and trying to assert their individuality, saying, "It's a break from Mom and Dad—to show that 'I'm different' they go to Wicca" (Catholic). Chaplain Drozdov also thought so: "Sometimes they get into things just to be different, and just to see how much they can get away with." He later added that "my theory is they're disgruntled Christians who just haven't discovered Orthodox Christianity yet" (Eastern Orthodox). Throughout his interview, Chaplain Michaud raised the same themes:

> I don't think you can call them a faith group. When we say *a faith group* that generally means that they have a level of education which would allow them to sponsor a chaplain. And they don't have that. [. . .] Many of the Wiccans we would see in the military were very young people, had just come into the military, and it was something novel for them. Or it was a way for them to express themselves in various ways [. . .] Of course they're not going to college, they're looking for adventure, they're looking for something different, they're experimenting. This is something that's really different, it's antiestablishment. (Baptist General Conference)

Chaplain Squires also thought Wiccans were ignorant about what they really wanted, positing that "it satisfies a need, perhaps a desire for ritual or belonging" and that "those who think they're Wiccan—they really don't know that much about it" (Catholic). Like Chaplain Drozdov, Chaplain Squires seemed to think that what Wiccans *really* wanted was what his church had to offer. Notice that to him, Wiccan is something you think you are, not something you really are.

This condescending attitude, that so-called Wiccans are merely trying to resolve some developmental crisis of childhood or adolescence, cut across religious traditions. So did another version of the argument that Wicca doesn't really have to be taken seriously, wherein Wicca is just self-indulgent defiance of other people or the military. According to Chaplain Chance, "It's like, 'We have freedom of religion, so I'm going to pick something that's generally seen as not a good thing because I have the right to do it. And I don't have any documentation to prove that.' I wonder if sometimes it's not more personality driven than honestly faith driven, but that's just my opinion" (ELCA).

Chaplain Timu thought some Wiccans were "wanna-bes" while "others use it just as a scare tactic to keep people away or isolate themselves from the world." In general, he said, "there are very few true Wiccans" (Disciples of Christ). Chaplain Farrow also thought true Wiccans are rare. He said,

> I have yet to run into a real Wiccan. I really have. In all my years, dealing with a lot of them—most, I find them in one of two categories. Usually they're somebody that is looking for something and this is just a stopping-off point, theologically. They're just kind of searching. It's just a novelty, it's a stopping-off point, it's a respite, it's something to hold on to, it's a way to be different. Or the other category, a lot of these are the guys who are a royal pain in the you know what to the command. And the command has

> been a pain to them, so they want to be a pain back to the command. So they're going to pull out all the stops and start writing their senator about free exercise of religion. (Catholic)

The literature on why people choose to affiliate with one religious group or another actually does include spite or "antipathy" as a real motivation. According to one sociologist, most participants in Neo-Pagan or Satanist movements "seem to relish the negative impact their blasphemy has on devout Christians," which implies that Wicca is more a negative reaction against something than an affirmative, valid option in and of itself.[62] Whether this characterization is ultimately "true" is not just an empirical question but also a matter of definition. It depends on what religion "really" is.

The contrast with Islam is stark. Not one chaplain argued that Muslims, or any other major faith group, were "just experimenting," rebelling against their parents, "stopping off" somewhere in their search for the chaplain's own faith group, or simply trying to be a "pain in the you know what" to the military. Such attempts to diminish an entire belief system were reserved for Wicca alone. Yes, there were scattered concerns about Muslims trying to use Islam to get out of a deployment or to get money for separate rations. But these cases were always described as departures from the norm of "real" Muslims who are sincere about their faith. Among Wiccans, it's sincere faith that is the exception according to the chaplains.

Despite this difference, there is one similarity worth pointing out because it highlights the importance of the military as an institutional context. The military ethos is pragmatic and activist. It celebrates problem solving, hard work, and a can-do attitude. According to the chaplains, conformity to this "Protestant work ethic" is a key to inclusion for any religious minority. Speaking of Muslims, Chaplain Farrow said it was the "good, solid sailors" who always got taken care of (Catholic). Chaplain Townsend said, "If they work hard and do a good job their religion is really a nonissue" and went on to praise a Muslim sailor who had the "best Personal Fitness Test scores," was considered "the hardest worker" and "the number one performer" in his shop, and was a good singer to boot (Reformed Episcopalian). Chaplain Tzilker thought Muslims would be accepted as long as "they serve like anybody else, they take their lumps like anybody else" (Jewish). Chaplain Hamoud unapologetically stated, "In my opinion a Muslim is a better soldier, a better marine, from the get-go. Better airman, better sailor. Because the discipline is built into him or her" (Muslim).

Chaplain Hamoud recognized good military character in Wiccans, too, saying of one that "he was a good worker, a very nice worker." Chaplain

Chance knew a Wiccan who was "not just a nice guy, but a very capable petty officer, too" (ELCA). Chaplain Street said that even though the Wiccans "get the eye raised, maybe the head scratched," that "perception does not hinder these marines and sailors from doing their job" because "religion and performance" were "two different issue altogether" (African Methodist Episcopal). Even Chaplain Illera, who was suspicious of Wiccans, admitted that those he worked with kept "kinda quiet," "never asked for much," "did their jobs," "were on time," and "were always neat and clean" (Catholic). This reinforces the primacy of the military's needs over religious claims, as described in the previous chapter.

CONCLUSION

My interviews with the chaplains confirm a claim made by Diana Eck, leader of the Pluralism Project at Harvard University, that the military provides "no-nonsense support for religious pluralism."[63] Because the chaplains have a more positive view of Islam than of Wicca, Muslims are probably more likely to benefit from the "support" and Wiccans more likely to be dismissed as "nonsense."

Wicca provokes confusion, suspicion, condescension, fear, exasperation, and contempt. Many chaplains hope and even try to avoid witches. Islam is engaged actively, inspires respect and caution, and is taken seriously. The same geopolitical conflicts that fuel hatred of Muslims also increase knowledge of Islam and have made fair and respectful treatment of Muslims a vital part of US policy. Although American Muslims are harassed and discriminated against, the military chaplains made it clear that there are many things they can and will do to facilitate their religious needs. Furthermore, the military seems to be getting better at accommodating Muslims in its ranks as knowledge about Islam spreads and the practicalities of providing prayer breaks, allowing for fasting, supplying appropriate food, and ordering prayer rugs are routinized. A proper comparison of facilitation outcomes for Islam and Wicca would require research on the experiences of Muslim and Wiccan enlisted, and some promising work is being done on the Muslim side.[64] What can be suggested here is that Islam is in the process of being accepted while Wiccans seem stuck in the category of irritating "whackos" who are either malevolent or silly.

The death of Patrick Stewart occasioned a poignant example of resistance to Wicca. Stewart, a member of the Nevada Army National Guard, was killed when the helicopter he was in was shot down in Afghanistan in 2005. His widow wanted to have a pentagram on his grave marker as a symbol of his Wiccan faith, but her request was denied by the Department of Veterans Affairs. The VA had a list of dozens of approved symbols for grave markers, including stars of David for Jews and various crosses for Christians, but the pentagram was not among them. In the end, state-level officials in Nevada asserted their jurisdiction over Stewart's grave and permitted the symbol, and intervention by Americans United for Separation of Church and State and the American Civil Liberties Union successfully got the VA to include pentagrams as permissible grave markers.[65] Had the Wiccans been better institutionalized, with a recognized endorsing agent to liaison with the military, educate decision makers, and assert its members' rights, Patrick Stewart may have been laid to rest more easily. Wiccan religious needs are not yet accommodated as a matter of routine.

In addition to Muslims being better organized, they have another advantage over the Wiccans in that they are rapidly adapting to American society while Wiccans are reacting against it.[66] Within Neo-Paganism, debates about whether their spiritual paths should or even can be codified and organized into forms resembling denominations take place against a backdrop of dramatic and increasing internal diversity.[67] At the same time, Diana Eck's prediction that Islam would begin to transcend its ethnic and even sectarian differences in the American context was validated by at least one of my subjects, Chaplain Grams: "My Muslim lay reader . . . his form of Islam, he's typically American. He describes himself as an American Muslim. Meaning he doesn't subscribe allegedly to the Shi'a or Sunni persuasion. He's pure Koran. He sounds like one of the Christians we had—'I'm just a Bible-believing Christian.' Well, he's a Koran-believing Muslim" (Presbyterian).

The chaplains' ability to make such direct comparisons between Muslims and members of their own faith is yet another advantage Muslims have over Wiccans. Sure, some chaplains appreciate the Wiccans' interest in ritual. But the Muslims have a book. They acknowledge Jesus as a prophet. They are patriarchal. What's more, without having to bicker among themselves about the nature of a Trinity, they can claim to out-monotheist Christians. Chaplain Irons, while estimating that "ninety nine point nine nine nine nine et cetera percent" of chaplains fell under what he called "the Judeo-Christian umbrella," argued that the exception he knew, the Muslim imam, still fit in because "even the Islamic ethic has the same background" (Southern Baptist). I mentioned a magazine cover I once saw featuring the three Abrahamic religions, at which he enthusiastically adopted the new term: "Abrahamic! Very good! Good term!"

Wicca is much harder for the Christian, or even Abrahamic, majority to comprehend. The same Chaplain Irons complained that "they don't have any body of teachings" and they are "very adverse to theism and

Judeo-Christian principles." Applying a "sociological" perspective, Chaplain Gunvant listed all the things Wicca lacked: "It doesn't have a hierarchy, it doesn't have an empowerment ceremony of some sort, it doesn't have a holy book or universally used holy book of some sort, it doesn't have a liturgy as far as we know" (Catholic). Mormon Chaplain Frantz explained that Wicca became "difficult" and a "challenge" because it was a different "type" and "philosophy" of religion, one that "most of us are unfamiliar with." That the broader New Age movement that Wicca is part of challenges Protestant moral commitments and Protestantism's traditional cultural hegemony compounds the organizational disadvantage of Wicca.

Some of the cultural resistance to Wicca may be rooted precisely in deeply held anxieties about the religious meaning and nature of the United States. Historians have traced Americans' religious self-conception as it has evolved from Protestant through Christian to Judeo-Christian, and now maybe even Abrahamic.[68] Wiccans, "nones," and adherent of religions such as Buddhism and Hinduism threaten to burst that conception before it's even fully formed. According to Hutcheson, a former military chaplain, this trend toward greater diversity has caused "a growing sense throughout American society of a breakdown in the *public moral consensus*, a collapse of generally accepted standards for making moral decisions." As a result of this, he believes "the basic moral issue confronting our society is how a religiously and culturally pluralistic nation can find a common core of beliefs about reality and values, on which to base its common life."[69] Muslims and Wiccans in the military raise precisely this issue.

Most chaplains and most commanding officers are part of the cultural consensus that is being challenged by increasing religious diversity. As civilians, some of them might have been sympathetic to what Hutchison has called the "counterpluralist impulse," which yearns for an older approach to diversity—namely, assimilationism—or which dreams of telling "all these nice other people that this is a Christian country."[70] As military chaplains, they may not act on such sentiments even if they had them, which raises the questions guiding the next chapter: what do the chaplains make of the diversity they encounter and how do they maintain their own identity against it?

The final point to make about Islam and Wicca, however, has to do with something deeper than organization and looking familiar to the majority. Whatever the chaplains make of Islam as a religion, they recognize it as precisely that—a religion. As shown in the preceding pages, chaplains don't always consider Wicca to "really" be a religion. The sociological maxim applies: what is perceived as a real religion has real consequences. More is at stake than mere semantics. To the extent that Wiccans reject "patriarchal monotheisms and the depiction of God as solely male"[71] and to the extent that their "movement ideology" is fundamentally committed to "individual religious authority,"[72] they risk defining themselves out of the category of religion altogether. What's more, this is often a very deliberate and celebrated move. Many Wiccans prefer to describe themselves as spiritual rather than religious and associate "organized religion" with conformity and oppression.

Even while remaining committed to an expressive, feminist, and ecological spirituality, some Wiccans have had experiences in the military and elsewhere that highlight for them the advantages of developing toward the denominational form. Tax-exempt status is one such advantage, but so is freedom of religion. To put a fine point on it: to assert religious rights you have to convince people that you are the kind of thing that those rights attach to. The dilemma for Wiccans is that often the people who need the most convincing are Wiccans themselves. Is it worth it to seek protection under a label you reject?

Whenever a group seeks protection as a religion, the courts face a dilemma. Precisely because you have to have "religion" before you can have "religious freedom," Winifred Fallers Sullivan argues the courts are faced with an "impossible" task:

> A fundamental definitional ambiguity inheres in all religion cases. Whatever law is being applied in a particular case, whether statutory or constitutional, all religion cases in the United States require a finding that the activity in questions qualifies as "religion." Such cases put courts in a difficult position. On the one hand, they are required by the use of the word "religion" in statutes and in the Constitution to inquire into its meaning, to draw lines between "religion" and not-"religion." On the other hand, there is much law in the United States saying that judges cannot enter into disputes regarding religious orthodoxy. The definition of religion for legal purposes in this country remains, as a result, profoundly unsettled.[73]

During the controversy that erupted over Wiccan worship at Fort Hood in the 1990s, a Catholic woman called Chaplain Russ Gunter of the Armed Forces Chaplains Board and demanded to know if the Department of Defense recognized Wicca. He answered, "It may come as a shock to you, madam, that the Department of Defense does not recognize the Roman Catholic Church!" His position was that keeping a list of approved ecclesiastical endorsers was something different than "recognition," so that Wicca and Catholicism had the same status as far as the Department of Defense was concerned. As he explained to a symposium audience, "the Department of Defense does not evaluate, judge, or officially sanction any religious faith."[74] However tenable or untenable the position may be, it shows how careful senior military chaplains are about steering clear of establishment charges.

With the Wiccans ambivalent about being a "religion," the courts supposed to be neutral, and the Department of Defense not in the business of "sanctioning" religion, who *does* decide if Wicca is "legitimate" as a religion? Formally, it is the commanding officers. But on what basis do they decide? They certainly rely on convention. Few commanders would doubt that a Catholic mass, a Jewish wedding, or a Baptist Bible study is something "religious." Occasionally they decide based on prejudice. According to the chaplains, a conservative Protestant commander can always find a "good order and discipline" reason to deny accommodation to a group he or she dislikes, even if it does hurt career, morale, or public relations (which it very well may not). In most cases, and especially in ambiguous ones, the commanding officers will rely on their chaplain's advice. According to Chaplain Frantz, "when the ships do ask me questions, they're basic questions about 'Is this a legitimate request that this sailor is making?" (Mormon)

Those chaplains who do recognize Wicca as a religion, as the kind of thing that guarantees rights like free exercise, know they are professionally bound to facilitate for it and would justify reasonable requests for accommodation to their commanding officers. The contrary and common view, that Wicca isn't really a religion, can cut two ways. If the chaplain is an inclusive type, the notion that Wiccans aren't really serious or are just passing through a phase in their search for something more real means they might as well be facilitated for. No lasting harm is likely to be done by them by letting them worship as they please. The Wiccans might even "get over" their phase and realize that the chaplains, and by extension the Christian majority, aren't so mean and nasty after all. If the chaplain is not inclined to be inclusive, infantilizing Wicca or describing it as a contrived expression of psychological needs or personality problems rather than sincere spiritual yearning justifies withholding the facilitation that is due all religious groups, large or small.

The chaplains' opinion of a minority faith group matters not only because they can speak to the military culture with the voice of America's tolerant legal system but also because the chaplains are called on to speak in place of that legal system. Although it isn't their job on paper, in lived reality it often falls to chaplains to separate religion from nonreligion, which means deciding who deserves freedom of religion and who doesn't.

CHAPTER 4

MILITARY CHAPLAINS' EXPERIENCES WITH DIVERSITY

> We're not members of some homogeneous civil religion in which we're all crushed together. Instead, like a magnet, part of us connects to each other, and part of us most certainly does not.
>
> —Reformed Episcopalian chaplain

THUS FAR I HAVE SHOWED HOW THE military manages religious diversity in accordance with US law, traditional American values, Department of Defense policy, and the need to maintain a Chaplain Corps that can't be challenged on establishment grounds. I have also explained how chaplains can exert their agency within this institutional and cultural framework to facilitate and sometimes limit the free exercise of religion. The previous chapter described how two specific religious traditions, Islam and Wicca, fare in the military. I concluded that it's probably easier for Muslims to have their religious needs met because they are easier for chaplains to anticipate, because Islam resembles Christianity more than Wicca does, and because no one contests that Islam is the kind of thing that has free exercise rights, a religion. This chapter is more directly about the chaplains themselves. How do the chaplains feel about religious diversity? How pluralistic can the military make its chaplains be? How are the chaplains' self-conception, theological outlook, and relationships with religious "others" affected by the increasing religious diversity they encounter?

The military wants its chaplains to serve the religious needs of all its members, within limits. In other words, they are expected to bracket their own religious particularity in service of other people's religious particularities. Although I have thus far explained the military's approach to religious diversity in defensive terms, in terms of its desire to avoid lawsuits, there are more affirmative perspectives that can be applied. Historian Anne C. Loveland views the military's preference for a general approach and ecumenical solutions to religious accommodation as an expression of what she calls "the plural ideal." The plural ideal has three component parts. First, it recognizes religious diversity as an empirical fact. Second, it assumes secularism. Although the military permits religious expression, it is itself a secular and neutral environment within which religiosity is a private matter. Third, free exercise of religion should only be limited by necessity.[1]

The institutionalization of the plural ideal means that the Department of Defense endorses a model of religious interaction and work that Richard G. Hutcheson calls "cooperative pluralism." Chaplains are supposed to work together in harmony to achieve as much free exercise of religion as is practicable, always being mindful of minorities' needs. Hutcheson, himself a former chaplain, emphasizes the collective nature of this effort because chaplains can only do so much acting alone. Teams of chaplains with "mutual responsibility" to each other and their commands can accomplish much more.[2]

Although Loveland and Hutcheson together describe the way things "ought to be," both are aware of tensions. Loveland, for example, articulates a rival perspective to the plural ideal, which she calls "the sectarian ideal," which there will be occasion to look at more closely in the next chapter. Hutcheson, for his part, raises the possibility of tension between chaplains and their sponsoring churches without seeming to think that it's a serious problem. In this, he may have been too optimistic, because many churches have profound objections to pluralism. Not all faith groups approve of how general the military expects the clergy they endorse for the chaplaincy to be.

In Chapter 2, I described religious accommodation in terms of a tension between "facilitation" and "good order and discipline." This was an artificial pairing that I made for analytical purposes. This chapter will also describe a tension, but this time it is a natural one. Chaplains often refer to and utter the motto "cooperation without compromise" when they describe their work. The largest umbrella organization of endorsing agents, the National Conference on Ministry to the Armed Forces (NCMAF), has a Covenant and Code of Ethics that speaks directly to the need for cooperation. Here are two relevant excerpts:

> I understand as a chaplain in the Armed Forces that I must function in a pluralistic environment with chaplains of other religious bodies to provide for ministry to all military personnel and their families entrusted to my care.

> I will seek to provide pastoral care and ministry to persons of religious bodies other than my own within my area of responsibility with the same investment of myself as I give to members of my own religious body. I will work collegially with chaplains of religious bodies other than my own as together we seek to provide as full a ministry as possible to our people. I will respect the beliefs and traditions of my colleagues and those to whom I minister. When conducting services of worship that include persons of other than my religious body I will draw upon those beliefs, principles, and practices that we have in common.[3]

The NCMAF Covenant and Code of ethics also includes statements that recognize the right of chaplains not to have to compromise their own religious beliefs, or ignore the requirements of their faith groups:

> "I will hold in trust the traditions and practices of my religious body."
>
> "I will carefully adhere to whatever direction may be conveyed to me by my endorsing body for maintenance of my endorsement."
>
> "I will, if [in] a supervisory position, respect the practices and beliefs of each chaplain I supervise, and exercise care not to require of them any service or practice that would be in violation of the faith practices of their particular religious body."[4]

In his description of the military chaplaincy, Hutcheson treats "cooperation without compromise" as a solution to the tension between churches and chaplains. I take a different and more critical approach in which the meaning of both terms depends on how chaplains understand, interpret, and apply them. I asked the chaplains to explain "cooperation" to me and to give me examples of both good and bad cooperation. I asked them in which faith groups they found their closest colleagues. My purpose was to give the chaplains a chance to discuss what they liked about their work, to talk about their friends, and also to find out how they rationalized working in a pluralistic environment while representing specific faith groups.

I also asked questions designed to uncover problems the chaplains might encounter as they tried to put the ideals of "cooperation without compromise" into practice. I asked them to define "compromise" and discuss whether they had ever had to compromise themselves or what they would do if pressured to do so. To discover the limits of facilitation, I asked if there were groups they would uncomfortable or unwilling to facilitate for. I also asked questions intended to elicit comments about conflicts among chaplains. Which faith groups do they tend not to get along with? Finally, I asked questions about the way each individual chaplain maintained his denominational identity in a diverse environment, how his own faith group fit into pluralistic setting, and how diversity had informed his ministry.

Taken together, the chaplains' answers let me tell two distinct stories. One story is good news for the military chaplaincy. It is about the many ways in which chaplains enjoy diversity, work well together, form genuine friendships, learn from one another, and don't feel that their own religious commitments are threatened at all. The other story is one where diversity grates on the chaplains, where rivalries and prejudice get in the way of effective cooperation, and individual chaplains feel disrespected or unappreciated. I'll tell both.

COOPERATION

Although every chaplain agreed that cooperation is important, they gave divergent answers as to why and to what it meant to cooperate. I found five different themes in their explanations: (1) cooperation as working well with other chaplains, (2) cooperation as meeting command needs, (3) cooperation as downplaying religious particularity, (4) cooperation as facilitation, and (5) cooperation as nurturing faith. These themes aren't exclusive of each other conceptually or in practice, but they do reveal that "cooperation" has no single, agreed-upon meaning among chaplains and that different chaplains will be oriented toward different needs and issues.

The most straightforward meaning of cooperation was of course that chaplains should cooperate with each other. Chaplain Irons spoke in terms of "collegiality in the Chaplain Corps" and "working together on a common mission," for example by making sure that Catholics in his battalion knew they had an "outlet for counseling" in him even though he was a Southern Baptist. Chaplain Squires talked about "professionalism in your calling" and "serving those you work with," which to him meant "you work together with other members of the clergy, other chaplains" (Catholic). Although Chaplain Tzilker said he "hated" the phrase "cooperation without compromise," he explained it as "to be an enabler, to allow other chaplains to do their ministry up to the point where it impinges on your faith's traditions" (Jewish). What all these statements have in common is that they refer to other chaplains.

Others referred more directly to the command. Chaplain Farrow, a senior chaplain, thought cooperation was all about matching religious needs with available religious expertise, saying, "So you look at ministry as a whole in an area or chaplain support in an area as a whole, and that's what cooperation and collaboration say. We're supposed to as a team go across and look at all the command needs and try to serve those needs as best as we can with the assets that we have, considering that there are different diversities and religious and support and that sort of stuff" (Catholic). Another experienced priest, Chaplain Dyren, agreed that cooperation was less about the inclinations and particularities of individual chaplains and more about what the command needed:

> Yes, we're here to take care of our own, but we're also here to take care of anyone. And you can talk to everyone in the command and they'll tell you, generals and admirals who I've known and grown up with, colonels, and through the years have said, "Take care of my people," things like that. What that means is, it's sort of a code word, "I want you to be there for everybody." Don't just be there for the Catholics or different denominations, Protestants or Jewish. All the personnel here are in a sense God's people, as we sort of define it.

It's possible that command needs are more salient to higher ranking chaplains who have more administrative responsibilities. To them, other chaplains may literally be human resources that they must distribute throughout the military. For lower-ranking chaplains, there is likely more attention to the details of counseling and worship and "running programs" about marriage, transitioning back to civilian life, or recognizing warning signs of suicide. Whether the chaplains resent being burdened with such "collateral duties" or welcome them as chances to score "points" toward promotion, they do provide chances to cooperate. Chaplain Feteris spoke of projects that chaplains could work on together in spite of religious differences, even under compulsion: "There are things that enhance the family of the community that we can work on together. And in those things we can cooperate, we can work hand in hand. Or we're ordered to work hand in hand; sometimes it's not a want, sometimes it's you will. Which is fine. Which I enjoy" (Presbyterian).

Chaplain Kanaridis (Conservative Baptist) wasn't willing to "send people to another denominational meeting where I know they're going to hear what I feel is false doctrine," but he would advertise programs such as "a conference on suicide," a "pot luck," a "group coming in to sing," a class on "how to handle stress," or programs for dependent youth, even if the chaplain running the program had "doctrinal stands" he was "completely opposed to." In other words, Chaplain Kanaridis was willing to cooperate on matters that didn't touch directly on theology. Like Chaplain Feteris, he interpreted cooperation in terms of tasks that had to be accomplished rather than the quality of relationships among colleagues.

Chaplain Cugrijus thought it was important to be "able to look at our similarities rather than your differences and work within your similarities rather than trying to dwell on your differences" (Mormon). Chaplain Beard agreed and elaborated:

> Cooperation would be to do things together that you're allowed to do by your religious faith. To look for similarities. And to not emphasize differences. For instance, a good example of that would be vacation Bible school. We would do Catholic and Protestant vacation Bible schools together. And we just left the divisive issues alone, we just never talked about them. So cooperation would be working together in a positive way, looking for similarities. Doing the things that we can to together. [. . .] I think the role of chaplain could be nondenominational completely, in that you really don't care what denomination a person is when they walk into your office, to do your job. Unless they're looking for particular sacramental act of some sort. (Southern Baptist)

Another Mormon, Chaplain Moore, said his endorsing agent had made his job "pretty clear" in that "he says I'm a chaplain endorsed by the LDS church, but I'm not a chaplain specifically for the LDS. My job is to be a chaplain, not an LDS chaplain." Chaplain Dyren talked about denominations as unions that required all chaplains to pay their union "dues" while keeping the needs of the larger project in mind. As he put it, "we have to realize that we are in an institution, and institutional ministry, it's not necessarily focused on our own unique perspective" (Catholic).

Chaplain Bowmaker (Presbyterian) defined cooperation as "being flexible enough to accommodate a variety of religious beliefs . . . realizing that a lot of religious beliefs that are slightly different from your own don't exclude the validity of your own." As discussed earlier, flexibility is necessary for effective facilitation, which in turn strengthens the chaplaincy's claim to be about free exercise rather than establishment. Several chaplains went straight for examples about facilitation when I asked them about cooperation. Referring to Wiccans, Muslims, and Jews, Chaplain Giraldo from the Evangelical Church Alliance, said that "there may seem that there's not a lot that I can do for them, but as a chaplain I can facilitate so that their freedom of religion rights, according to the Constitution of the United States, can still be protected by facilitating." Chaplain Townsend combined the emphasis on setting aside particularities with the one on getting facilitation done:

> We're not pounding on each other's heads, saying, "You'd better believe what I believe or you're going to hell." We may believe that, but we're not going to say it. What we say is things like, "Who is going to cover this church service, who is going to take care of things while I'm on leave, how are we going to handle this that or the other thing? When a person comes

> in and says, "I have a religious question" and it turns out they're Roman Catholic, I'm picking up the phone and calling Father [name] and saying, "I have another one for you, come and get him." Or if it's LDS or what have you, I'll say talk to Chaplain Cugrijus. If we need something that really looks like a Baptist, we'll get a Baptist chaplain to take care of that. (Reformed Episcopalian)

Facilitating this way, by connecting religious people to the right clergy member for them, means that you're strengthening another person in a faith that's different from yours. This actually requires some restraint, as many chaplains are deeply committed to the teachings of their own faith group. Some chaplains might view this as an unfortunate side effect derived from the legal framework of constitutional law and Department of Defense policy, perhaps rationalizing that it's the price of admittance to take care of those who do belong to your faith. But several chaplains seemed to think that nurturing other faiths was the very essence of cooperation.

One of the Catholic priests, Chaplain Squires, said cooperation meant "if the sailor is Jewish or Lutheran or Muslim, to make them the best in their faith group," adding that he both hoped and expected that "any other chaplain would do the same for Catholics, make them good Catholics." Chaplain Clement said he would do whatever he was allowed to do "in good conscience with my denominational faith group, to assist you to those same things so that you can have a great spiritual experience" (United Methodist). Chaplain Timu gave bringing a Mormon chaplain to his base to train Mormon lay leaders as his example of cooperation.

The norm of reciprocity among chaplains was sometimes justified in explicitly religious terms. When Chaplain Gunvant started explaining cooperation, he started with, "I suppose the Golden Rule. I would want to do for members of other faiths what I would expect to be done for members of my own" (Catholic). Another chaplain who defended supporting someone else's faith in religious terms was Chaplain Townsend. He said giving "the Muslim person a hard time" was neither appropriate "nor very Christian" in his opinion, because "as a Christian what I'm supposed to do is love my neighbor. Well, that makes my job real easy, because my job is to take care of everybody" (Reformed Episcopalian).

Unlike chaplains who look at religious others as rivals, enemies, lost souls, or servants of the devil, those who believe the "neighbor" the Bible tells them to love refers to other faiths wouldn't need laws and policies to spur them to facilitate. Two of the more conservative chaplains, Metzger and Illera, saw nurturing other faiths as a religious duty as well. Chaplain Metzger said, "I am compelled by the love of Christ to assist them [other faith groups] even though I do not worship with them" (Chaplaincy of Full Gospel Churches), and Chaplain Illera told me that chaplains' "main care as a whole always should be to care for each other as brothers in Christ and Yahweh, and/or Mohammed or whatever the case might be, so we can care for the needs of all" (Catholic). Chaplain Metzger went to the Jewish service occasionally and would "recommend" that Jewish personnel he met go, too. Chaplain Illera went further. He would "challenge" Jews to go. If he met Jews who weren't attending the Jewish service, he'd demand to know why not and give them the rabbi's contact information so that they couldn't use ignorance as an excuse. According to Illera, the rabbi sought him out to ask how he was getting so many Jews to come to his service and to thank him for "sending me my lost sheep." According to a Lutheran chaplain I interviewed separately from this study, Judaism is easy for Christians to facilitate because there's nothing in it that contradicts Christianity, except that Christians would say "so much more." I don't know with certainty whether Chaplains Illera and Metzger would be as proactive about sending Wiccans to their covens, but their efforts on behalf of Judaism are impressive either way.

These last two understandings of cooperation, as facilitation and as nurturing faith, show that chaplains pay a lot of attention to what sociologists call the "demand side" of religion.[5] Their focus is on the needs of military personnel as "consumers" of religion, on giving lay people what they want more than what the chaplain thinks is best. Chaplain Clement's desire to give everyone a "great spiritual experience" illustrates the point, which is significant because chaplains are by definition closely associated with the main "suppliers" of religion in America, churches and other institutionalized faith groups. For some chaplains, cooperation means putting the free exercise rights of individual sailors and marines above interests that the churches might have, such as doctrinal purity or maintaining membership numbers. A Lutheran should not be expected to do anything that is contrary to Lutheran teachings but routinely is expected to help others do non-Lutheran things.

Cooperation thus means accepting the religious commitments of sailors and marines and helping them follow up on them, rather than trying to persuade them to choose differently. When Chaplain Squires said cooperation was about helping people be the "the best in their faith group," he sounded a lot like the old Army recruiting slogan, "Be All You Can Be," which was inspired by humanistic psychology and its celebration of the self. Theologically, the rise of "the self" in American culture has brought with it "an individualistic ethos, a therapeutic mentality, and a growing consumerism," according to Wade Clark Roof.[6] In both democratic politics and capitalist business, *freedom* means freedom to choose. With regards to religion, that means "people choose whether or not to go to church. They choose the kind of church that appeals to them. They choose what to believe."[7] Religion has been reduced to a bunch of individual "preferences" that the chaplains are expected to respect.

Conservative theologians and cultural commentators bemoan this development. Religion as "preference" signals a subjection of ultimate truth claims to idiosyncratic taste, urgently felt need, or mere whim. Under such circumstances, religious commitment is less robust and less communal and loses both moral and political clout. There's a risk that the culture of choice marginalizes and trivializes faith. Such is the conservative lament. This lament is heard among military chaplains, too, because the military necessarily buys into the culture of choice in order to dodge accusations of establishment. In simple terms, the military assumes and expects that chaplains will accept other people's religious preferences and agree to be ecumenical and inclusive in their ministry. Unfortunately, this is an unrealistic assumption—and to some chaplains an unfair expectation as well.

The fact is that many chaplains are not comfortable with ecumenism, whether as individuals or as faithful representatives of their ecclesiastical endorsers. Despite many examples of seemingly effortless cooperation across religions, some boundaries are harder to negotiate than others. For example, there is a sharp line between the Evangelical Lutheran Church in America (ELCA) and the Church of Jesus Christ of Latter Day Saints (LDS or Mormon). Chaplain Chance, who belonged to the former, said, "The ELCA doesn't even recognize the LDS as a Christian Church." This caused him some consternation when he had to work for a new senior chaplain, who was Mormon. In fact, it was Chaplain Cugrijus. Despite differences in theology and rank, the two became friends. Chaplain Cugrijus described Chaplain Chance as "a great guy," while Chaplain Chance didn't hold back at all in his praise of Chaplain Cugrijus: "I gotta say this, of all the people I ever worked with, he was the most Christ-like man I ever worked with in the sense of being selfless and loving and caring for your neighbor. He was a fellow, a servant leader in the best sense of Isaiah the Prophet. He was the senior guy, and he would always volunteer to do the hard stuff."

Friendship still left them with the thorny issue of how to conduct religious services as copastors at their duty station. According to Chaplain Cugrijus, "actually it was kinda ugly when I got there," because he was replacing a chaplain who seemed to dislike him personally and because when Chaplain Chance called his endorsing agency they "told him that we couldn't concelebrate." Instead of avoiding each other or trying to organize separate worship services, neither of which would have worked very well, they sat down and discussed the format of the Protestant worship service together.[8] As the senior officer, Chaplain Cugrijus took the lead:

> And so, what I did when I got there was I sat down with Chaplain Chance and said, "OK give me a copy of your service bulletin." So he gave me a copy of his service bulletin and I looked at it. There are certain things as Latter Day Saints that we don't do. We don't do creeds and we don't wear robes, we don't do open communion, so . . . There are some prayers that people say that I'm not really comfortable with. We're not Trinitarian, so there's a problem with some of those kind of things. But I took his service bulletin and said, "OK, this is all fine. You're doing the Nicene Creed. I can't do that so I'll take the Nicene Creed out of the service." And there was a prayer I didn't feel comfortable with, so I took that out. And pretty much everything else was OK. So I took his service bulletin and said, "When it's my Sunday, do this one, when it's his Sunday do this one." And that seemed to work pretty well, that to me was cooperating. (LDS)

The two chaplains agreed it should make as little difference as possible whose Sunday it was to conduct the service. Military congregations are already transient in both membership and leadership, so sudden changes in worship style can be unwelcome. Imagine a community used to high liturgy, solemn music, and plenty of time to pray quietly suddenly being given a hellfire-and-brimstone sermon by a pastor in a business suit who exhorts them to sway and clap their hands as they sing!

Knowing that some colleagues would have a problem with his presence at their services, Chaplain Cugrijus tried to fit in as best he could. He worked with one Baptist chaplain who had zero interest in liturgy and "just wanted to preach," so he "did everything else" (LDS). He added that his colleague's sermons were "good stuff." Chaplain Cugrijus had also worked with other chaplains who didn't want him in the pulpit at all: "They wanted me sitting in the congregation if they were going to preach. That's fine with me. I was good to go and all that" (LDS).

I don't know whether Chaplain Chance or the ELCA had any qualms about the Protestant service being run without a Nicene Creed every other Sunday or not. Another Mormon's experience also shows that dealing with religious boundaries, which are always about inclusion and exclusion, can be tricky. Chaplain Moore had less institutional clout than Chaplain Cugrijus while serving as one of a handful of chaplains on a ship. "One of the guys," he remembered, "said he could not work with me because I was LDS." As he recalled the incident, it was

> not that they couldn't work with me specifically, but they couldn't "share the pulpit," I guess was the way he phrased it. And it was not from their personal background, but I guess it was a denominational thing. But the one guy that said that to me [. . .] he said that his particular denomination did not allow him to share the pulpit. But, he ended up being my best friend during the cruise. And we did share the pulpit. What I consider sharing the pulpit. I don't know exactly what that means to him.

In practice, what the two chaplains did was take turns in the pulpit, not every other week as Chaplains Chance and Cugrijus had, but by standing in the pulpit at different times during the same service. Chaplain Moore would say the invocation and then the other chaplain would preach. Chaplain Moore also played the piano to accompany the other chaplain, who sang because "he was the best singer" of the two. The other chaplains' qualms did not bother chaplain Moore as much as the other chaplain's denomination's qualms about working with Mormons. "I was not offended because I knew it wasn't anything personal, but I was disappointed that that would exist between denominations," he said, adding that "from my point of view, we shared [the pulpit]."

According to Chaplain Moore, then, the meaning of religious requirements, in this case a denominational imperative not to "share the pulpit," can be open to subjective interpretation. The abstract idea of ritual separation from Mormons didn't tell Chaplain Chance or Chaplain Moore's colleague exactly how to draw the boundary in practice. That was something that had to be worked out on the ground, or in Chaplain Moore's case at sea. As for the boundary between Protestantism and Mormonism, it is not necessarily symmetrical. Can you share the pulpit with a Mormon while not sharing the pulpit with a Mormon? Yes, if you and the Mormon have different definitions of what that means. Friendly personal relationships help when negotiating such religious boundaries. This, of course, was another understanding of cooperation.

COMPROMISE

When I asked chaplains to define and explain "compromise," they often brought up the ritual aspects of their faiths, such as communion. It is possible to have two separate communions during the same service. Chaplain Oberlin (ELCA) had conducted a service with a Baptist colleague where one served wine and the other grape juice, because they had different views on the appropriateness of alcohol. Chaplain Bowmaker (Presbyterian) had participated in a joint Protestant/Catholic communion where the chaplains stood at separate tables. When the time came for the Eucharist, "people divide and they go to whatever table they want to, and then they come back together to celebrate." Chaplain Bowmaker added that "that doesn't compromise my Protestantism at all, my Presbyterianism." Chaplain Drozdov was among the chaplains who could not participate in or offer such multidenominational communions, explaining, "Obviously, in the Orthodox churches, intercommunion, we don't practice that. It's closed communion. It's only for the Orthodox, and if they would say, well we want you to make communion available to all the members of your battalion because you're the only chaplain, then that's compromise. It's a question that's been posed to me. And not by chaplains. By commanders who say what kind of service would you do, and would you be able to have communion for everybody here, or just for your own?" (Eastern Orthodox).

Neither Mormons nor Missouri Synod Lutherans are allowed to serve communion to outsiders, either. Chaplain Frantz (LDS) said, "I'm only permitted to bless and pass the communion for my own church" and Chaplain Cugrijus would sit down and have "two members of the congregation come forward and do the communion part of the service" (LDS). Chaplain Szmatula did something similar: "We cannot serve communion to just anybody. They can only be Lutherans. And so we're in a chapel setting, what we do is on the first Sunday of the month when communion is given during the General Protestant Service, we will have someone who can give communion step in. And that's how we cooperate without compromising ourselves" (Missouri Synod).

Presbyterian Chaplain Bowmaker thought the reason he didn't worry about compromise much was because of his "relatively open, liberal theology," but he actually had compromised slightly on his theology when confronted with a "tricky" situation, described as follows: "Some of our people who come here for service on occasion are from the alcohol rehab down the street. I'm a believer of using wine in religious services, but knowing that's part of my community, I don't feel really comfortable doling out wine on Sunday morning (chuckles). So I took the step back and said, 'You know they need the grape juice more then they need the wine.' It's symbolic so . . . It might not be exactly what I believe is appropriate, but it's what they need, so . . ."

A few chaplains raised the issue of women in the ministry as a possible source of compromise. Chaplain Beard said that "women ministers are not acceptable for some faith groups, so their faith group doesn't allow them to do a service with a woman chaplain." As a result, chaplains from those faith groups "can't be expected to do that" (Southern Baptist). Chaplain Koch looked at the issue from the woman's point of view, and then claimed that if any senior Protestant chaplain refused to let a woman from his denomination, the United Methodist Church, preach "that chaplain would have a very short time remaining on active duty as a chaplain, because the institution requires that we accommodate." He believed it was mostly "conservative evangelical Protestant religions" that don't recognize the ordination of women. That the Catholic Church doesn't either didn't draw much comment at all, probably because there aren't any female Catholic priests asking to celebrate mass in the military.

Three of the chaplains I interviewed had special dietary requirements from their religions, Chaplain Hamoud (Muslim), Chaplain Tzilker (Jewish), and Chaplain Mace (Seventh Day Adventist). Chaplain Tzilker and Chaplain Mace brought up food as an area where they had to exercise caution so as not to compromise themselves. Chaplain Hamoud didn't in this context, possibly because he had already discussed when I asked him about facilitation. Instead, Chaplain Hamoud's example of compromise was that he couldn't be asked to perform a baptism, not that he thought he ever would, although he was perfectly willing to help someone find a chaplain who could. Chaplain Moore (LDS) and Chaplain Metzger (Chaplaincy of Full Gospel Churches) also raised the issue of baptism in their answers about compromise, each making the point that chaplains who only baptize adults can't be required to baptize an infant.

Only two chaplains brought up topics related to the ethics or morality of war when asked to discuss compromise. Chaplain Grams meditated at quite some length on the question of whether his mere presence in the military was an endorsement of war, musing, "By my being here, am I part of it?" Addressing me again, he explained this was a "conversation I have within the Presbyterian Church." He said he wasn't a pacifist and didn't think anyone who was could serve in the military in any capacity because such a person would be "ethically compelled to work against the military as an institution." Ultimately, he didn't think his ministry serving "our nation's military and military men and women who are called upon by the state" amounted to "a compromise of my opposition to war" (Presbyterian). Furrowing his brow and shrugging, he didn't seem quite satisfied with his own answer, but he clearly disagreed with those civilian Presbyterians who assumed he was "prowar."

Chaplain Squires's concern about compromise was less introspective. Instead of agonizing over his own role in the military, he told me how he'd had to assert himself in order to avoid the sanctity of the chapel being compromised. "In a large Marine Corps base, there was a chapel. Sometimes they would use it to brief the marines on different subjects and [on] a number of occasions I said, 'You can't use it, you're teaching them war, fighting skills; you can't do it within the chapel. That very structure itself represents something that is peaceful.' We do not give into or are meant to support the actual taking of life" (Catholic).

With so many young people in the military, it's no surprise that marriage was another big area of concern raised by the chaplains when discussing compromise. Like communion, marriage is an important ritual, and although it isn't a sacrament to Protestants as it is to Catholics, Chaplain Beard described it as if it was: "If someone asked me to marry them and they were not Christian nor would they even consider the claims of Christ. For me marriage is almost a sacrament, and when I marry, when I ask God's blessing on someone I have to believe that God will truly bless the marriage and if neither of them acknowledge God I can't believe that God will do that, so I would refuse that" (Southern Baptist).

Chaplain Illera had helped a Roman Catholic/Greek Orthodox couple coordinate their marriage. To satisfy both churches and both sets of parents, they had a civil marriage, a Greek Orthodox wedding, and finally a Catholic wedding. At the Greek Orthodox wedding, Chaplain Illera "didn't facilitate, but I went as a guest, and I extended my hand at one particular point, said a prayer, which was totally acceptable" and in the end the couple was "very, very, very well married" (Catholic).

Chaplain Chance was about to willfully, and apparently happily, violate his church's teachings, until he was stopped. He explained that a "girl got pregnant, local Lutheran girl, I knew the family, so I was gonna do it on Holy Saturday, which you're not supposed to do. But I mean the girl is pregnant, and I think 'serve the people.' What's the Sabbath for? Are people for the Sabbath or is the Sabbath for the people? And he [Chaplain Chance's endorsing agent] was gonna basically force me to not do it" (ELCA).

As it turns out, religious affiliation is not the chaplains' biggest concern when it comes to enlisted personnel marrying: speed is. Chaplain Kanaridis (Conservative Baptist) explained that the military has problems with young men marrying foreign women much too quickly, because these women often see the man as a chance to escape poverty and come to America. Hastily arranged marriages can come with severe cultural misunderstandings, which can be compounded for the women by physical isolation on military bases and social isolation because of language barriers. Taken together, these create a risk for marital discord and domestic violence, which of course often end up in the chaplain's office.[9]

Another force driving couples to marry fast is lust, especially male lust, according to Chaplain Kanaridis. With parents too far away to counsel restraint, young couples make a dash for the courthouse, or worse, the chaplain: "Joe Blow and Susie Q meet each other on the pier and fall in love, and that week they want to get married. And they have no training, no counseling, nothing." This is why Chaplain Kanaridis wouldn't marry anyone unless he had counseled them for at least four months. Although this wasn't a requirement of his denomination, "my church backs me on it," he said. Chaplain Clement, loath to feel as if he could have done more if a couple divorced, also had a private requirement separate from his church. He insisted on six weeks of counseling. The Catholic chaplains did follow their church's requirements. "We cannot marry at the drop of a hat," one told me, "whereas, if Private Schmuckatelli and the woman he loves, that he'd met last night wants to get married, I dare say we could find a chaplain on this base who could marry them in a week or two weeks" (Catholic). Part of the problem was that some chaplains seem to really enjoy marrying people.

Chaplain Kanaridis provided one of the few examples of compromise that was not hypothetical or easily solved with some education. He had been pressured to compromise his counseling policy by a commanding officer whom he otherwise got along with very well. In fact, the CO was "a very good Christian" and part of Kanaridis's congregation. When the commander insisted that Kanaridis marry a junior officer and his betrothed without all that counseling, it took a long time for the chaplain to get the disappointed commander to relent. Chaplain Kanaridis's position was, "I'm not a justice of the peace; I'm a minister" (Conservative Baptist).

CONSCIENCE AND DENOMINATIONAL RESTRICTIONS

For some chaplains, the requirements of their denomination didn't limit them much at all. Chaplain Timu, for example, said that compromise was "hard to define from my perspective because the Disciples believe everybody is OK. So it's very hard for me to compromise my beliefs. We are very unique in that regard. We believe Jews are OK, Mormons are OK, Muslims are OK." When I pressed him to think of a way he might still compromise himself, he concluded that he'd only be "in violation of what my church believes" if he himself "became intolerant of other religions" (Disciples of Christ).

For most chaplains, however, there are denominationally specific limitations on what they can do. Combined with personal convictions, these mark the boundaries of cooperation. Baptists were especially eager to discuss this. Chaplain Beard said, "Compromise is that we should never be asked to do what our conscience does not allow us to do. We have the freedom to be true to our faith; endorsing agents and our own faith tenets. And we're not expected to change or alter those just for the sake of cooperation" (Southern Baptist).

Chaplain Kanaridis feigned disbelief when I first brought up compromise: "Compromise? I don't do a lot of compromising!" Having chuckled at his own dramatic flair, he continued in a serious tone that he thought many chaplains were too dogmatic and would pick fights about unimportant things. As he grew older, he said, he found fewer and fewer things to fight about, although he'd still stand up for himself if Scripture was directly challenged:

> I can compromise in things that aren't doctrinal. I can compromise in anything that's not doctrinal. If it's not written in the Book, then I don't care. But if it's written in the Book, you're gonna have a problem. [. . .] Our first responsibility is to God, our second responsibility is to the church that sponsors us, and our third responsibility is to the military. That's the hierarchy, if you will. And so we can only do what our church allows us to do, in ministering to people. We facilitate for others but we minister to our own. (Kanaridis, Conservative Baptist)

The Lutheran Church, Missouri Synod (LCMS) had a reputation among other chaplains for being uncompromising. Chaplain Farrow, a Catholic priest, said, "We're having a real problem in the Chaplain Corps" because Missouri Synod Lutherans were being sent to provide "Protestant coverage" even though they couldn't offer communion to anyone but other members of the LCMS. Recognizing that they had a right to stay true to their church's teachings, he still thought they were less useful to the military than more inclusive Protestants because they were so "strict" in their theological demands. As Chaplain Farrow saw it, the matter boiled down to a question of "How do you really stay true to your faith but still serve the needs of the military?" Chaplain Kojic, who was LCMS, still thought he could contribute, though: "If we're going to have an ecumenical Easter service obviously I . . . By reason of my faith, I can't actually participate in them. In the worship or the liturgy. Outside of being a member in the parish. But what I can do is do all of the things that would get the thing going. Send out the flyers, set up the chapel, make sure all of the extra things are taken care of."

If the Missouri Synod Lutherans were the group considered least able to do compromising, most chaplains thought Mormons were the group least likely to be compromised with. Both liberal and conservative Protestants ran into prohibitions against working too closely with members of the Church of Jesus Christ of Latter Day Saints. Chaplain Cransveld, from the Foursquare Gospel Churches, thought it was "an unfair burden on everyone" for Mormons to be "superimposed" on military congregations because of their "difference in theology." Although Chaplain Feteris didn't have anything against Mormons personally, he still thought it was a problem that the military would put Mormons in the same category as Protestants. He said,

> The military doesn't study theology so sometimes they will lump groups together, who I don't . . . I can't worship with Latter Day Saints. As a denomination, we have a statement that says we will do mission with them, we will work alongside them, but we cannot worship with them, because of the difference in theology of understanding who Jesus Christ is. And while I have great friends in the Chaplain Corps who are LDS, I won't be in a worship service with them. If they do a worship service, I will be outside that worship service. If I do a worship service, then they are free to come in and participate. But they won't be preaching at the one where I'm presiding. So I won't compromise on that. Even if ordered to do so, that might be one of the few times I might be forced to call my endorsing agent and say I need some help.

Calling the endorsing agent for help is one recourse for chaplains who run into trouble with military authorities over matters of faith. Before it comes to that, there are a few other things they can do. Both Chaplains Dyren (Catholic) and Drozdov (Eastern Orthodox) described how their first response is to "educate" the person insisting they do something inappropriate, typically a commanding officer. If education doesn't work, chaplains can go to the senior chaplain for their base or region, whose higher rank commands more attention. Learning when to stand up to a commander for oneself and when to bring in a senior chaplain is a matter of judgment that junior chaplains have to learn. If both education and the Chaplain Corps hierarchy come up short, there may be no option left but to contact the endorsing agent.

The endorsing agent can appeal to difficult commanders on behalf of the faith group, hoping it's easier to change someone's mind when they're dealing with a representative of an entire church than with an isolated chaplain. The endorsers can also express concerns about policies or practices that cause their chaplains problems to military and civilian authorities. In extreme cases, the endorsing agency can "rescue" the chaplain by revoking their ecclesiastical endorsement, meaning that the chaplain in question ceases to be one. The exact effect this has on the officer's commission remains unclear: does a chaplain without an ecclesiastical endorsement still have all the rights and responsibilities of an officer? The easiest solutions are for the chaplain to find a new endorsing agent or for the military to give the (former) chaplain an honorable discharge.

There's no consensus about what "endorsement" means. Israel Drazin and Cecil Currey, part of the team that defended the Army chaplaincy against charges it was unconstitutional on establishment grounds in the 1980s, write that if chaplains were official representatives of their churches or synagogues in the military, then that would be a violation of the Constitution because it would create an "excessive entanglement" between church and state.[10] "By definition," they argue, the endorsement is "nothing more than a statement or affidavit by a recognized religious body that the applicant is a member of the clergy" and that the chaplain's relationship with the endorsing agent is merely a "personal and unofficial choice." Richard Hutcheson disagrees with this position.[11] He argues that it is an antiquated understanding of endorsement from "a century past." To Hutcheson chaplains are obviously and necessarily "representatives" of their faith groups: "There is no such things as a generic 'member of the clergy' available to do whatever military authorities may order. There are only Catholic priests, Baptist ministers, Jewish rabbis, or Muslim imams, and their ecclesiastical and liturgical functions are controlled entirely by their religious bodies. To say that a Catholic priest's ability to celebrate mass or a Baptist minister's inability to baptize infants is based on a 'personal and unofficial' relationship is, from a chaplain's point of view, absurd."[12] Unlike Drazin and Currey, Hutcheson argues that ecclesiastical endorsement is more than a matter of professional licensing, analogous to the credentials given legal and medical professionals by the American Bar Association and American Medical Association. "Denominations are qualitatively different" than mere professional associations, he writes, because lay people can be members of them and because they concern themselves with good of all of society, not just their own congregants.[13] Hutcheson's thesis in both editions of his book is that chaplains are full-fledged members of both the military and their faith groups, and it is up to each chaplain to "interpret the dual relationship." Part of his underlying concern is that military chaplains should not be thought of as clergy who have left their churches for the military.

To try to sort the matter out empirically, I asked the chaplains questions about how they "interpreted" their relationship to their faith groups. Not surprisingly, they didn't all agree, either. Chaplain Irons thought his "primary mission" was to be a Southern Baptist chaplain, saying that "compromise means essentially forgetting who you are first and foremost. And as chaplains we are endorsed by specific faith bodies to represent fully the teachings of our bodies to our people. OK?" Chaplain Irons believed the setting he worked in created challenges to maintaining his particular identity, with its temptations to fall into a kind of "go along to get along" attitude that should not be allowed to spill over into questions of ultimate truth:

> But I think any chaplain who is in an institution; it can become very easy to live by the sort of wagon wheel philosophy. Which says that all roads lead to God, and because we're all here part of the institution, what really matters is that . . . What happens is they essentially turn their back on the very teachings of their own faith group. And they can do it in kind of a silent way, but they don't . . . They're not anymore Christian missionaries, as it were. They are, they're very much sort of religious, civil . . . civil ministers, if that makes sense. Civil religion. Does that make sense? (Southern Baptist)

Several other chaplains asserted the importance of maintaining religious boundaries and not watering down beliefs in pursuit of a spiritual lowest common denominator. "We're not trying to produce a new religion out of, by mixing together Catholic, Lutheran, Muslim, Jewish, and every other denomination, or all the Christian denominations into a sort of amorphous blob of generic faith," said Catholic Chaplain Squires. He continued, "As a chaplain, I am expected to be authentic, true to my faith beliefs, so you don't compromise." When I asked Chaplain Townsend about compromise, he thought that would happen if he and a Mormon chaplain pretended to have identical beliefs even though they don't. Instead, both should hold true to their church's teachings. "I don't cease to be who I am," he said. "He doesn't cease to be who he is. We're not members of some homogeneous civil religion in which we're all crushed together. Instead, like a magnet, part of us connects to each other, and part of us most certainly does not" (Reformed Episcopalian).

Chaplain Dyren, however, worried about what he called "hyperdenominationalism," which he thought was especially prevalent in the Chaplain Corps because "we see it all eroding before us" (Catholic). He was referring to the decline of denominations in civilian life but also to the military's assumption that "a chaplain is a chaplain is a chaplain" regardless of denominational flavor. This "lessening of the boundaries" made some chaplains, who felt they were being forced to "compromise the integrity of their faith traditions," all the more defensive and rigid in defense of their particularity. Chaplain Dyren worried that chaplains making young people who approached them "jump through all these hoops" or "impose all kinds of restrictions" would make people who needed someone to talk to turn their backs and walk away.

How often young people are turned off by "hyperdenominationalism" is an open question. That prayer is the flashpoint of controversy over compromise in the military is not. When standing before their congregations on a Sunday morning, chaplains are probably perceived as clergy first and those in attendance are all volunteers. But when the occasion is obviously military and attendance is mandatory for all practical intents and purposes, the chaplains are more likely to be perceived as officers first, and the words they choose as reflecting the military's world view or preferences. Consequently, the Navy and Marine corps require that "absent extraordinary circumstances" prayers said at command functions "should be non-sectarian in nature."[14] Chaplain Drozdov explained the reasoning behind the policy, "If you invite someone to pray with you, and it turns out that they're a Jew, and then you end your prayer 'in Jesus' name we pray,' you have at best excluded that person from that prayer. And at worst, not only have you offended them, but you have encroached upon their religious privacy. To believe differently than you and even to reject Jesus Christ" (Eastern Orthodox).

Chaplain Hamoud, the imam, repeatedly voiced his conviction that the Navy and its Chaplain Corps were sincerely trying to be inclusive and making progress at it, but nevertheless admitted that he had felt excluded "on a couple of occasions chaplains have prayed in the name of Jesus even though maybe a rabbi is there or I am there also." Over time, he got used to it and decided to be patient, viewing the incidents as symptoms of the "military as a subset of society going through a transformation in terms of awareness of other faith groups." He even expressed sympathy for those who offered noninclusive, sectarian prayers: "I know from their perspective, it's difficult for them to give up praying in the name of Jesus, and I appreciate that and I can understand, because this is how they grow. They're growing up. They just can't detach themselves right away" (Muslim).

Most chaplains "don't have a problem" with offering nonsectarian prayers, according to Chaplain Feteris (Presbyterian), but he did personally know one retired chaplain who had refused to pray any other way than in Jesus' name.

It's mostly older and more theologically conservative Christian chaplains who insist on their right to pray in Jesus' name, according to Chaplain Dyren:

> They tend to be more evangelical, and they will not want to do public prayer. We do a lot of things that you could probably call social religion or civic religion. And they pretty much don't want to do it because you get up, like on the ship or something, you pray and you sum up the thoughts of the day: "Lord God, hear the prayers of us all, bla bla bla." Whatever the issue. And we pray for either specific or sort of general things. And then we sum up without using "in Christ's name" or something like that. But I

know there are some senior guys who definitely are having problems with that. They hate that. (Catholic)

Although it is up to the commanding officer whether an assembly should have a religious element or not,[15] the chaplain's participation is often expected as a matter of tradition. Technically, the Navy does not require that any given chaplain offer a nonsectarian prayer, because the same instruction that says command function prayers should be nonsectarian also says chaplains can refuse to participate without repercussion. The simplest solution is for the commander or reluctant chaplain to ask a different chaplain to do it, but this still puts the first one asked in a position of having to say no to a superior.

The issue of nonsectarian prayer is exacerbated by some chaplains believing that it is only Christians who are encouraged to be inclusive. Chaplain Geschka, a Catholic priest at the start of his military career, said that chaplain school candidates would sarcastically say "Mary's son" instead of "the J-word" in public prayers, in order not to offend non-Christians. He revealed some resentment toward Muslims when he added, "All that boils down to is we can't say Jesus and they can say Allah until the cows come home." Chaplain Cransveld shared this sentiment: "There's a high point of stress when rabbis are able to pray in their faith tradition, Muslims are able to pray in their faith tradition, and Christians very often are not allowed to pray in our faith tradition" (Foursquare Gospel Church).

As far as I can tell, this belief is erroneous and seems to assume that the God of Muslims, Jews, and Christians is not the same. An invocation of "Allah" should not be considered a sectarian and exclusive statement, since it is the Arabic word for "God." Neither Chaplain Hamoud (Muslim) nor Chaplain Tzilker (Jewish) expressed any reservations about being inclusive in their own prayers, the imam explicitly saying that the name of the deity doesn't matter. Still, chaplains such as Geschka believe the requirement to pray inclusively to be an example of both political correctness and senior chaplains' timidity.

Chaplain Drozdov felt very strongly about the nature of prayer at military functions. He conceded that "public events are not the time to win people's souls" but still advocated a strategy of pragmatic inclusion: "There are things you can say before you pray, that would make it palatable even to people who believe otherwise and will not accept the exact words that you use. For instance, 'I invite you to pray along with me' and, "We are going to pray for this, and I will ask you to pray in the manner of your faith even as I pray as a Christian would.' Without changing the words to the prayer itself—sort of a preface" (Eastern Orthodox).

This approach still excludes atheists, of course, but avoids watering prayer down to such a low common denominator that prayer has to be addressed "to whom it may concern."

Controversies about prayer in public are not limited to the military, of course. They happen in legislatures, schools, and other settings. At stake in all of them is the balance between the First Amendment's two religion clauses. To be sure, public prayer by taxpayer-funded officials does risk running afoul of the Establishment Clause. But trying to limit or dictate the contents of such prayer may violate the Free Exercise Clause, as well as the right to free speech. Even Chaplain Drozdov, who was willing to stretch himself far to be inclusive and described Navy policies regarding ceremonial prayer as "prudent," had his limits: "What I take exception to is when they say the appropriate word to use instead of 'Jesus' name' is 'Lord.' And I say, 'You can't tell us how we're supposed to pray.' You cannot, as someone who doesn't believe in Jesus Christ, or believe as strongly as I do, tell me how and when and in what manner I should invoke or refrain from invoking the name of Christ" (Eastern Orthodox).

The most public incident in the debate over sectarian versus inclusive prayer has been the case of former chaplain Gordon J. Klingenschmitt. After serving as a chaplain for the Evangelical Episcopal Church in the Air Force and then in the Navy for more than a decade, Klingenschmitt turned activist. He alleged that he had been personally persecuted by a line officer for praying in Jesus' name and that chaplains in general were pressured to offer bland, nonsectarian prayers by the military. He appealed to members of Congress, asked President George W. Bush for an executive order that would allow Christians to pray in Jesus' name, and gained the admiration of many religious conservatives. In 2006, he staged a hunger strike in front of the White House, held a press conference where he complained about lack of action by President Bush, and attended a political rally in Washington, DC. He would appear at these events in his chaplain's uniform, even after being ordered not to. As a result he was reprimanded, fined, and involuntarily separated from the Navy. As of late 2011, he was suing to have his conviction overturned and pension reinstated.[16]

MAINTAINING IDENTITY IN A PLURALISTIC SETTING

A recurring problem for chaplains is that the military doesn't make as fine a distinction between Christian denominations as the chaplains do. The extreme case is where all chaplains are considered interchangeable—the "a chaplain is a chaplain is a chaplain" attitude mentioned earlier. Even when some diversity is acknowledged, the military might be operating with crude or outdated categories, such as Herberg's "Protestant-Catholic-Jew" typology from the 1950s.[17] According to that logic, if you're not Catholic or Jewish, you must be a Protestant, so why not lump the Mormons in with them whether they're welcome or not? As for the Greek or Russian Orthodox, they risk being considered "some kind of Catholic" for administrative purposes.

My impression from the interviews is that chaplains from small religious groups were more likely to subsume their religious particularity and accept the military's assumption that chaplains are, or ideally should be, generic religious functionaries within the armed forces. Chaplain Hamoud, for example, described himself like this: "I am a chaplain, and I am chaplain first and an Islamic chaplain later." He reiterated, "I am a chaplain who happens to be Islamic" for emphasis. One of the Mormons, Chaplain Frantz, interrupted one of my questions on a different topic to correct me, because I had referred to him as "an LDS chaplain." He said, "I'm gonna split hairs here. I'm not an LDS chaplain. I'm a Marine Corps chaplain. So my job is always essentially the same wherever I'm at: provide worship services, counseling, consultation. I think that's the essence of what I do wherever I'm at."

Chaplain Cugrijus, however, who is also a Mormon, frequently emphasized his religious uniqueness, so my impression could be wrong. Then again, Chaplain Cugrijus outranked both Chaplain Hamoud and Chaplain Frantz, so it's possible that religious minorities do downplay their distinctiveness, but only until they achieve a certain rank and feel safer in the military hierarchy. My data cannot resolve this question, but it would be worth pursuing with a different research design that makes a larger sample possible.

Protestants seemed far more likely to assert their particularities and object to being thought of or treated as ministers of "mere" civil religion. "I'm expected to be a Presbyterian minister," Chaplain Feteris said. "That's why the Navy gave me a commission." Chaplain Beard, a Southern Baptist, said he took "a very open approach to what I do" that minimized the risk of compromise and gave him "generally speaking, a good ride" in the Navy. Nevertheless, the "biggest example of conflict" he'd had as a chaplain had to do with Mormons:

> See, Mormon chaplains in the Navy are considered Protestant. My faith group will disagree with that. And most Protestant groups would, most evangelical groups would also disagree with that. And I was in a situation where a command was trying to force a [Mormon[18]] chaplain to take charge of a Protestant chapel. And the congregation was objecting to that. And so there was some conflict with that chaplain, in that regard. His

> approach was that we were generic chaplains. That if I told anyone he was a Mormon it would be discriminating against him. And my approach was, "No, we're not generic chaplains. We are endorsed by particular faith groups. And it would be negligent of me not to tell somebody. Because our faith groups are so different in what they believe." He was hiding behind the Protestant label. (Southern Baptist)

For some chaplains, then, avoiding compromise means resisting pressures from the military and from other chaplains to be too broad in their theology and ministry. That's why I specifically asked them how they maintained their religious identity while in the military chaplaincy and how they thought their own group fit in. Of all the chaplains, the one who reported the most difficulty was the rabbi, Chaplain Tzilker: "Well, you know, we fit in well only because we've got the short end of the stick as far as compromising . . . You know, the military is not a good place for someone who wants to be an observant Jew." He did acknowledge progress. Adopting an alphabetical scale of "steps" toward inclusion, he thought Protestants and Catholics were at "step Z" (fitting in effortlessly) while Jews were at "step C" (with much distance to cover). He added that Muslims, who face many similar issues as Jews, were probably at "step B" and Buddhists at "step A." His assessment contrasts with Chaplain Hamoud's, described in the previous chapter. The imam admired how well Jews were accepted and looked forward to the day when Muslims arrived at the same point, a point that the rabbi thought was just one step ahead. It's possible that the military pays more attention to being accommodating of Muslims given geopolitical realities, while it takes Jews for granted. It's also possible also that Judaism is less flexible in its demands than Islam. Chaplain Tzilker described one of the obstacles to fitting in: "The big one is ignorance of the holidays. They don't understand the concept of what a holy day is . . . They don't understand the concept that there's a commandment to observe the holiday and that commandment is binding. And you can't just say, 'Well you can't observe the Sabbath today, why don't you observe it on Tuesday?' You know, this type of thing."

There might well be insensitivity to religious holidays in the military, but the different assessments given by the one rabbi and one imam I interviewed might also be expressions of different personalities. Chaplain Hamoud seemed to be a generally sunny guy, compared to a wearier Chaplain Tzilker. I might also have caught Chaplain Tzilker on a bad day or provided him with a chance to vent about things that had grated on him over time. Whatever the reason, Chaplain Tzilker said he had to exert a lot of energy to maintain his identity. He said, "You gotta work at it very, very hard. You gotta constantly remind yourself and remind others of who you are. And you can't be afraid to speak your mind. And in a military setting you can't be afraid to suffer the consequences of speaking your mind. You can't be in it for the promotions. And I was passed over for promotion and I think one of the reasons why is because I'm not a shy person. I'll tell people how it is" (Tzilker, Jewish).

Chaplain Cransveld also discussed the importance of assertiveness, describing himself as someone who stood up for other people's religious needs rather than his own. He even believed he would have advanced higher in the ranks if he had been content to be one of the "chaplains that will refuse to get involved or do anything that might hurt their career" (Foursquare Gospel Churches). This seems strange because facilitating for other faith groups is rewarded in the Chaplain Corps, not punished, and because Chaplain Cransveld was one of the chaplains who had the most and deepest objections to other faiths, Chaplains Illera, Kanaridis, and Mace being the others. For Chaplain Cransveld, Mormons were the biggest challenge.

"We're not always viewed as being a Christian Church," said Chaplain Frantz (LDS). Although he hadn't had any unpleasant experiences based on that personally, he knew the attitude was out there. He considered himself lucky. Warned by his church that he would cause and face controversy from the beginning, the more experienced Chaplain Cugrijus had no illusions about his presence offending other chaplains but still thought he had "a great advantage over other chaplains" when he joined the corps: "I think I was at a great advantage over other chaplains. In that sense. Many chaplains assume that they are homogenous. They are in a homogenous environment. I came in knowing that I was not. I know that we have some differences. To me that was a big advantage. I didn't assume anything. I don't assume that we have anything in common. And so I knew that I would have to make appropriate adjustments. And my church told me that was the expectation" (LDS).

Because he was part of a small religious group, Chaplain Cugrijus was often isolated so that he had to give up some of his normal religious practices. At sea "there was no other worthy LDS priesthood holder aboard ship so I was unable to take sacrament, or communion, for six months" (LDS). While the military can accommodate needs for material objects, space to meet in, and time for worship, if what you need is a coreligionist you may be out of luck.

Other chaplains mentioned their relationship to their endorsing agent as central to fitting in to the military and to maintaining their identity while there. Chaplain Gunvant believed Catholics benefited from their church's "strong institutional sense," saying,

> Catholics, because we have a larger institutional sense there are certain requirements we are obliged to do—for example, sending reports to our endorsing agents. His interaction with us, usually at least once a year. And of course there are daily requirements that Catholic priests are expected to observe. The celebration of mass, for instance; the praying of the hours, the liturgical hours, the spiritual preparation for Mass and for Sundays, of course. And specific times of the year, advent, lent, and so on. So I think our identity, there's a large institutional element to that, that people grow into and that becomes part of your, almost your daily life. So I don't see a great deal of wandering around "Well, what is my identity?" It's fairly, fairly structured.

Chaplain Gunvant thought other chaplains often envied "the order and rhythm" provided by the Catholic church and that it was a "very good thing" when they tried to imitate it "because you can lose your way in this organization." Chaplain Koch, however, thought it was his denomination's lack of structure that helped him fit into a pluralistic setting: "Fortunately, because I'm in an inclusive, fairly inclusive Protestant tradition, it means a lot of folks can come to my service. My communion is open" (United Methodist).

As a Missouri Synod Lutheran, Chaplain Szmatula's communion was not open. He said his church tacitly acknowledged that he faced unique challenges in the military and gave him and other LCMS chaplains "a little bit more freedom as missionaries than the local pastors get." For example, he had been allowed to give communion to Episcopalian personnel while at sea because they had nowhere else to go and "because they believe that the bread and the wine is the body and blood of Christ, as I do." On another occasion, he avoided a "no" from his denomination by not asking permission in the first place: "To be honest, I don't know if my church would agree with this, but on the ship, the two Protestants—one was a Southern Baptist and one was me, a Lutheran—and we believed, he and I, that it would be better for us to give a united Christian front, than to be divided. So one Sunday he would preach and I would do the liturgy, the next Sunday we'd reverse." He thought his church would be OK with it, given the circumstances, whereas "a local pastor would be strung up if he preached in a Baptist Church" (LCMS). Chaplain Bowmaker did not have to contend with any figurative ecclesiastical lynch mobs, because he was Presbyterian. No matter where he went, his services would be "Presbyterian-like" although he could "flex it a little bit, be more casual or more formal," depending on the needs of the congregation. In other words, he would adapt them rather than insist they adapt to him. In his opinion, his "balanced" relationship with his endorsing agent helped him maintain his identity: "I'll go to a Presbyterian meeting, couple times a year, to touch base with my own denomination. [. . .] The endorsing agent will come out and visit. See how we're doing. I send them reports every quarter so they know I'm alive and functioning somehow. They don't micromanage me, but they're always interested and concerned about how I'm doing."

Staying in touch with the "home church" can be done in a number of ways, aside from receiving visitors and sending reports. Chaplain Timu's church, the Disciples of Christ, required that he affiliate with the nearest civilian congregation no matter where he goes, so he can attend it when not preaching himself. Chaplain Szmatula also made sure that no matter where he was stationed, he and his family had an LCMS church "in town" to go to. This was especially important to him because it meant there would be a "Lutheran pastor and congregation to watch over" his family whenever he deployed. The LCMS also brought its chaplains from the different branches of the armed forces together for regular gatherings where they could study the Bible together, exchange experiences, and encourage each other. In this, he thought they were similar to the Catholics, "so that helps us keep our identity."

Southern Baptist Chaplain Irons maintained his identity by meeting with other Baptists in local churches and at conferences that also brought in chaplains from hospitals and prisons. He also relied on his "personal prayer and devotional life . . . my spiritual disciplines" to remind him who and what he was. Chaplain Cransveld had found mentors in an informal support group and also drew strength from a regular Bible study group. In addition, "during worship, I engage in a lot of types of liturgy that express my own particular denominational, my own particular spiritual persuasion" (Foursquare Gospel Churches).

Chaplain Mace found it easier to be a Seventh Day Adventist and get his proper Sabbath day off work because "we've come into this heightened sense of pluralism" in the Chaplain Corps even though his own appreciation of pluralism didn't extend to Islam. To maintain his identity, he read from a series of books about his tradition every Saturday and tried to keep his "mind on the hope of a second coming." He articulated his church's contribution in simple and modest terms: "I believe God has given the seventh Day Adventist church to the Christian community at large just to say, 'Hey wait a minute, there's a couple teachings within the Christian tradition that I don't want you to lose sight of.' So these two teachings [the Sabbath and the second coming]that are pointed out in our title, or in our name, are there to keep before the public as perceived elements of Christianity that ought not be forgotten."

Chaplain Mace's belief that each Christian church had something unique to offer was shared by Chaplain Street, who said this about his own African Methodist Episcopal Church: "Like every other denomination, we bring a lot to the table. We bring the ability to be prophetic. To be pastoral. To be compassionate. To speak truth to power when need be. We bring an array of gifts to the table. I think we are an asset to many commands. An asset to any base. And we bring joy, given the opportunities."

The Catholic Church's contribution was slightly different, according to Chaplain Gunvant. "We know what discrimination is like because we were there," he said, so that

> to me it is the great tribute to Roman Catholicism that, because it is substantially represented in the military, certainly in the military academies, Roman Catholicism has become the protector, and is known to be so, of Jewish folk, of Mormons, who have not received with acclamation [. . .] Mormon chaplains! We know what discrimination is like because we were there. So when these new groups come along and experience it, we know what that's like. And now that we are more a part of the institution we can do things that would protect and enhance them.

FRIENDSHIPS IN THE CORPS

Chaplain Gunvant's pride in Catholics being looked on as defenders of minority faiths was vindicated when I asked the chaplains to describe the faith group of their closest colleagues. Two of the three Mormon chaplains (Moore and Frantz) said their closest friends in the Chaplain Corps were priests, as did Chaplain Tzilker. As a rabbi, he appreciated how the Catholics had a similar understanding of liturgy and ritual, especially the "timeliness of ritual." That's why he said, "I've kind of gravitated to the Roman Catholic priests socially and friend-wise" (Jewish).

Mainline Protestants and Catholics described friendships both within and between their groups, and both also described warm feelings toward conservative Protestants, Mormons, and non-Christian groups. The only pattern that seemed to emerge was in the answers given by conservative Protestants, none of whom listed mainline Protestants or Mormons as their "closest colleagues," only Catholics and other conservative Protestants. This is consistent with what sociologists know about conservative Protestant's boundary maintenance. After studying a fundamentalist church, Nancy Ammerman concluded that its "most well-defended boundaries are those that divide it from their closest neighbors, those with whom it would seem to have the most in common."[19] Mainline Protestantism is a threat because it has a similar theology, while Mormons' lifestyle and commitment to "family values" make them a social rival despite great theological differences.

Many chaplains refused to answer the question, at least at first, claiming to get along with everyone or listing friends in so many different groups as to make the same point. Chaplain Gunvant's closest relationships had been "across the board" (Catholic), Chaplain Koch's "across the spectrum" (United Methodist), Chaplain Cugrijus' had run "the gamut; I haven't met anyone I can't get along with" (Mormon) and Chaplain Szmatula said, "Denomination doesn't make a whole lot of difference socially with us" (LCMS). Chaplain Szmatula did, however, find some groups more congenial theologically. Specifically, he liked Baptists because they understood atonement the same way he did and Catholics because they were close to Lutherans in their understanding of grace.

Chaplains don't always have much of a choice in who they associate with. According to Chaplain Giraldo, "It depends on who you're working with." He then listed the three other chaplains in his command as his closet colleagues: "those are my colleagues and they become my support group" (Evangelical Church Alliance). Chaplain Irons came to the same conclusion differently. After listing his five closest colleagues, he realized they were all "right here," which led him to conclude that "a lot of it is geography, to be honest with you" (Southern Baptist). Chaplain Bowmaker pointed out that most jobs for Marine Corps chaplains were "pretty much in isolation." Even if there were "another battalion down the road, you don't really interact with them that much" if you're responsible for more than a thousand marines of your own. When other chaplains were around, Chaplain Bowmaker said he would usually "end up hanging out with the priests" (Presbyterian).

For better and worse, celibacy affects the social life of Catholic priests. They tend to rely more on each other and form cliques that attract non-Catholic chaplains who are separated from their families. Several Protestants mentioned the priests' reputation for sociability. If you're new to a command and want to have a beer with a good bunch of guys or find out where the best food in town is, tag along with the Catholics. However, if a priest is assigned to an area where all the other chaplains have families to go home to at the end of the day, he might have to look farther afield for community.

Chaplain Szmatula's claim that denomination didn't matter was common, although I witnessed one clear incident of actions not matching words. Shortly after Chaplain Kanaridis told me he didn't care and sometimes didn't even know what denomination other chaplains were, our interview was interrupted by a phone call from a reserve chaplain who was being called up to active duty. Chaplain Kanaridis's very first question was what faith group the other chaplain belonged to. Chaplain Bartley started with a protest, exclaiming that he could "not answer that question" about closest colleagues. He then proceeded to answer it anyway:

> The same groups of people that I got along well with would be the same kinds of people from similar faith backgrounds that I didn't get along with. It really depended on the person. Because I can think of a great Southern Baptist chaplain that I have tremendous respect for, and a great Catholic chaplain, boy, that I got along well with. Then on the flip side there was a Southern Baptist chaplain I just would not want to work with, a Catholic chaplain I would never want to see in my life (chuckles). The struggle was not the faith walk that they had, it was personality.

By the end of the answer he had changed his mind, adding "it's a good question" (Church of God in Christ). Catholic Chaplain Gunvant (who said, "It's more about personality") and Eastern Orthodox Chaplain Drozdov (who said, "It's based more on their personal piety and their personality") both downplayed the importance of denomination and theology. Chaplain Feteris thought that when there was enmity between chaplains, that was a function of individual traits and demeanors just as friendships were: "I think most of that stuff is personality-driven rather than theologically driven" (Presbyterian). Chaplain after chaplain shifted the question I asked away from religion and onto psychology. More or less consciously, they covered up denominational particularity by individualizing the rationales for their social relationships. Given the importance of cooperation, it's a sensible strategy.

THE JOYS OF DIVERSITY

If the chaplains resisted the idea that their friendships might be based on religious affiliations, they were all the more eager to answer the question, "How has religious diversity informed your ministry or affected you as a person?" Some reported they had been profoundly changed by their experience in the Chaplain Corps. "It has opened my eyes to the fact that God is much bigger than I could have ever thought," said Chaplain Timu (Disciples of Christ). In similar terms, Chaplain Metzger said, "It's enhanced me. It has shown me how big God is. As I said earlier, I left college with a myopic view that God was only concerned with my denomination. Seminary and all the years of serving on active duty in the Navy has shown me that God is much bigger than I once perceived Him to be. And I think the diversity has helped me see that" (Chaplaincy of Full Gospel Churches).

Presbyterian Chaplain Feteris thought he had become "even more appreciative of other traditions" than he had been before, and LDS Chaplain Frantz said "I think I'm more accepting, less judgmental" than before joining the military. Chaplain Giraldo found that he had benefitted from diversity because, he said, "I think it has broadened my horizon" and "my view of understanding God." He drew a contrast to how narrow his world view used to be:

> I think coming into the Chaplain Corps, that became very clear to me, that my role as a clergymen is expanded to be inclusive. Very inclusive. Something that, in my civilian ministry, I was not . . . I didn't have to face that, that much, it seems. It was simply because the community I ministered to for the most part came to me . . . To minister here, is more one-on-one evangelism, it's more one of seeking out . . . And in such a pluralistic and secular environment, at least I find that I minister to individuals differently. I find it to be very exciting. Pretty exciting on different levels. Encountering ministers of different faith groups, interacting with them and getting to know them. Not only as people, as individuals, but also understanding more of their faith traditions. (Evangelical Church Alliance)

Chaplain Bartley thought diversity was "frightening" because "you have to live in conflict," but this challenge of diversity was something he thought he was well prepared for. He had lived in conflict all his life, he said, so tension was "normal" to him. Warming to his topic, he explained why he had even been a bit disappointed by the chaplaincy:

> It was exciting for me to come into a situation where the notion of diversity would be discussed. I don't think that as chaplains we feel as comfortable as we should, to delve into that. See, that takes work. [laughs] It really does. It takes intentionality to be diverse. It does! And I don't think that has been met. For me. In terms of satisfaction. I wish that we were a little more involved in that. In a more intentional way. But the pressure of promotion, the pressures of assignments and going different places, makes it very difficult for us to move in that direction. (Church of God in Christ)

For Chaplain Bartley, then, structural aspects of the military left him wishing for more exposure to diversity. Other chaplains were nevertheless able to confront diversity in intentional ways. Chaplain Townsend from the Reformed Episcopalian Church had a regular "scripture study" with one Mormon and one Catholic colleague whom he felt very close to. He considered the Mormon "more of a spiritual leader to me than many of the official spiritual leaders I've dealt with" and the Catholic priest "one of my most dear friends on all the earth." In the Chaplain Corps, he "learned something every day" because the other chaplains "will say the most absolutely profound things that you could possibly imagine. And I really, really mean that. [. . .] Religiously we're not very close to each other in many regards, but the reality of our chaplain experience, the reality of what it means, has to me just absolutely been delightful. Absolutely delightful. How can I say enough good things about being a Navy chaplain?" (Reformed Episcopalian).

More somberly, Chaplain Gunvant (Catholic) remembered the intentional efforts of an orthodox rabbi after a Catholic sailor died. Although this Jewish chaplain "loved sailors" and "dealt with sailors better than any other chaplain of any faith group I know, including my own," he had a bad reputation among some colleagues for being a "jerk and not a team player." In the aftermath of the fatality, the rabbi went to great lengths to support Chaplain Gunvant and other members of the command. He even compromised his own faith to go with Chaplain Gunvant to the funeral home the night before the burial: "The remains were present. In Orthodox Judaism you just can't do this. You just can't be present with the remains" (Catholic). When Chaplain Gunvant celebrated mass for the young sailor, he felt the presence of his Jewish colleague: "I still can remember that, at the portion of the mass which is most related to the Passover, that I had every sense that he understood better what was happening than anyone else present because of his own sense of Judaism, and that rebounded to me. Then I suddenly began to realize that the ties were not superficial at all, they were very profound. And perhaps deeper than either of us realized." Based on this experience, Chaplain Gunvant realized the rabbi's reputation was unfair. He answered his own hypothetical question "What did we receive?" by saying, "Well, we received a rich, living Old Testament" (Catholic). Added to earlier statements about what each faith group has to offer, this anecdote illustrates the values of honest, respectful, and intentional pluralism.

Broader horizons were a recurring denominator for what chaplains gained from diversity. Greater security in, appreciation of, and commitment to one's own tradition was another. Chaplain Tzilker said, "If anything, [diversity has] given me more of a passion to pursue who I am and try to spread that to other Jews." Chaplain Michaud had also had a good experience with diversity: "It's given me a depth of understanding of all the major religious groups, has helped to firm up my own beliefs, my own understanding. Given me much more depth of understanding of what I value. [. . .] One of the reasons I came in was to have the association with other pastors and religious leaders. I wanted the exposure and the enrichment that that brings. And so I really have not been threatened at all, or have felt threatened by any other beliefs" (Baptist General Conference).

Chaplain Szmatula said that "the great thing about military ministry is interacting with other people" because "it strengthens your own faith." He thought he had become more "solid" in his beliefs (LCMS). Chaplain Squires had had to develop skills and gained appreciation for other faiths that together had "made me a better priest." Another Catholic, Chaplain Dyren, who had helped Wiccans develop rituals, doubted that he would have been able to function in "the little straightjacket" of his diocese. He considered the chaplaincy a "blessing" and the military a "great place for me as a priest" where,

> I've learned to see everybody as having the spark of God. Now, they may not have my tradition, or they may not have my view and my upbringing and things like that, but each in their own way is endeavoring toward that what is most deep and sacred inside themselves. [. . .] I think I needed something, and this is a beautiful, wonderful way to serve. [. . .] What I thought was diversity, I found it even larger. It's always a strain in sense to open yourselves even wider, to recognize the wonder and the beauty in everybody.

Although he occasionally sounded like a New Age type, he reassured me (and maybe himself) that he was able to remain true to his Mother Church: "I'm a Catholic priest; I've got my union card." Depending on just how narrow his home diocese was, it's possible the military rescued it from him as much as him from it. He wasn't the only priest with an expansive view of truth, though. Chaplain Geschka recalled annoying a bishop who was later made cardinal, and thus "pretty high up there in our food chain," by arguing that Catholics didn't have all the answers: "I say, 'You know, bishop, when it's all over and done with we're going to find out we made most of this stuff up.' He hits me, for some strange reason. We're all gonna get there [the afterlife]. And when we do, it's gonna be a whole lot of, 'Oh my goodness, they were right! He was right" (Geschka, Catholic).

The chaplain with the most to say on the issue of truth and diversity was Chaplain Irons. Intense and thoughtful, he seized every chance he had to turn his answers to this topic and spoke at length. During one exposition, he blamed me: "I'm preaching, now. You put a microphone in front of a Baptist preacher and that's what you get." Although diversity had broadened his "perspective of God and his grace and mercy" it had also "forced me to make sure I know what I believe." Arguing for the importance of both toleration and truth in encounters with diversity, he said chaplains weren't just around to serve as role models for toleration. They should also be able to provide sailors and marines with answers. It was this latter effort that he found somewhat lacking in the Chaplain Corps because what he found most "exciting" about his job was the opportunity to "sit around a beer" debating other chaplains on theological matters. What he disliked most about his job was the frequent relativism and lack of confidence he encountered in it. He said he was drawn to colleagues able to take and defend a stand:

> I'm not called to be just an ambiguous chaplain. I'm called to be a Baptist chaplain. And the Mormon chaplain, he needs to be the very best Mormon chaplain he can be. And I would expect nothing less of him. And the rabbi needs to be the very best rabbi he can be. Now, do I believe that my beliefs are true? Yes, certainly. Would I sit down with an LDS chaplain and talk about that? Absolutely. And expect him to fully describe to me why he believes that . . . See where I'm going with that? So as a Southern Baptist coming into this institution, I think it's exciting because I'm not being asked to deny anything, and many lay persons in Baptist churches think that. (Southern Baptist)

Chaplain Irons considered himself "suited for diversity" because of an ecumenical outlook and because he was "gifted in areas of communication." Like so many others, he was attributing his comfort and effectiveness in the Chaplain Corps to personality traits as well as to denominational affiliation. Chaplain Grams (Presbyterian) also thought he had an aptitude for working in a diverse environment, explaining it in musical terms: "I prefer the orchestra of voices of religion rather than the one instrument." He did accept that there were "prophetic cries of exclusive understanding" that claimed to uniquely possess the whole truth but said, "I can't listen to that comfortably." That's why he thought "chaplain work is very interesting."

Chaplain Oberlin believed it was necessary "to come down to ground level and say, 'This is what I believe and this is what I don't believe'" in order to avoid compromise. Despite having serious conversations with other chaplains, his favorite religious thinker had been one of the enlisted:

> I can certainly understand and I can see the sincerity of another person's belief. And I can understand how their belief system can say that I'm wrong. That's fair. Because you believe they're wrong, on some points. [. . .] We finally wind up looking at Scripture itself. Look at the same words and see that you're interpreting in one way and I'm interpreting it . . . We're looking at the same words, even. With a different understanding. The greatest theologian I've run across was a sergeant in the Marine Corps who was sitting out there in the middle of the desert, and she said, "God uses bandwidth, the whole spectrum." [chuckles] OK! Got it! I find my theologians in the desert. [Interviewer: "Good place to look!"] Yeah, exactly. What do you think Moses was doing out there? (ELCA)

While Chaplain Irons focused on the need to assert individual beliefs with conviction and Chaplains Dyren, Geschka, Grams, and Oberlin all found ways to suggest that every group had something valuable to offer, Chaplain Chance took a different approach entirely: he joked that all religions were equally ridiculous. Speaking of Mormons, he said, "The theology is pretty far out there, if you ask me, but we believe a guy rose from the dead, so it's all pretty crazy I guess, when you think about it in hard and fast terms" (ELCA).

Chaplain Cugrijus (LDS) had had "rewarding and enriching" encounters with other faiths in the military, making "wonderful friends" and learning "a lot about Judaism that I wasn't aware of." He suggested that military chaplaincy made clergy more moderate, saying, "I've experienced that chaplains who tend to be really liberal when they come in, if they're very successful they tend to be far more conservative when they leave, and those who are extremely conservative tend to be far more liberal when they leave. Become the middle. Many chaplains get out and they find they are totally out of touch with the denomination they left twenty years ago. It's fascinating I haven't experienced that personally."

If Chaplain Cugrijus is right in his hypothesis, which would be worth testing empirically, then it would make sense that chaplains would generally get along well and enjoy their time in the Chaplain Corps. As I warned from the outset, though, this is far from the complete story. There may be things about the Chaplain Corps and its members' background that cause conflict. The issue of how to pray is just one illustration among many.

INTERPERSONAL CONFLICTS IN THE CHAPLAIN CORPS

There is much evidence to support that "cooperative pluralism" happens in the military and that chaplains really do stretch themselves far in service of the "plural ideal" without feeling that they have to compromise themselves very much. Based on my sample of chaplains, this is the common and normative reality of military chaplaincy. However, any norm can be transgressed, so I asked the chaplains questions designed to explore the limits of cooperation and pluralism. Most were simple reversals of the immediately preceding positive question—that is, I would ask for an example of poor cooperation right after I asked about good cooperation, and I would ask about which faith groups they had trouble working with right after asking about their closest colleagues.

There were different kinds of answers to the question about difficulty working with other chaplains. One consisted of chaplains telling me they didn't have problems with anyone, as Chaplains Street (African Methodist

Episcopal), Townsend (Reformed Episcopal), and Irons (Southern Baptist) all did. Chaplain Cransveld joked, "all of them" to make the same point (Foursquare Gospel Churches). Interestingly, only Protestants denied having trouble getting along with anyone. Maybe it's easy to be a Protestant?

Another common answer was chaplains telling me that conservative Protestants, variously labeled, were hard to work with.[20] Chaplain Tzilker called them "evangelical Christians" and didn't like how they would try to "save" him (Jewish). Chaplain Grams described those he struggled to get along with as "under the umbrella of radical conservatives," by which he meant "people that just are a little quicker than I am to move to moral absolutes regarding religious beliefs" (Presbyterian). He much preferred people with more of a "critical mind" about their own and others' beliefs than conservatives who, in his opinion, took the Bible too literally.

Another Presbyterian, Chaplain Bowmaker, said he had more trouble working with "really proselytizing or rigid fundamentalists" than he did with Wiccans. He also didn't think he'd get along with anyone preaching hate or racism. This was exactly the problem Chaplain Timu had with "some Southern Baptists." He said, "Some of them are what I consider very evangelical. [chuckles] Very little tolerance. Plus, I've found that the racial prejudice I've faced in the past comes from some of them. [. . .] You get denominations that are white male, then they have difficulty dealing with women clergy or people of color. Because they have never had that experience" (Disciples of Christ).

Chaplain Timu was much more concerned about racism than most of the other chaplains. I didn't ask questions specifically about race relations, but he brought the issue up several times. In Chaplain Timu's view racism hurt people's chances for advancement in the military and was still widespread in "sophisticated" rather than overt forms. Surprisingly, given that virtually all religious groups preach racial equality, he thought racism was a bigger problem in the Chaplain Corps than in the rest of the military.

Carefully making sure I understood he had wonderful friends among them, Chaplain Cugrijus also mentioned evangelical Protestants because they had a problem with him:

> There are faith groups who are more anti-Mormon than others. Baptist tends to be. Some Baptists tend to be. It tends to be more evangelical groups. People that don't like Catholics, don't like Mormons, don't like Jews. That make sense to you? That's my experience. It's the whole fascinating thing about the word *Christian*. For many, the term *Christian* is a fence. To keep you out. Me out. I don't believe Christ ever built a fence like that. If you build a fence you'll keep us all in. To me that's the bottom line.

> Biblically and every other way there is no basis of any kind for religious persecution. If you can show me a litmus test in the Bible for what a Christian is, I'll empty my wallet for you. There isn't one! (LDS)

The "fanaticism" Chaplain Cugrijus objected to also bothered Chaplain Dyren. Advanced enough in rank to supervise other chaplains, he didn't like how the "evangelical guys" were irritable and prone to adopt an adversarial "us-versus-them type of thing." He didn't associate much with them, but did worry. He found it "scary" that "in the end the real fight that will happen in the world will be the fight of the rest of the world against Christian Fundamentalism. 'This is my piece of earth, and it's God-given to me, and it's more important than yours, and therefore, since I can't share it with anybody else by faith, and I can't share that the world is pluralistic, I can castigate everybody else as devils and evil.' And that's a danger. In the Navy we have to fight against that" (Catholic).

Clearly, in Chaplain Dyren's opinion, the military had no place for that kind of particularism, and he was not alone. Conservative Protestants were perceived by at least some other chaplains as judgmental and uncivil, narrow-minded and rigid, stridently averse to pluralism, and occasionally even racist.

Every conservative Protestant I interviewed claimed he didn't have any problems with any particular faith groups, except Chaplain Mace. Validating Chaplain Cugrijus's perception, Chaplain Mace said he might have trouble working with Jews: "It would be a total challenge. I mean, you can have a relationship with . . . But when it comes to the Scriptures and how they interpret the Scriptures, and how they totally reject Christ as the messiah, to me just blows my mind. So that might be a possible difficulty" (Seventh Day Adventist).

While conservative Protestants deny difficulty working with others, many of their peers find it hard to work with them. Not one chaplain I interviewed claimed it was hard getting along with mainline Protestants, and the only chaplain who said he had trouble getting along with Catholics was a Catholic priest himself, Chaplain Squires.

As they did when discussing who they were close to, chaplains described interpersonal conflicts in terms of personality, rather than theology. Chaplain Koch, for example, had had problems with some individuals but "wouldn't say it is distinguished based on faith" (United Methodist). Chaplain Giraldo from the Evangelical Church Alliance didn't think so either: "I think a lot of the challenges we face as chaplains, stressful challenges, with colleagues has to do with personality and temperament in my opinion." Interestingly, some of those who reported problems with conservative Protestants made a connection between personality and theology. Chaplain

Chance thought that "a lot of the time certain kinds of personality types are drawn to certain kinds of faith groups." He hadn't been close friends with any "fundamentalist evangelicals" precisely because "they tend to be so dogmatic and so closed-minded in their thinking in general" (ELCA). Not content to connect theology to personality, Chaplain Cugrijus implied there might be a personality disorder involved:

> I think that evangelicals are human beings. I mean, I'm concerned for some of them. Not because of who they are, but because of how they are. Anybody that foams at the mouth has a problem. And I don't mean that disparagingly. There are people who I think are attracted to that because they're not well, I don't mean that in any bad way toward any particular church, I think there are people attracted by a church because they are not well. [long pause] I don't think . . . I don't know how to say this and sound right. (LDS)

I'm not sure if there's a nondisparaging way to describe someone as "foaming at the mouth." Chaplain Cugrijus wasn't just saying evangelicals were wrong; he was suggesting there was something wrong with them, at least with some of them. In so doing, he was providing another illustration of chaplains individualizing personal conflicts. As a group, they seemed to want to persuade me that communal obligations and commitments, such as their belonging to faith groups, didn't impinge on the relationships they formed within the corps. The exception was with conservative Protestants, variously described as "evangelicals" or "fundamentalists." Significantly, those chaplains who felt a need to "explain" the conservative Protestants in terms of personality were doing to them what the conservative Protestants often did to the Wiccans: discounting the sincerity and validity of their religious commitments. Apparently, both Wiccans and conservative Protestants risk coming across as "difficult" when they assert their beliefs too strenuously.

Poor Cooperation and Failures of Facilitation

Notwithstanding an unconvincing denial from United Methodist Chaplain Clement ("No, because we're Navy chaplains and we always cooperate, we're perfect."), most chaplains were able to give examples of poor or ineffective cooperation. Many of the problems were structural in origin, derived from features of the military as an organization. Chaplain Street was theatrically evasive as he explained,

> Not on this base, because poor cooperation *never* occurs on this base, for the record. But I've been told, and I guess in *other* locations I have

> experienced, I guess when you see chaplains more concerned about making rank than doing ministry, and they are on an ego trip, then you see poor cooperation. It's "either my way or the highway." Granted, we are in an outfit where rank has its privileges. But when rank trumps, derails cooperation, it can equal bad news. I don't want to give you a precise example, but trust me it's out there when egos and rank go before ministry. (African Methodist Episcopal)

Chaplain Kanaridis had run into the "my way or the highway" attitude, too, when he ran into "unbelievable" walls set up by chaplains envious of a program he had designed to help the enlisted. "They didn't come up with it and they didn't feel it was important, and it wouldn't work where they are, because they had their own programs that they were doing" (Conservative Baptist). Chaplain Chance had a conflict with a supervising chaplain who canceled a wedding he had scheduled simply because he hadn't sought the supervisor's approval beforehand. In Chaplain Chance's version of events, there was no conflict about having the wedding on a Saturday at two; the problem was simply bureaucratic spite by a supervisor who was a "horse's you-know-what" (ELCA). Things came to such a head that the commanding officer had to step in and adjudicate between the two chaplains on his staff. Chaplain Illera expressed his irritation with colleagues who were "lazy" or "jealous" or "lived by the clock" (Catholic). Motivated purely by their paychecks, these kinds of chaplains would essentially hide in their offices, never seeking out sailors and marines to offer them help, and leave as soon as the work day was over.

Friction between chaplains is embarrassing to the Chaplain Corps, especially when it comes to the attention of line officers or the enlisted. Clergy are supposed to be righteous and forgiving, after all. Even when promotions and paychecks aren't at stake, the realities of bureaucratic organization, horse's asses and all, cause friction and competition in the military chaplaincy as they do in any other professional setting. Several chaplains thought the love of money, or budgeting, was the root of all evil in the Chaplain Corps. Chaplain Hamoud spoke hypothetically of situations in which one religious group would "take the lion's share" of the budget for its programs even though base chapel funds are supposed to be for everyone. Chaplain Squires had actual experience with this when he served as the only Catholic priest on a large base. Before he learned how the budgeting process worked, he went to the command chaplain, who was "of a different faith group" and asked for money for hymnals and other supplies. He was told there wasn't any money left for "the Catholic program" even though, as he learned later, the funds weren't parceled out that way and there actually had been money to spare.

In addition to bureaucracy and money, another common answer to questions about poor cooperation had to do with not being pluralistic enough and neglecting the needs of religious minorities. Chaplain Hawthorne said "being closed" and unwilling to understand others was a common cause of ineffective cooperation (Southern Baptist). Another Southern Baptist, Chaplain Beard, believed taking "a very isolated and restrictive approach" was a problem, especially with the Catholic priests, but that "sometimes it happens with the more fundamental elements of the Protestant religion, too." Chaplain Dyren also thought many of his colleagues were too "parochial" and rigid:

> In fact, the one thing that I have found in the Chaplain Corps that doesn't happen out in local ministry is the emphasis that we sometimes have here, and maybe it's artificially induced about us, what's Catholic and what's not Catholic and who's in and who's out. We all talk about each group as if they were still going on with the Reformation. And the Reformation has been over for 400 years, but we're still fighting in there in the Chaplain Corps. There are times when I think what we do is we see each other as somewhat wary, as adversaries, that we have to hold to our own specific unique denominational tradition and understanding and not make enough room for everyone else. That can be a problem. And that holds us back. (Catholic)

Chaplain Irons seemed to think Chaplain Dyren's concerns were well founded. There was a "temptation" for a chaplain "to not reach out to members of his command who are of other faith groups." Although he tried his best to care for the Catholics, Mormons, and Muslims he was responsible for, he did concede that "it would be very easy for me to simply forget about them" (Southern Baptist). When Chaplain Mace (Seventh Day Adventist) said poor cooperation would be "not finding out what background people have" so they can't be put in touch with others from the same group and when Chaplain Timu (Disciples of Christ) described it as "sabotaging the efforts to facilitate free exercise of religion" when there was a known need to meet, both seemed to have specific instances in mind.

Evasiveness about failures to facilitate was understandable given the importance of free exercise to the chaplains' mission and corporate legitimacy. Another reason it was a sensitive topic was that discussing failures of cooperation or facilitation could mean criticizing both peers and superiors. When I interviewed Chaplain Tzilker, for example, we left his office door open for ventilation. During our conversation, he would occasionally scoot his chair over to the doorway so he could look down the hallway, and nothing in his demeanor suggested it was a dramatic flourish. His body language left no doubt that his example of poor cooperation was far from hypothetical: "A Protestant battalion chaplain not caring about his Jewish sailors, not providing them with prayer books or kosher food or even lifting a finger to do anything for them" (Jewish).

Chaplain Koch (United Methodist) also thought Judaism wasn't accommodated as well as it should be, because the military almost always considered Christian holidays when scheduling exercises but almost never remembered Jewish or Muslim ones. Chaplain Gunvant had seen another chaplain give a briefing to newly arrived personnel and fail "to mention that there is a Jewish service" available to those who might want to attend. "I would take great offense and believe it to be constitutionally inappropriate if someone did that to my faith," he added (Catholic).

Chaplain Cugrijus had a whole list of problem areas when I asked him about poor cooperation. One was other chaplains who would "hunt for" and try to "head off" sailors and marines who might be interested in the Mormon faith, or who would try to convert Mormon "kids" to their version of Christianity. Sometimes they would lecture both LDS enlisted personnel and Chaplain Cugrijus himself about what Mormons "really" believe and stand for. "That happens frequently, frankly," he said. The incident that had most aggravated him was when a devout Southern Baptist general ordered him not to take his turn preaching at a general Protestant service because some members of the congregation had gone "whacko" after he taught the children's sermon. This congregation was apparently quite picky, having objected to a female chaplain as well. Chaplain Cugrijus wanted to know why some kinds of discrimination were OK and others weren't: "What if a black pastor had come in? Do you think they'd thrown her, thrown him out of the pulpit?"

To shift attention away from good order and discipline as a limit on facilitation, I asked the chaplains if there were any groups that they personally would feel uncomfortable facilitating for. Half the chaplains said there weren't any. Chaplain Street thought chaplains who couldn't facilitate for others were insecure about their own beliefs, whereas he knew "who I am, whose I am, and where I'm going" so that he didn't have any qualms about anyone. Chaplain Kojic was "fine" with "any group recognized by the US Navy" (Missouri Synod Lutheran), and Chaplain Hamoud pointed out that if he refused to facilitate for someone "that would be negating the First Amendment, the freedom of religion" (Muslim).

Some chaplains mentioned Wicca in this context. Chaplain Beard, who had surprised Wiccans by facilitating for them and then had to ask them to stop sending Wiccan jokes to his email, said, "The only group that I've had conscious conscience problems with would be the Wiccan group, who is becoming more popular in the military. However, I've done it" (Southern Baptist). Chaplain Illera also mentioned them: "Yes, definitely not comfortable facilitating for Muslims. [corrects himself] Not Muslims. Wiccans! Just not interested. I shouldn't say not interested. I would send them to someone. I would try to help them go to someone. But that is something I just don't feel comfortable with because it kind of cuts all across what I believe as a Christian" (Catholic). Like Chaplain Beard, then, Chaplain Illera would facilitate a bit even if he preferred not to. "I'd be courteous with them," even though "it would be a bit of an awkward situation," he concluded.

If any group really "cuts all across" what all the chaplains I interviewed believe, it's Satanism. This was Chaplain Timu's one-word answer when I asked who he wouldn't facilitate for. When I asked why, he explained, "Because it goes against what I believe human beings were created for" (Disciples of Christ). Similarly, the only time Chaplain Koch (United Methodist) would "hesitate" to facilitate would be if a Satanist came to him, "because Satanist is absolutely the antithesis of what I believe." Still, he said he'd do what he could, even though it would be difficult. Seeming to reassure himself as much as me, he ended his answer, "but the person who makes the ultimate decision is the commanding officer." Clearly, it was a decision he'd rather not have to make. Chaplain Michaud also brought up the commanding officer. First, he explained his reservations: "Um, yes. I'd have trouble with anything of the occult. Because it's, I see it as being completely opposite of what I stand for, what I believe. And I think that's a fairly common understanding. [. . .] In no way am I going to support Satan worship. At all." When I probed, asking if he'd try to get the Satanist to go to another chaplain, he revealed that he thought the military actually could coerce him to do it himself: "Well, no. Not if the commanding officer orders me to [facilitate]. I would have to do that. Am I violating religious convictions? No, I don't see that as a violation of what I believe in. Because it's not asking me to change my beliefs at all. Am I condoning, am I supporting it? [pause] Well, I guess you are to a certain extent, yeah" (Baptist General Conference).

Chaplain Bartley mentioned Satanists, but then laughed as if the very idea was ludicrous: "I haven't seen any come forth" (Church of God in Christ). Chaplain Clement, however, actually had facilitated for Satanists because "that's what my charge is" even though it had made him "a little uncomfortable" (United Methodist). Chaplain Kanaridis had also encountered a Satanist. He was a young man who had been "caught" and put under guard after lighting candles near "millions of gallons of fuel."

Ignoring the guards' "looks that could kill," Chaplain Kanaridis went to the Satanist and talked to him:

> I got really close to him and I went up to him and said, "Listen, before we go any further I want you to understand something." And I said, "The guy that you were worshipping, I hate. The guy I'm worshipping, you probably hate. So I want to make sure we got that real clear before we move forward." And I sat back like this [relaxed] and I said, "Now, I'm your chaplain, how can I help you?" He said, "I want to worship my god." I said, "There's no problem with that. You can worship whoever, I don't care. You can worship a rock. I care, but I don't care, you know what I mean? It's up to you what you worship." (Conservative Baptist)

Having impressed the importance of safety rules on the kid, the "problem" with this Satanist was solved.

The most restrictive chaplain, Chaplain Cransveld, said that in addition to Wicca he would "to one degree or another struggle with any group that's not Trinitarian, orthodox Christian" (Foursquare Gospel Churches). Other than Satanism and Wicca, however, few specific groups were mentioned. Not one chaplain said he'd have trouble facilitating for Mormons, Muslims, or Jews. Buddhists, Hindus, and Sikhs weren't mentioned at all. Chaplain Beard (Southern Baptist) wouldn't facilitate for the Nation of Islam and Chaplain Tzilker (Jewish) wouldn't facilitate for any white supremacists groups because both men opposed racism. Nor would Chaplain Tzilker assist evangelical Protestants if what they wanted to do was try to convert Jews or distribute anti-Jewish or anti-Catholic tracts. Then his answer would be "not only no, but hell no!" Chaplain Oberlin (ELCA) was a bit distressed by "the New Age and that stuff" but would facilitate as a constitutional right. He could only think of one thing he was sure he'd never facilitate: "Definitely, I would say no to human sacrifice." I resisted the temptation to ask if that wasn't an unavoidable part of any war.

CONCLUSION

The evidence presented in this chapter shows that the plural ideal is alive and well in the military Chaplain Corps. At their best, chaplains feel personally enriched working in a diverse environment and celebrate each religious tradition for its unique contribution to the spiritual life of the command. They make friends, learn from each other, and facilitate as many religious needs as they can—and maybe then some. They find ways around denominational restrictions and are creative in putting together interfaith events such as weddings, communions, and memorial services. As a group, chaplains embrace Muslims and Jews and at least shake hands with Mormons. Wiccans get a mixed reception and only Satanists and racists are clearly beyond the pale. The cooperation, goodwill and esprit de corps of the military's chaplains is more than an ideal or an institutional party line: I have seen it in practice.

Individualism pervades their work and their outlook. Facilitating free exercise means taking the religious "preferences" of atomized religious "consumers" at face value and respecting them. If the friendships and rivalries that happen between chaplains aren't coincidences born of circumstance, they're caused by personality. Religious commitments are not supposed to determine social relationships. Avoiding friendship with someone because of differences in faith is wrong. Being friends with someone just because of religious affiliation is also inappropriate, with an exception for the celibate fraternity of the Catholic priests.

The chaplains think in such individualistic ways for many reasons. Most importantly, they are Americans and partake of a deeply individualistic culture that celebrates autonomy. They are well versed in the discourses of "rights," which attach to individuals, not groups. Individualism may also serve as a kind of professional defense mechanism because explanations couched in individual or psychological terms deflect attention from communal commitments, established traditions, and collective sentiments. In other words, individualism can exonerate religion when there are problems and conflicts, and that is good for the soul, the career, and the corps. Because things do go wrong.

Chaplains quarrel. Sometimes it is about money and bureaucratic turf, but sometimes it really is about religion. Not all chaplains are equally happy about diversity. Although aware of the plural ideal, they don't really like it. They resent institutional rules that require them to be broad and general, even while following them. They worry about a trend toward a generic, hollowed-out civil religion. While enjoying some aspects of religious diversity, they fear the pursuit of truth has been abandoned in favor of inoffensive, relativistic platitudes. They facilitate for others more because it's a job requirement than because it's a chance to express their own commitment to pluralism. The counterpluralist impulse is real in the military chaplaincy, too.

It's mostly conservative Protestants who admit to having reservations about diversity. Other chaplains find them difficult to work with. They manufacture scandals. Chaplain Klingenschmitt's career-ending prayer crusade was just one example. They are insensitive and combative as they draw religious boundaries against Mormons and take stands against liberal, mainline Protestant wishy-washiness. At the same time, other chaplains seem to be drawing boundaries against *them*. The subtext of all the complaints against them is that evangelicals and fundamentalists don't really fit in; they don't quite belong in the Chaplain Corps.

When Richard Hutcheson updated his 1975 book about the military chaplaincy 22 years later, he wrote that one important change for chaplains during the interval had been the decline of denominations and denominational identity. Although he still thought chaplains should maintain close ties to their churches to avoid being swallowed up by the military, he conceded that physical separation from endorsing agents and the financial security of a government paycheck gives chaplains a lot of freedom from their denominations. This chapter has shown that he need not worry too much. Chaplains still have to remain in good standing with the people who send them into the military, and many say their first loyalty is to their church. They reject the military's wish that they be "all things to all people" and view themselves as emissaries, even missionaries, from their churches. They also rely on their ecclesiastical endorsers to go to bat for them if they're ever faced with a compromising situation.

Religious particularity can be taken too far. The counterpluralist impulse is not welcome in the military chaplaincy. The next chapter shows that it is nevertheless strong and explains the significance of that strength. The military chaplaincy is one of many battlegrounds in the so-called culture war.

CHAPTER 5

CULTURE WAR IN THE CHAPLAIN CORPS

> I've had my theology, integrity, and call all challenged by evangelical Protestants. They've tried to proselytize me!
>
> —ELCA chaplain

THE MILITARY PREFERS A CHAPLAINCY THAT IS ecumenical and staffed by flexible and open-minded people. Broad, generic chaplains can meet more religious needs than narrower ones can. Ecumenically minded chaplains are less likely to be distracted by theological bickering. Also, an ecumenical chaplaincy is easier to justify constitutionally. From the military's point of view, particularistic doctrine and sharp theological distinctions are irrelevant at best and disruptive at worst.

The chaplains look at particularity in very different ways. Some believe their tradition is one among many valid ones and take it as a point of departure for dialogue in pursuit of truth. Others believe their tradition already has the final truth and thus should be defended from corruption and proclaimed to as many as possible. The latter position is more common among evangelicals than other groups and has consequences for the way they perceive and interact with others. For example, evangelicals are most likely to disagree with the statement that they can trust someone "regardless of their religious beliefs."[1] A recent report on how positively religious groups view one another shows that no one likes Buddhists and Muslims less than evangelicals, that only the nonreligious view Catholics with less warmth than evangelicals do, and that evangelicals also rate Mormons low. Evangelicals do have a high opinion of mainline Protestants and Jews, although the Jews don't reciprocate, as they only rate Muslims lower than the evangelicals.[2]

The general outlines of the evangelicals' rise to power in American life are quite well known. In the nineteenth century, American Protestantism split in its response to modernity. Theological modernists accommodated religious teachings to the emerging scientific discoveries and market economy of their day. Placing less emphasis on miracles so as not to offend reason and less emphasis on judgment and Hell so as not to offend their congregants, the liberal theologians promoted a Christianity in which Jesus was love and the Bible a source of morally uplifting stories and inspiring examples. The aim was to keep Christianity relevant to the needs of real people in the real world. Critics, however, saw it as selling out. At the beginning of the twentieth century these critics were given a name by the publication of a series of books called "The Fundamentals," which listed and defended essential doctrines that could not be abandoned and must not be compromised. Modernists and fundamentalists struggled for control over congregations, mission boards, publishing houses, schools, and entire denominations. The most famous clash between the two happened in the 1925 "Scopes Monkey Trial," about the teaching of evolution in Tennessee schools.[3] Although the fundamentalists won the case (Scopes was convicted and fined for teaching evolution), they lost the public relations battle and retreated from public life.

The post-Scopes generation of conservative Protestants put most of their efforts into circling the wagons to protect what they had left and to organize. After World War II, a new generation was ready to abandon this defensive posture and work to reclaim America for Jesus. Led by Billy Graham and other celebrity preachers, the evangelical movement emerged out of the fundamentalist retreat.[4] The difference between the fundamentalists and their evangelical heirs is thus less theological than strategic. The theological modernist heirs are called "mainline" Protestants today.[5] Thanks to effective institution-building and birth rates higher than the general population, the evangelical movement had achieved such a degree of political and cultural power by the 1980s that liberals were alarmed and academics working on the assumption of inexorable secularization were thrown into confusion.[6] Not only was religion supposed to have retreated into the "private" sphere of family and church, but the content of what the evangelicals proclaimed also didn't fit the modern world as it was supposed to be. So what is evangelicalism all about?

Sociologists generally agree on four defining characteristics of evangelicalism. First, they take—or at least claim to take—the Bible as "literally true," which means they accept that supernatural events happen, are skeptical about scientific claims about how the world came into being and where people came from, and hold the Bible up as the final authority on moral matters. Evangelicals often describe their lives or their churches as "Bible-based" and evaluate actions and beliefs in terms of whether they're "biblical" or not. Second, evangelicals believe that everyone must undergo a "born-again" experience: an intensely emotional event where they decisively surrender their lives to Jesus. This is when a person becomes "saved," and evangelicals celebrate the ability to give verbal testimonies that divide a person's life into "before" and "after" being born again. They also provide opportunities during worship services to approach the front of the congregation and "give your life to Jesus." Appeals to do so are called "altar calls." Third, evangelicals evangelize. They feel personally responsible for converting others to Christianity, one person at a time. It is not enough to leave this to designated missionaries, although they have those, too: everyone should seize opportunities to "share" the Gospel and bear "witness" to the joys of life with Jesus. There are books and courses that instruct people in how to do this—for example, by cultivating friendships at work and then using those as frameworks for influencing people. Finally, evangelicals insist on strict behavioral norms, especially those relating to sex, but they also frown on vices such as drinking, swearing, and gambling.[7]

Taken together, these characteristics describe a sociological "ideal type" of evangelicalism. Although individuals vary, the characteristics just described tend to occur together and reinforce one another. Even though not everyone who fits the sociological definition would self-identify as "evangelical," preferring to simply think of themselves as simply "Christian," classifying people based on their answers to indicator questions and by denominational affiliation shows that approximately 30 percent of Americans can be counted as evangelicals, making them a larger group than Catholics.[8] Obviously, as with any other religious group, some evangelicals are more fervent than others. However, given their view of the Bible and their behavioral norms, there is a solid core of evangelicals who believe theirs is the only true religion. Even other people who consider themselves Christian aren't really "saved," and non-Christian religions are simply false. They draw sharp boundaries against others and come across as rude and inappropriate in secular, pluralist society when they do what flows naturally from their world view: pass judgment and act on their convictions. This leads to real religious conflicts.

In 1991, James Davidson Hunter published a book arguing that there was a "culture war" in America. The two sides were separated by "different systems of moral understanding," which he called "orthodox" and "progressive." Each system provides adherents with a sense of meaning, purpose, and solidarity. The fundamental split between the orthodox and the progressive flows from a deep disagreement about the nature and basis for moral authority. In the orthodox view, moral authority is "external, definable, and transcendent," so that it provides a "consistent, unchangeable measure of value, purpose, goodness, and identity"[9] for both individuals and the country as a whole. In the progressive view, moral authority reflects the spirit of the times, so that truth is both subjective and constantly unfolding. Progressives don't expect everyone to arrive at the same answers or believe that any answer is necessarily final. They resent the orthodox for trying to impose their view on them, while the orthodox react strongly against the progressives for abandoning what few real standards that are left.

Importantly, Hunter argues that this split cuts across denominational boundaries. Religious conflict in America is no longer between Protestants, Catholics, and Jews. Rather, conflict now happens within each tradition, with progressive Protestants pitted against orthodox Protestants and orthodox Catholics and Jews struggling against the progressives in their traditions. Both orthodox and progressive religious people find political and cultural allies in other faiths. For example, orthodox Protestants, Jews, and Catholics make common cause against abortion and homosexuality. The 2012 presidential candidacy of Rick Santorum provided a vivid illustration of this when his opponents unearthed a speech he gave in 2008 describing mainline Protestantism as "in a shambles" and "gone from the world of Christianity as I see it."[10] What's interesting is that even though his comments sound like ones a Protestant fundamentalist would make (he also argues that Satan is trying to destroy America and is making inroads in academia), Santorum is in fact a Catholic.

Critics have accused Hunter of overstating his case, pointing out that most Americans are quite moderate on religious and moral issues and backing that up with both qualitative and quantitative data.[11] Hunter answers such charges by clarifying that the culture war is not a matter of "popular opinion but rather of deeper normative systems manifested within and defended by powerful cultural institutions and elites who represent them."[12] These elites have influence far beyond their numbers and it is they who struggle for control of the courts, educational institutions, local and national politics, and the media. Each side tries to assert its view of moral authority and its vision of America. My argument in this chapter is that as clergy and officers, military chaplains are part of the elite that participates in the culture war and that the military itself is a battlefield in it.

EVANGELICALS IN THE MILITARY: THE SECTARIAN IDEAL AND THE DECLINE OF THE "GENERAL PROTESTANT"

The best account of evangelicals' rise to influence in the military is that of historian Anne Loveland. The paragraphs that follow draw on her work extensively. As recently as the 1950s and 1960s, most military leaders, including most chaplains, belonged to mainline Protestant groups. Evangelicals were few, were considered outsiders, and were wary of the military establishment. Evangelical denominations objected to the military chaplaincy lumping all Protestants together and offering "General Protestant" worship services. A countervailing force was at work, however, because evangelicals were becoming more comfortable with the military as a whole and discovering opportunities to evangelize outside Sunday church hours through counseling, character education classes, religious retreats, Bible study groups, and spiritual revivals. By the time controversy raged about the war in Vietnam, many mainline chaplains were accused of being warmongers by their own churches, while the evangelicals could tell their sponsors that they were "missionaries in uniform." Since then, the representation of mainline denominations in the military chaplaincy has declined.

Civilian groups such as the Full Gospel Businessmen's Fellowship International supported evangelical chaplains with publications they could distribute to military personnel. Many high-ranking officers and well-placed officials at the Pentagon became converts to evangelicalism, which gained entry into national politics and gained status within the military because of its support for the Vietnam War and opposition to atheist communism. Loveland provides detailed case studies of senior line officers (i.e., not chaplains) who unabashedly proclaimed their faith from their positions of power, gathered like-minded junior officers around them, and used their influence to create an institutional climate friendly to evangelical religious expression. From the evangelical point of view, there were some setbacks. Compulsory chapel attendance was ended at the military academies in 1972, more and more recruits declined to state a religious preference, and military authorities had become "increasingly apprehensive about the possibility of a challenge to the constitutionality of the Chaplain Corps" long before it actually materialized in *Katcoff v. Marsh* in the 1980s.[13]

Although brief, this summary introduces two of the important conflicts plaguing the military chaplaincy today: proselytization and the military's preference for ecumenical "general Protestants" over stridently particularistic ones. According to Loveland, it was the controversy about homosexuality in the military during the Clinton Presidency that really galvanized the two sides. Moral conservatives, including chaplains, were outraged by Bill Clinton's apparent disregard for traditional sexual morality, and decided it was time to take a stand against a culture and a corps in decline.

From the evangelical point of view, accommodation of homosexuality was but one more instance of liberals selling out Biblical truth, one more concession to a secular world run over by political falsehood (socialism), scientific falsehood (evolution), and religious falsehood (competing faith groups). From a strict evangelical point of view, pluralism amounts to a celebration of lies. Although few ordinary Americans would go to the extreme and condemn everyone who disagrees with them as unbelievers, chaplains are not ordinary Americans: they are clergy, and as such, they are more likely to embrace doctrinal stands fiercely. Putnam and Campbell illustrate this "clergy-laity disconnect" with an anecdote about what happened when Putnam spoke to a meeting of Missouri Synod Lutheran theologians.[14] They were "shocked" to learn how high the percentage of Americans who thought there were many ways to get to Heaven was and "stunned into silence" when Putnam was able to pull data up from his laptop indicating "that 86 percent of Missouri Synod Lutherans said that a good person who is not of their faith could indeed go to heaven." Remember, the culture war is about elites.

Rejecting the plural ideal, evangelical elites have articulated a rival worldview, which Loveland calls "the sectarian ideal." In her analysis, it has three component parts: sectarianism, moral absolutism, and custodial responsibility. *Sectarianism* means limiting ecumenism. In 1990, for example, the National Association of Evangelicals warned against "broader forms of worship," which prompted some endorsing agencies to insist that their chaplains remain loyal to their doctrines while simultaneously promising them legal assistance should they need it.[15] *Sectarianism* also means that for evangelicals, freedom of religion means freedom to be particular, to cling to and proclaim their own uniqueness rather than toning it down to avoid giving offense. *Moral absolutism* refers to the rejection of relativism and of religion as mere "preference." This is the part of the sectarian ideal that intersects with the "orthodox" position in the culture war thesis. Finally, *custodial responsibility* means that chaplains must preach truth and oppose falsehood wherever they go. The combination of particularity and custodial responsibility makes life difficult for evangelicals in the military. It frequently makes them annoying to the progressives and problematic for the military as well because the sectarian ideal undermines cooperative pluralism.

Sociologists, clergy, and the military don't organize the religious world into the same categories. Not only do many clergy who fit sociological definitions of fundamentalism reject that label, but some mainline chaplains who would be "progressive" in Hunter's scheme would claim the label "evangelical" for perfectly sound historical and theological reasons that nevertheless contradict sociological usage. This was the case with one of the Evangelical Lutheran Church of America chaplains I interviewed, for example. When I describe one group of chaplains (for example Mace, Kanaridis, Cransveld, and Irons) as "evangelical" or "conservative" and another group (for example Grams, Timu, and Chance) as "mainline" or "liberal," I am doing so in the sociological sense. I relied on several clues when categorizing them. I asked each chaplain to describe his own "theological perspective," name his ecclesiastical endorser, and to explain whether they thought they were more conservative or liberal than other members of their denomination. When I asked questions about evangelicals, I noted whether they spoke of "them" or "us" in their answers. And of course I listened to them at length as they discussed issues germane to the mainline/evangelical split.

The military has its own approach to classifying chaplains, being far more interested in what a chaplain can do than in theological niceties. What kind of worship services can he or she lead? How many and what kinds of religious needs can he or she facilitate for? To answer these questions, the military works with three major categories: Catholics, "liturgical" Protestants, and "nonliturgical" Protestants. Thanks to the institutional penchant for abbreviation and acronym, the Protestant groups are referred to as LitProts and NonLitProts. LitProts tend to come from denominations where the clergy wear vestments, whose worship follows a set order, and where worship is typically solemn and peaceful. They include Episcopalians, most Lutherans, and many Methodists. They are sometimes jokingly referred to as "the frozen chosen" and their services described as "smells and bells" because some of the most ceremonially inclined groups use incense. They are also called "baby-baptizers" and tend to be progressive in Hunter's terms. NonLitProts are more likely to preach in a business suit than robes and to conduct spontaneous worship services that are enthusiastic, even boisterous. They include the Assemblies of God and most Baptists. Jokingly, they are described as the "Jesus-hallelujah-amen crowd" or the "praise-the-Lord" people. They are called "non–baby-baptizers," and I consider it a near miracle that no one has reduced this to NonBabBap. Chaplains do, however, appropriate and use the terms *LitProt* and *NonLitProt* and use the latter interchangeably with *evangelical.*

The military's interest is to provide religious "coverage" to as many of its members as possible. For chaplains representing small religious groups, such as Islam, Judaism, or one of the Eastern Orthodox churches, that means typically assigning them to large bases where there's a greater likelihood that they will be able to sustain and serve a stable congregation. Because most members of the military are Christian, however, coverage generally means trying to make sure each ship, base, or area has a priest for the Catholics, a LitProt to baptize babies and offer a "high church" styles of worship service, and a NonLitProt to baptize adults and offer a more "low church" style of worship. A base or ship large enough to have three chaplains is likely to be assigned one of each. Many evangelicals believe the Chaplain Corps inappropriately promotes and retains chaplains to serve this "thirds system," overstating the need for LitProts and not adequately recognizing the enlisted demand for NonLitProts.

This recognition of a split within Protestantism is relatively new. Historically, Navy officers tended to be "gentlemen" from the upper class of Eastern seaboard cities, and the collateral duties Navy chaplains were expected to perform were ones that presupposed a certain degree of education, like teaching literacy and navigation.[16] The evangelical movement flourished on the less affluent and less educated frontier.[17] That's how the Navy chaplaincy and its institutional culture came to be dominated by mainline denominations, much more so and for longer, than the Army or Air Force chaplaincies. "High church" liturgy also fits well with the Navy's tradition of elaborate ceremony. During World War II, the Navy used three letters on its dog tags to identify sailors' religion: "C" for Catholic, "J" for Jewish, and "P" for Protestants. The Protestant "P" was treated as a catch-all category for everyone who wasn't Jewish or Catholic. Even the Russian Orthodox were counted as "P."[18]

Although the military has, reluctantly, conceded that there are different kinds of Protestants, some of the older chaplains I interviewed could remember there being a single "General Protestant Service" early in their careers. One of the Catholics recalled, "We did not have all these services that you see now. If Lutherans wanted to have their own service this was considered disloyal to Protestantism because you know you had three groups! You had Protestants, Catholics, Jews. 'What's the matter with you? Why do you want to have this kind of things?' And Episcopalian the same way. 'We have the Protestant service and it's at this time and you're Protestant, right? Well, then get with the program.'" (Catholic)

By now, a generic Protestant service is usually offered alongside several more specialized Protestant services. Evangelicals, who object to the concept of a "general Protestant" on sectarian grounds, are especially likely to advertise worship formats that appeal to the military's young demographic. Chaplain Frantz (LDS) described the proliferation of Sunday options for sailors:

> A lot of people would say that holding services on ships would be something that could unify a large part of the crew, but it doesn't always. Because you may have a very liturgical group of Christians who want to practice. And another group may want to have a very free-style evangelical Pentecostal type service. And you may have a middle group that is more reserved than the evangelical and yet a little more free style than the liturgical churches. And you may have a gospel group, too. You may have four or five or six Christian services on one ship. (LDS)

On smaller bases and ships, where there aren't enough chaplains to provide such variety, the Protestant service still resembles the old "General Protestant" model. Chaplain Drozdov thought the Navy still made "efforts to have a Navy worship service, where the ten o'clock Protestant service is the Navy worship service, and this is a basic generic Protestant service, and anybody can come to that" (Eastern Orthodox). What has changed institutionally seems to be a shift in emphasis. A worship service that by necessity has to appeal to a wide range of Protestants is now offered as "a" general Protestant service rather than "the" General Protestant Service of the institution. The term and category "general Protestant," however, is still commonly used among working chaplains.

The most general service I heard of was advertised as "nondenominational" and featured a Muslim, Chaplain Hamoud, preaching to Christians out of the Bible, with one or two Muslims in attendance as well. "I used the Bible," he said, "because as a Muslim I believed in the Scripture." He would carefully choose passages he thought would be relevant to the daily experiences of his little congregation and enjoyed "seeing their eyes open and the light bulb come on in their eyes" as he explained how the texts could be applied to them.

A Muslim preaching to Christians might be a nightmare to some, but it was probably an exceptional arrangement. There aren't that many Muslim chaplains, and any base large enough to assigned one is likely large enough to have several Christian chaplains as well. A much more common "problem" for supporters of the sectarian ideal involves Mormons. Presbyterian Chaplain Bowmaker discussed the different groups in the military: "It's not like [facilitating for] a Muslim, where I know I'm kinda fish out of water talking to them. I can listen and try to be whatever help I can. But the perception is that I should be able to at least help the Protestants. The Navy considers Mormons general Protestants. There's basically Catholic, liturgical Protestants, and nonliturgical Protestants. Baby-baptizers and non–baby-baptizers, and the Muslims. Those are the big dividing points. And Jewish" (Presbyterian).

Sociological research has shown that older and younger congregations do different things during their weekly worship service and that there are also variations by education and race. Older and more educated congregations are more likely to have an organ, follow along in a written program, and have plenty of time set aside for quiet prayer. Drums, jumping, speaking in tongues, and calling out "amen" during sermons are characteristics of younger and less educated congregations.[19] And that is exactly what the military provides. Military demographics thus make sure there's a demand for less ceremonial and more enthusiastic styles of worship, which is what evangelicals specialize in. Evangelical chaplains and endorsing agents have told me they consider the Navy chaplaincy to be an unjustified "jobs program for mainline churches," whose theology and style of worship aren't really in demand. Chaplain Chance, from the ELCA, was well aware of the younger generation's preferences:

> I come from the Liturgical background. You're a Baptist, but you were raised in Norway, so you know these Lutherans services. The "frozen chosen" kind of stuff. That's the big joke. That is not the kind of religion that Americans, by and large like today. They like this guitar stuff and rock and roll. They got a service like that here. We got a brochure for it. And that's what people like. Lot of people like. And you look at all the church growth movements, that's the kind of church they do. (ELCA)

Chaplains often make good faith efforts to offer services that appeal to the whole congregation, aware that the people in it come from different backgrounds and have different expectations about what "church" should be like. Although clearly an evangelical, Chaplain Metzger was willing to be flexible: "Of course, I naturally lean toward a more Free Church format, and yet I want to maintain liturgical elements within the Protestant service so that all people will feel that they're being ministered to" (Chaplaincy of Full Gospel Churches).

Not everyone was as willing or able to be accommodating, though. "I can see that being hard for them," said Catholic Chaplain Farrow about evangelicals who were "forced into this broader concept from their faith tradition," but this was a difficulty mainline LitProts faced, too: "I can see it hard for an Episcopal priest in the military to be doing a General Protestant service that's nonliturgically oriented, so to speak. It's just Scripture and preaching and that sort of thing. I can understand that. So there's a lot of rough edges here as far as that whole thing working" (Catholic).

It's not hard to imagine how awkward each chaplain might feel trying to adjust his style to that of a military congregation, but it is necessary. A "fire and brimstone" Baptist preacher might frighten any Episcopalians in his pews, while a "frozen chosen" Lutheran might put Assemblies of God congregants to sleep. Interestingly, Chaplain Beard thought it was easier to move in one direction than the other: "I think evangelicals are less likely to go to a high church service than a high church person might be to go the other way. I think it's harder. They just don't understand it. It looks too Catholic. [. . .] I think it's easier to adapt to a low service" (Southern Baptist). Chaplain Beard also said, "I think that my beef with the Chaplain Corps or the Navy chapel setting is that it's been predominantly high church" and pointed out that some Navy chapels had a literally built-in mainline bias. While Baptists preach from the middle of the church, the older "high church" denominations put the pulpit off to one side, which is where it located in some of the older chapels. He was glad some of the newer chapels had a baptistery for full immersion, a decidedly important feature for a Baptist. In the big picture, he was pretty happy: "On a personal level, I've never been in a position where I've been told that I had to conduct that kind of worship. I know chaplains who have. I've just done worship like I wanted to do worship, and I've had very good success with that" (Southern Baptist).

Chaplain Chance admitted that when he led a General Protestant service it ended up "looking peculiarly like" a Lutheran service, even though he is "not out there trying to force the small catechism down people's throats and turn them into Lutherans." He reverted to the Lutheran format because "that's what I know and that's what I'm familiar with." Besides, he didn't think the liturgical style bothered anyone: "Now, there's nothing in the Lutheran church that is particularly offensive to, that I'm aware of, to Catholics or even non-Catholics, or new evangelicals. It's not free worship the way they're used to but there's nothing offensive in it" (ELCA).

The NCMAF Covenant and Code of Ethics for chaplains states, "When conducting services of worship that include persons of other than my religious body I will draw upon those beliefs, principles, and practices that we have in common."[20] The consequence of this is that some worship elements, such as a sermon and congregational singing, will be perfectly fine and uncontroversial, while others probably don't belong in a general Protestant service. Chaplain Michaud described one such element: "Well, an example of where there's been difficulty in the military. You have some conservatives; I guess you can classify them as evangelical, Christian evangelical conservatives; that believe in an altar call. And that, at least early on, became a real issue when I came into the military originally. Many of your mainline senior chaplains, Lutherans, Presbyterian, Methodist, would not allow a Baptist chaplain or an evangelical free chaplain to have an altar call. They felt that was proselytizing. And there has been controversy, major controversy over that" (Baptist General Conference).

Chaplain Drozdov explained why the altar call was so controversial, with an example from his own experience. He had given a lay volunteer permission to organize an alcohol-free dance for a youth group under the auspices of the base chapel. The event had been advertised with flyers, but

> what he didn't advertise in these flyers was that the music that they played would basically be Christian rock, which didn't bother many people, but that there would be an altar call. At some point. At least a call up to the stage, and an invitation to accept Christ. Well! It upset a lot of people. And the individual who set this up came to me for help, because he felt that he was very unfairly persecuted. He says, "Well, I don't understand why they would object to some of this." I said, "Believe it or not, most of the people who objected to what you did are Christian parents. Because some of them, first of all, they might come from liturgical backgrounds that wouldn't consider themselves evangelical and say, 'Well, we believe in salvation differently than you. And that is not an instantaneous thing, it is something that is learned, and the children are nurtured. So therefore we object to you trying to turn them from that.' And there are other people who were evangelical who said, 'My kid's already saved, what are you trying to do here?'" (Eastern Orthodox)

Chaplain Szmatula witnessed a different intrusion of something very particular into a General Protestant service. Having arranged for a younger chaplain he was mentoring to preach one Sunday, he was surprised by the format he chose: "[He] gets in there, a new chaplain, and has a healing service! At the general Protestant service! And so I brought him in the next day and I said, 'You know, if you want to have a healing service as a charismatic, you can hold a charismatic service on Sunday night. Call it that, call it a healing service, and you can do that. But in the General Protestant Service you must—everything must be in common with what is generally believed in Protestant Christendom'" (LCMS).

While Chaplain Szmatula thought healing had to be relegated to a more specialized and separately advertised service, there were elements he insisted had to be included in general Protestant services. Without the Lord's Prayer or the Nicene Creed, he thought too many liturgical sailors and marines would be unfulfilled.

FROM A LITURGICAL TO A LITIGIOUS CHAPLAINCY

A number of lawsuits have been filed against the Navy, several of them coordinated by an attorney named Arthur Schulcz, who maintains a well-organized website dedicated to "Chaplain Reform" where he provides updates and rationales for the litigation.[21] His positions are consistent with the sectarian ideal as described by Loveland. For example, he objects to ecumenism and argues that real free exercise of religion requires freedom to assert religious particularity. My interest here is not to comment on the merits or status of each of the half-dozen cases at their various stages but to describe how the active-duty chaplains I interviewed responded when I asked them, first, what they thought "motivated the lawsuits" and, second, whether they thought the allegations made had merit. I learned that many chaplains felt very deeply about these questions, and while both sides would probably prefer a long exposition of their side of the story, I will limit myself to a sketch of the evangelicals' grievances.

The various lawsuits allege that the Navy is biased against evangelicals and in favor of Catholics and mainline Protestants. Worship formats and programs that are mainline and ecumenical are promoted, celebrated, and rewarded, while evangelical worship styles and programs are discouraged and "shut down" and the chaplains who offer them punished. They also argue that the Navy uses an unconstitutional "thirds system" to try to recruit and promote one-third liturgical chaplains, one-third nonliturgical chaplains, and one-third Catholic chaplains, even though the Navy denies that it does or ever did. The "thirds system" is unfair, they say, because the mainline churches have so few members in the armed forces that they don't deserve as many slots as they get in what the evangelicals believe is a de facto quota system. This makes it harder for many evangelicals to enter the military. It also leads to discrimination against evangelical chaplains in promotions.[22] The running joke among evangelical chaplains was that for a baby-baptizer to get promoted, he only needed to be able to chew gum and walk at the same time. A non-baby-baptizer on the other hand would have to be able to chew gum and walk . . . on water.

Navy chaplains are evaluated approximately every five years and promoted from lieutenant through lieutenant commander and commander to captain in part on the basis of "fitness reports" that are examined by a "promotion board." To achieve the highest ranks of the Chaplain Corps, it is also necessary to have served in a variety of different commands and thereby to have been exposed to many different tasks and conditions. The most prestigious positions are of course chief of chaplains and assistant chief of chaplains, but chaplain recruiter is also very sought after. Because some assignments are de facto prerequisites for promotion to these jobs, the position of detailer, which involves assigning chaplains to different commands, is also important. Chaplains are very aware that there's no standing still in the military hierarchy. Anyone passed over for promotion twice has to leave, which means even chaplains who aren't personally inclined to be ambitious have to compete for promotion to keep their jobs.

As a group, the chaplains I interviewed were skeptical of the lawsuits.[23] Only 4 of the 34 were certain that evangelicals were discriminated against, with another 2 saying they thought it was probably true. All the six chaplains who thought it likely that the nonliturgicals' grievances had merit were Protestants: Chaplains Michaud and Irons (Southern Baptists), Cransveld (Foursquare Gospel Churches), Metzger (Chaplaincy of Full Gospel Churches), Bartley (Church of God in Christ), and Chance (ELCA). Eight chaplains were sure there was no discrimination against evangelicals. This was the position of Chaplains Drozdov (Eastern Orthodox), Tzilker (Jewish), Cugrijus (LDS), and two of the Catholics, Squires and Dyren. Three Protestants also said there wasn't any antievangelical bias, with two of the more conservative chaplains in my sample, Mace (Seventh Day Adventist) and Kanaridis (Conservative Baptist), joining Chaplain Szmatula (Missouri Synod Lutheran). The remaining twenty chaplains either couldn't or wouldn't offer an opinion on the lawsuits. Some said they'd barely heard of the cases. Others pled that they didn't know the facts well enough to offer an opinion, although most of them discussed the issues and speculated about causes anyway, without taking a position.

Addressing the allegation that LitProts and Catholics sabotaged NonLitProt careers by denying them necessary assignments, Chaplain Metzger from the Chaplaincy of Full Gospel Churches shared this perception:

> Kim, I noticed that people from my faith group can only go so far as chaplains. To date, none of our chaplains have ever been promoted above the rank of lieutenant commander. Also we're never really received any of the, let's say prime assignments, such as assignments to one of the academies, Naval Academy, Coast Guard Academy. We've never been assigned to the chief of chaplains office. I don't know that we've had any recruiters. We've never been assigned a chaplain recruiter. So I've seen strong indicators that my church has been discriminated against. (Chaplaincy of Full Gospel Churches)

Chaplain Geschka countered that the reason some faith groups didn't ascend the ladder as easily as others had to do with legitimate military needs, not discrimination. He applied a version of the same logic the evangelicals do in their lawsuits, both arguing that the shape of the Chaplain Corps should reflect the composition and needs of the military population. The difference is that while the evangelical lawsuits take a macroscopic view and claim there shouldn't be as many liturgical Protestants as there are, Chaplain Geschka argued for a case-by-case evaluation of what a base or ship needed. Using a small installation in Alaska as an example, he said the military had to consider the needs of the people there: "For instance, in Alaska, you're gonna need a Catholic priest, and you're going to need a Protestant that baptizes babies. Just to meet the needs of the community. So more than likely, you wouldn't send a Baptist to Alaska, and there's probably a couple of other little sites where you wouldn't send just a Baptist unto themselves. And I guess that's kind of off-putting, because you don't have the opportunity to serve in that particular assignment and get that check on your, your ticket punched, that's what we say" (Catholic). Although Chaplain Kanaridis didn't agree with the lawsuits, he wasn't persuaded by this kind of "military needs" argument either: "I see the logic behind it. But I can also see that that's an O-5, O-6 billet that other people might want, and just because I'm not a Lutheran, I can't get that billet? That's not right" (Conservative Baptist).

It wasn't just Protestants who objected to assigning chaplains this way. The residual category of chaplains who don't fit into the scheme of Catholic, liturgical, and nonliturgicals, sometimes referred to as "Special Worship," risked missing out on opportunities, too. Because there are few of them, it doesn't make sense for the Navy to assign them to small bases or ships, because they wouldn't be able to provide as much "coverage" there. Chaplain Drozdov complained, "When I'm told by the detailer, 'We don't send Orthodox to the Naval Academy,' or, 'We don't put Orthodox on board ship.' Would they dare say that, 'Well we don't send people of certain races here, or certain genders here'? But somehow we can have that hurled at us and nothing comes of it" (Orthodox).

The lawsuits allege, and a few chaplains still believe, that LitProts and Catholics conspired to control assignments and promotions in past and still do so today. Worried about cliques of chaplains organizing in secret to manipulate the system to their own faith groups' advantage, Chaplain Chance thought there was a bias because so few evangelicals had held the highest positions in the Chaplain Corps in modern times: "And something is not right there. I mean, their schools are every bit as good. I mean, they're theologically different, but they're endorsed by . . . I think there is denominational bias. It's all done in office doors between senior people. And you can't . . . O-6 chaplains tell me this, if you get a bad name among Catholic Priests in the Navy chaplains corps, you're done" (ELCA).

The Catholic faction Chaplain Chance referred to is sometimes called the "Boston mafia" because at one point there was a glut of senior Catholic chaplains from that city. Others invoke, jokingly and not, the existence of a "Lutheran mafia." Chaplain Chance quipped, "Yeah, I always tell people it hasn't served me very well," because he had at one point been passed over for promotion himself. Chaplain Feteris found the idea that the Lutherans were secretly in control ludicrous. One reason was that the version of the rumor he had heard implied that ELCA and Missouri Synod chaplains were in cahoots even though "It's like, they hate each other!" Laughing hard, he somewhat composed himself and added, "I also objected because if anybody is going to politically outmaneuver other denominations, I was insulted that the Presbyterians weren't named in that suit. We're political animals, so by nature, if . . . If anyone is going to be getting in on the inside track, I want it to be Presbyterians politically maneuvering themselves in. That I can understand. Lutherans? Don't have a clue!" (Presbyterian).

According to Loveland's history of evangelicals in the military, such denominational Machiavellianism wasn't limited to the Catholics or the mainline. Discussing the last two decades of the twentieth century, she says there "is evidence that some evangelical leaders allowed their sectarian commitment to influence decisions regarding performance evaluations, duty assignments, promotions, and the like." These leaders were not necessarily chaplains. Staff officers, line officers, and well-placed civilian officials in the Department of Defense joined evangelical organizations and officers' clubs such as the Navigators. One anonymous officer complained about superiors who used attendance at Bible studies as a criterion in official evaluations, and a service school commandant was rumored to be "placing 'born-again friends' in administrative positions" in the early 1990s.[24] Apparently, evangelicals aren't immune to the temptations of promoting their own either.

The chaplains who reacted most negatively to the lawsuits were those from the "Special Worship" category. Rattling off a long list of key positions that had never been held by a Jewish chaplain, Chaplain Tzilker said, "I can't feel bad" for evangelicals who were dissatisfied. "You know, boo hoo hoo. I don't buy that. I don't buy that" (Jewish). Chaplain Drozdov also thought his group was more disadvantaged than those filing the suits:

> I've heard all kinds of faith groups bemoan the fact that they haven't had a chief of chaplains, from their own, in the last 15 or 20 years. And I say it's hard for me to get emotionally involved in this conversation, because I know we will never have an Orthodox chief of chaplains. [. . .] I really

> would challenge them to walk in my shoes. Because I come from one of the minorities that's not recognized as a minority. And we withstand all kinds of unintentional discrimination. At least the chaplains do. (Orthodox)

One of the Mormon chaplains willingly answered my question about what motivated the lawsuits, but when I asked if he thought there was any merit to them he dismissed the question: "I won't even comment. If anybody has a right to claim discrimination, I certainly do. I can demonstrate it. Whatever." He later explained that he had heard through contacts that denominational prejudice had adversely affected his performance evaluations.

Strangely, the website dedicated to reforming the chaplaincy to address discrimination against evangelicals partly supports the grievances of the Special Worship chaplains. A summary table that lists the rates of promotion by religious category (Liturgical, Nonliturgical, Catholic, and Special Worship) shows that of the four groups, the Special Worship chaplains historically have the highest rate of promotion from lieutenant to lieutenant commander in the Navy, but the second-lowest rate of promotion to commander, and the lowest rate of promotion to captain. As for nonliturgical chaplains, they have had a higher rate of promotion from lieutenant commander to commander than liturgical chaplains, the lowest rate of promotion to commander, and the second-lowest rate of promotion to captain. The evidence presented does suggest that Catholics and Liturgical Protestants promote at higher rates. However, the differences between the groups are so small that only one is statistically significant and unlikely to have happened by chance: Catholics do promote at a higher rate than the others from lieutenant commander to commander.[25]

Those chaplains who believed the lawsuits had merit and referred to real discrimination found the lawsuits both necessary and self-explanatory. The majority of chaplains who thought the lawsuits were wrong, or who weren't sure about their merits, offered three kinds of explanations for why they had happened. One group of explanations focused on individuals, specifically on the plaintiff's motivations, abilities, and qualifications. Another focused on the organization of the Chaplain Corps within the military, emphasizing its history, institutional culture, and assumptions. The third type of explanation was religious, about how evangelical chaplains come across to others. I will discuss these explanations in order.

INDIVIDUAL EXPLANATIONS FOR THE LAWSUITS

The most common and straightforward explanation offered for the lawsuits was that the plaintiffs were simply being self-serving and sued for personal financial gain or to salvage their self-esteem. Chaplain Timu explained the rewards of military chaplaincy: "The issue there is that the Chaplain Corps is very rewarding, both financially and professionally. And the chaplains can not see themselves outside the Chaplain Corps, because they love it so much" (Disciples of Christ).

Chaplain Squires thought unrealistic expectations were to blame and shared some "exceptionally insightful" advice that he had received with me: "almost everyone in the military at the end of their career was disappointed." The retired commander thinks he could and should have made captain, the retired captain that he could and should have made admiral, and so on until "the only one who seemed to really retire from the military and be satisfied was Dwight D. Eisenhower, because he then went on to become president" (Catholic). Chaplain Hamoud also spoke of how painful it must be to be passed over for promotion because "as a human being, yes, you do feel hurt" (Muslim). Chaplain Kojic thought the culture of the Chaplain Corps exacerbated these feelings and said he had prayed for the plaintiffs when he read some of the complaints in the lawsuits because what he saw was "pain. Yeah, pain. Pain and frustration. I think we can do a lot better job of communicating praise. We have a tendency to tear down rather than build up. We have a tendency to not go around and demonstrate just how important every chaplain in their role and their ministry is. I think we can do a much better job" (LCMS).

These chaplains who gave emotional explanations for the lawsuits were willing to identify with the plaintiffs, saying their desire to stay in the Chaplain Corps was rooted in common and admirable feelings of love or ambition. These three very different but equally blunt answers to what caused the lawsuits show that not all were as generous:

1. "In some cases it's money. Greed. In some cases it's narcissism." (Chaplain Szmatula, LCMS)
2. "I believe an inordinate emphasis on career success. And also delusion." (Chaplain Drozdov, Eastern Orthodox)
3. "Thirst for power. I'm serious!" (Chaplain Tzilker, Jewish).

Chaplain Illera also alleged that the plaintiffs had been in the chaplaincy for their own sake all along: "They were there, a lot of them, for what? For the salary, for the promotion, for the prestige, and the retirement. And when they didn't get what they wanted they were very angry and unhappy people" (Catholic). Chaplain Metzger, who was part of one of the lawsuits, also explained his motivation in terms of promotion, if not personal gain: "I was passed over twice for promotion. So I was months from being, from being removed from active duty. And I just didn't have a peace about leaving" (Chaplaincy of Full Gospel Churches). His point was that the desire for promotion wasn't necessarily selfish but could also be about wanting to continue to serve others. Other chaplains I spoke to thought he had been passed over because he wasn't doing a good job, but I personally had no doubts that he honestly wanted to be a good military chaplain for the men and women he was assigned to.

Another cluster of individual-level explanations were less about personal motivations than about aptitudes, training, and skills and how these fit into the military. Discussing one disgruntled colleague, Chaplain Szmatula said, "Well, it became very obvious why he wasn't promoted. He was incompetent! To the point where an admiral walked out of his worship service and said to the senior chaplain at that base, 'If he ever preaches here again, I'm never attending service here again!' [. . .] He couldn't preach well; he couldn't counsel well. He was inept. But if you talk to him, he thought he was the very best chaplain in the Navy" (LCMS). Chaplain Farrow thought "brain power," "capability," and "pastoral performance" were the decisive factors, along with education and past experience (Catholic). He thought a chaplain with a doctorate from a good school, extensive time in parish ministry, and experience working in a large bureaucracy would have obvious advantages over a less experienced pastor with a master's degree coming into the Navy straight from an obscure Bible college. Chaplain Oberlin was also convinced that he was working in a meritocracy: "It's so simple. The well-educated, the articulate, the athletic are getting promoted. Because that's what the country needs. And those are the people the country needs. If I'd been really bright I would have gotten my PhD twenty years ago. You know? I mean, it's fairly obvious. Have you taken the classes? Do you have the skills? Have those skills been recognized?"

Another explanation for the lawsuits was that the plaintiffs failed to accept that God was in control. Chaplain Clement said,

> I think sometimes God uses people to do his will. And sometimes we get passed over for promotion and it has nothing to do with us, it has nothing to do with the guy that's sitting on the board or the woman sitting on the board, it has to do with God is saying, "Hey, it's time for you to come home now, it's time for you to take this church, it's time for you to take another ministry." And I think sometimes we don't look at that as a supernatural event. And I think that's sad. [. . .] If I get passed over it's because God has something else for me. Unless, of course, I just messed up; then I gotta take ownership for that. (United Methodist)

The same sentiment was expressed by Chaplain Giraldo (Evangelical Church Alliance), who said God opened and closed doors for people, letting them know where they were supposed to serve Him. When I asked LDS Chaplain Cugrijus who thought that he, if anyone, had cause to sue, why he didn't, he said it would be "disrespectful to God" and asked rhetorically, "Who is in charge? Is God in control of my life? Or is this person who sat on my board that didn't like me?" Chaplain Feteris looked at the issue of God's will differently, saying some people confused it with their own ambitions:

> It's funny, one of the first things I ever read about someone that felt they were discriminated against was a chaplain, was an O-6. Saying how he had been discriminated against because he was an evangelical and not a liturgical Protestant and not Lutheran. And that it held him back. I was reading this as a brand new lieutenant, looking at my collar and going . . . He's got an eagle there! Unless he thought he was divinely appointed to be chief of chaplains, nothing held him back. So I had a little problem with, when it was done, when that was brought up by an O-6. (Presbyterian)

STRUCTURAL EXPLANATIONS FOR THE LAWSUITS

The military's attention to hierarchy, rank, and promotion is intense. What that means for chaplains is that they have to compete against each other while simultaneously being expected to get along and cooperate. Chaplain Geschka reminded me that chaplains wear their officer's rank on their right lapel and their religious device (e.g., cross for Christians, crescent moon for Muslims) on their left lapel: "Some of these people come into the system and they get caught up in what we call the right side of the collar, the rank, as opposed to the left side of the collar, which is ministry and what you know as a chaplain. And because they've decided, 'Well it's every man for himself now,' and that's where we lose this whole cooperation and collaboration thing; it's every person for themselves in order to get promoted" (Catholic). Under such working conditions, lawsuits are just a kind of advancement by other means for the competitive types.

Another feature of military culture is its vast bureaucracy. Many liturgical and Catholic chaplains thought nonliturgicals were less adept at the kind of teamwork institutional ministry requires: "It's the idea that people that are used to working within institutions do better in institutions than people who think they are The Pastor; they are The Leader of the congregation" (Reformed Episcopal). Chaplain Farrow (Catholic) described how frustrating it must be to not know how to navigate the Navy's bureaucracy very well:

> They don't have a big bureaucracy such as some of the mainstream religions such as Catholic or Episcopalian or Methodist or even the Lutherans. I mean, it's easy for a Catholic priest to come into the military as far as I'm concerned, bureaucratically, because we're used to dealing with a huge bureaucratic system. And we kinda see how we fit into that, and we kinda know how to work with the system in the sense. Or use the system to our advantage. Most of these chaplains that have never been experienced in this larger bureaucratic institutional stuff, especially institutional ministry, they're intimidated, they're threatened, they feel ill at ease, and they become on the attack mode rather than the solution mode. And that's once again where a lot of these lawsuits come from.

To return to the issue of promotions, many chaplains thought the system was broken. Chaplain Kojic complained about what teachers would call grade inflation in the fitness reports that supervising chaplains and commanding officers filled out:

> The folks that sit on the boards who will and who won't, what is the objective criteria that is used to delineate, and how do you distinguish? Does everyone become a water-walker[26] now? Does everyone score a five on all their fitness reps? In reality, what we're instigating here is, in order to stay above and beyond the normal tour, it's like everybody has to compromise on their personal integrity and write up all these glowing and glorious fit reps about themselves in order to stay alive. In order to stay within the scheme of things. (LCMS)

Chaplain Oberlin believed the chaplaincy was a meritocracy but that the lawsuits stemmed at least in part from disagreements about what counted as "merit" (ELCA). He was probably right about that, since the Navy definition of merit is informed by the same pluralist ideal that evangelicals reject. The composition of the promotion boards is also an issue in the lawsuits. The plaintiffs have documented that virtually all promotion boards have at least one and often two Catholic priests in addition to one liturgical Protestant.[27] They also claim to have proven statistically that promotion boards favor members of their own group, giving Catholics and liturgicals better chances of promotion. If that is accurate, then evangelical-controlled boards should favor evangelical careers. The chaplains I spoke with were, with a few exceptions, less interested in critiquing the plaintiffs' statistics[28] than with countering the less subtle claim that the Navy made sure Catholic chaplains got promoted because they were in short supply and hard to replace.

If scarcity made Catholic priests precious, the evangelicals were a dime a dozen. Chaplain Szmatula (LCMS) thought

> the problem with a lot of nonliturgicals is they have a lot of seminaries and they're producing more pastors than they've got churches. So you take a Southern Baptist, and you don't promote him, and you say, "You're going to have to get out of the Navy before you hit your twenty," he goes, "Where am I going to find a church? I'm going to have to start my own church, and probably work at a gas station." And so all of a sudden what happens is a great dependency develops on the Navy for that person. That "if I don't get promoted, how am I going to support my family?"

Chaplain Szmatula advised other chaplains not to become too dependent on the Navy, because there were too many contingencies. To survive in the Chaplain Corps you had to be "in the right place at the right time, with the right personality and the right programs," and only God could decide if you would be. Too often, he said, the competition to stay in and get promoted led chaplains to stab each other in the back.

Dependency on the Chaplain Corps was brought up by Chaplain Hamoud as well. He thought the lawsuits happened because of "everyone [having] put all their eggs in one basket, and then they suddenly see[ing] that basket taken away from them" (Muslim). He had received advice along the lines of what Chaplain Szmatula offered and described a fairly detailed plan he had for supporting his family by other means should his Navy career end, although he hoped it wouldn't any time soon. Chaplain Kanaridis had at one point started planning with his wife for life after military chaplaincy, and they were getting excited about the possibilities so that "when I got promoted I was a little bit disappointed, to be honest with you, Kim" (Conservative Baptist).

The Catholic priests have several advantages in the Chaplain Corps. They can be pretty sure there will be a fellow priest on their promotion boards, and they know the military needs them urgently to cover the sacramental needs of all the Catholic enlisted. The Navy grants waivers for priests who don't quite meet fitness or age requirements in order to recruit and retain enough Catholic chaplains, as it would for other clergy whose services are in high demand. They're not under as much pressure to be ecumenical because everyone knows they often have their hands full just taking care of all the Catholic "kids," nor is *ecumenism* necessarily a dirty word to them. They also know that if things don't work out for them in the military chaplaincy, the Catholic Church will have a new assignment for them in a matter of weeks. Unlike many of the others, all the Catholic chaplains are single. As one put it, "I don't have to go home and tell Mrs. Priest, 'Honey, I lost my job'" if things went wrong in the Navy. Catholic chaplains don't miss their children when deployed, either.

The situation for nonliturgicals is different. There's no shortage of evangelical pastors inside or outside the military chaplaincy. They don't all have a powerful church hierarchy backing them up and promising "steady work," but many of them have families to support and miss. The lawsuits allege that there are de facto quotas for recruitment and promotion, and that the nonliturgicals' share is too small. Even if it was bigger, though, there'd probably still be strong competition among them for promotion. That causes a lot of anxiety and pressure to conform to institutional norms, even ones they're theologically and morally uncomfortable with. If I were an evangelical military chaplain, I might resent the Catholic priests, too.

Religious Explanations for the Lawsuits

The last type of explanations for the lawsuits has to do with what evangelicals are like as a group. The same stereotypes I discussed earlier returned with a vengeance here. Evangelicals were more "dogmatic" than mainline chaplains, which makes them struggle more, according to Chaplain Feteris (Presbyterian). Chaplain Dyren described them as "hostile and resentful" and often coming across as having an "angry white male type of syndrome" (Catholic). Having met Chaplain Mace, I thought I knew what he had in mind. However, Chaplain Mace himself didn't think there was a basis to the lawsuits. Still riled up by my earlier question about Muslims, he explained angrily, "I think some people become sensitive to things, or they read into it something completely different and it has nothing to do with the fact that they're evangelical. That's another thing. It's kind of like racism. You have African Americans who don't get promoted and they'll call their supervisors racist! When race has nothing to do with it!" (Seventh Day Adventist).

Both Chaplain Koch (United Methodist) and Chaplain Cugrijus (LDS) thought evangelicals were paranoid and combative. Chaplain Koch said they had an "us-versus-them mentality" that made them quick to feel discriminated against and that this was probably what was driving the lawsuits. Sociologically speaking he has a point, since tension with the secular world and feelings of being embattled are hallmarks of the conservative Protestant world view.[29] Chaplain Cugrijus started out in a conciliatory tone, but gradually irked himself as he described the chaplains who often wouldn't acknowledge him as a fellow Christian:

> Evangelicals tend to be more fanatical. And that's not a bad statement. I'm not saying it as a bad statement. They just tend to be more fanatic in the way they see things. I don't use *fanatic* in the sense that they would use *cult* when they talk about me, because they belong to a cult, too. Christianity is a cult if you look at the definition. So if you say I'm in a cult, that's OK. I'm using *fanatic* as somebody who is just extremely dedicated to, almost to a fault . . . But when it comes to the point at which you have to say wait a minute, maybe Christ said by their fruit you shall know them? And you've got a lot of bad fruit hanging around? Everybody is going to get some bad fruit, it hangs on the tree and worms get in it. But if the majority of the fruit is bad? Hmmm! So anyway, I would speculate that people that tend toward a more fanatical view of things also tend toward feeling persecuted. (LDS)

Other chaplains complained about evangelical narrow-mindedness, too. Chaplain Oberlin said, "There's a lot of evangelical Christians out there who don't think Lutherans or Catholics are Christians" (ELCA). Chaplain Squires agreed with him: "I think we have to be honest. I think there is as a bigotry woven throughout these lawsuits. It's not very well hidden. It's fairly clear. And I have to be honest, too; I'm on the receiving end. I'm one of the groups that is the object of bigotry" (Catholic). The chaplain who became most agitated in discussing the lawsuits was Chaplain Townsend. They upset him because "I just think that it makes us look bad, makes us look like fools, makes us look like we don't know how to get along with each other." As he continued his answer, he rose from his chair and ended up yelling at me from across his desk, as if it was I who had filed the lawsuits: "As a Christian, I don't like Christians publically berating one another. It seems to me, if the Apostle Paul says, 'Wouldn't you rather be wronged?' [gets up] that the correct answer is *wouldn't you rather be wronged*?" (Reformed Episcopalian).

Of all the grievances liturgicals and Catholics have against nonliturgicals, by far the one that has received the most attention outside the military in the media and the courts, is that they are aggressive proselytizers.

PROSELYTIZATION

Not "stealing sheep" from other chaplains' flocks has been an established norm in the Chaplain Corps for generations. Proselytization raises a number of tricky questions. First of all, what exactly is proselytization? Which behaviors or circumstances count as stealing and which don't? Also, how do you know if a sheep is part of another chaplain's flock or not? Which military personnel are fair game and which are off limits, and how would you know? Finally, what do you do if a sheep comes to you by itself, if you sincerely believe your flock is the only safe one, or that another chaplain's flock needs to be saved from running into a lake of fire?

The controversies about proselytization in the military boil down to the social implications of the Great Commission in the Bible. Evangelical chaplains take it very seriously, believing that converting others to evangelical Christianity is an inherent and unavoidable part of their own free exercise of religion, whether it offends others or not. The institutional norms against proselytization were effective as long as the Chaplain Corps was dominated by mainline and Catholic clergy. The evangelicals, however, challenge it head on.

When I asked the chaplains what proselytizing meant, they generally agreed that that it was to "preach to the saved" (Chaplain Drozdov, Eastern Orthodox) or "recruiting for your faith" (Chaplain Frantz, LDS). High-pressure tactics were also considered proselytizing: Chaplain Bartley said it was "nagging" or "enforcement of my belief on someone that does not want to hear it" (Church of God in Christ), and Chaplain Cransveld said it was "forcing them through guilt or shame to believe in Christ" (Foursquare Gospel Churches). Most chaplains would support Chaplain Oberlin's explanation of when invitation crosses the line to proselytization: 'Well, I'd define it as taking a person who is confirmed in their beliefs, whatever they are, and try to get them to change their beliefs. [. . .] One offers, but when a person says, 'Thank you no,' it's to respect the 'thank you, no.'" (ELCA)

The exception to this general agreement would be evangelicals. Chaplain Beard, who held intermediate rank, discussed how short evangelicals' careers could be if they felt strongly about proselytizing: "Usually they'll last . . . They'll stay until they're about my rank now. When chaplains get to my rank now, they're making a decision. That they're either going to buy into the retirement, you know invest into the institution, or they're going to break away and do something else. And I've met more evangelical chaplains who have left at that point because they felt like they were more restricted" (Southern Baptist). The urge to proselytize was strong, according to Chaplain Oberlin: "Because their reason for being here, this is their mission field. People are dying to know the Lord. They're dying without the Lord. And that's the end of the story. It must not be that way" (ELCA).

Another reason to proselytize, which was very much on the mind of Chaplain Cransveld (Foursquare Gospel Churches), was to be able to "run up the numbers" of conversions and baptisms for the ecclesiastical endorser, and to be able to report a large and vibrant congregation to both religious and military superiors.

Some chaplains proselytized while calling it something else. Chaplain Kanaridis, for example, knew and accepted that proselytizing was off limits, but didn't feel it affected him much: "Well, I'm an evangelical. But I think it's the tradition of the church and a misunderstanding of what proselytizing is. I think some chaplains feel that proselytizing means that you can't share your faith. And if proselytizing is me not sharing my faith, then I have no reason to be in the military chaplaincy. So I've never had an issue with it" (Conservative Baptist). Chaplain Kanaridis distinguished proselytizing from "witnessing." To him, proselytizing meant trying to change someone's denomination, for example, from Methodist to Baptist. Witnessing, on the other hand, meant leading someone to salvation. That was something "totally different. You know, I can lead a Catholic to the Lord. I can lead a Mormon to the Lord. I can lead a Baptist to the Lord. I can lead anybody to the Lord. But I don't see that as proselytizing."

Chaplain Metzger from the Chaplaincy of Full Gospel Churches made the same distinction: "I've gotta say, Kim, that I've never been made aware of any prohibition against witnessing. I'll use that word instead of *proselytizing*. Because that entails just the expression of my religion beliefs and an invitation not for people to assume my beliefs, but an invitation for people to receive Jesus Christ as he is portrayed through Holy Scriptures." He explained the difference between belonging to a denomination and being saved very, very carefully:

> I think proselytizing in a strict sense for me, Kim, is to see the Lutheran who is attending a Lutheran service and say, "You need to come to my church instead." It's also referred to as sheep stealing. But witnessing for an evangelical Christian is just sharing what Christ is doing in their life and also giving the people the opportunity to receive Christ. So for me, let's use the example of the Lutheran again, I have no intentions of trying to take the Lutheran out of the Lutheran church. But as far as witnessing to that Lutheran, I would just ask them if they know Christ as their savior. I know that Lutherans are Christians and are born again, that they love the Lord and so . . . I would ask that person. I don't presume that the person just by the fact that they are a member of a church and attend a church that they have made a commitment to Christ. They could be nominal attendees, and so going back to that example I would ask if that person is born again, "Do you know Christ as your savior?" If not I would, in a very friendly, nonthreatening manner, I would share with them the gospel and invite them to receive Jesus Christ as their savior to totally commit their lives to Him. And if they do, I would encourage them to continue to attend the Lutheran church. (Chaplaincy of Full Gospel Churches)

Even though Chaplain Metzger was going to great pains to express his respect for Lutheranism, the action he described would certainly count as proselytizing members of another faith group. His distinction between being Lutheran and being saved is not one the Lutheran in question—or that Lutheran's pastor—would agree with. Where salvation for Chaplain Metzger has to occur with the individual making a "commitment to Christ" in an intense born-again experience, the Lutherans may hold that joining and attending a church regularly for years is just as valid a commitment.

Chaplain Irons predicted I'd get five different explanations of proselytizing if I asked five chaplains and certainly contributed to the variety with his own distinction between proselytizing and "evangelizing" (Southern Baptist). For him the key difference was the degree of coercion involved. He still thought the prohibition against proselytizing was harder for evangelicals to live with than for other faith groups because it didn't let them be themselves fully. He spelled out what he thought was the key for evangelical success in the Chaplain Corps:

> I think that to be a Southern Baptist chaplain in an institution like the United States Navy, you have to know who you are in terms of your faith background, your faith beliefs. You have to know what your ultimate mission is. In terms of being a Christian witness to these men and women. But you also have to know that the world is pluralistic. And you have voluntarily—no one has forced you to be a chaplain, come into an institution that's pluralistic in order that you be the best representation of your faith body. And that actually is motivating, that's not crippling. (Southern Baptist)

Chaplain Townsend thought that evangelicals did proselytize, but so did everyone else. No matter what they pretend, they were all "busily doing their best to evangelize their faith according to how they understand evangelization to be done" (Reformed Episcopalian). This didn't bother him at all, he said, as long as everyone was ready to change the subject to sports as soon as someone told them they weren't interested. Chaplain Townsend's point about chaplains having different understandings of evangelization was nicely illustrated by two of his colleagues, Chaplain Kojic (LCMS) and Chaplain Feteris (Presbyterian). In contrast to evangelicals who spoke of their own role in salvation in very active terms, such as "leading someone to Christ," these two chaplains described salvation in a more transcendent way that justifies restraint on their part. Chaplain Kojic thought evangelicals struggled with proselytization only because they misunderstood the word *evangelical*: "It's Pauline theology. If they believe that's something a man does, then well obviously yeah, they're going to be high and mighty on the issue. But if they believe it's something that God does, then obviously it's going to be within the preaching of the gospel" (LCMS).

Chaplain Feteris believed he could evangelize through the routine conversations and interactions he had with other people: "Form a Reformed Christian perspective I'm not someone that converts someone, that's God's job. My job is to share the message with them. And I've had a chance to do that with Buddhist personnel, with Jewish personnel, in a respectful dialogue. Not in any type of coercive, you know, hell-stone-and-damnation, brimstone-and-hellfire mode" (Presbyterian).

Together, Chaplains Kojic and Feteris articulated a theological rationale for the military norm of not proselytizing, at least not aggressively. Evangelicals have to rely mainly on institutional and legal rationales, which many of them did embrace wholeheartedly. Chaplain Irons, for example, recognized that the power chaplains wield over the enlisted as officers could lead to coercion in religious discussions unless they were handled with sensitivity. He also described the risk of religious establishment, enlisting me in his example:

> So whatever I say to you, sailor Kim, you're gonna be like, "Oh I gotta listen because this is the chaplain talking." Another good reason for that is [neither] the military nor the government can say, "This is the true religion," because the Constitution also says that we'll not have a state religion. And so for me to do that could be misconstrued as, "Oh he's representing the Navy, which is representing the government, so it's the United Methodist church that's the church of choice by the United States government." No it's not! So I can't proselytize like that. (Southern Baptist)

Chaplain Illera gave me several reasons why he thought proselytizing was bad: talk of hell might come across as menacing, sometimes evangelicals acted as if the people they were proselytizing weren't very bright, and "going around telling others that they're all wrong about their faith" is a threat to good order and discipline. He didn't mince words on the effect proselytization could have in a command: "That's absolutely wrong, that's absolutely false. It tears apart good command cohesiveness. It's wrong. And . . . that is very distasteful, to say the least. And disrespectful also. We don't proselytize" (Catholic). As it turned out, he was speaking from experience. During one deployment he had been approached by a much younger line officer who, like Chaplain Metzger, didn't assume someone was saved just because they belonged to a church—or was a member of the clergy, for that matter:

> And his first question to me, he just came up and said, "Hello chaplain, how are you doing? Are you saved?" And I stepped back and I said, "Young man, I think you're totally out of line and I think unless you can redirect this question we really don't have much to talk about." "But are you saved?" I said, "Well, what about you?" He said, "Yes." I said, "What does it mean to be saved?" and we started a discussion, and he didn't like the way the discussion went. (Catholic)

Having devoted his life to the church, Chaplain Illera found his faith questioned by a layman who might have been in diapers when he gave up marriage and children to serve God. Chaplain Oberlin had had several similar encounters: "I've had my theology, integrity, and call all challenged by evangelical Protestants. They've tried to proselytize me! And I think we've both, or that all of us have grown from it" (ELCA).

The three Presbyterians I interviewed had all had issues with evangelicals. Chaplain Feteris said evangelicals insisted on having their own, separate worship services because "they didn't recognize that the Presbyterian was a true Christian." Chaplain Grams thought he was "generally liked" by the enlisted because he was good at providing them with programs and tried to be nonjudgmental. The exception was the evangelicals. "Now, my evangelicals, "he said. "They think I'm like Satan or something like that. And the way they actually deal with me is, I'm the chaplain. I'm not a preacher. I'm the chaplain. So that's OK. My job is to give them space and time so that they can be Christian. In fact I had one guy's girlfriend once say, 'Well he may be a chaplain but he's not a Christian.' Because she didn't approve of some of the things that I'm tolerant of" (Presbyterian). He also related a story about Navy pilot in training who had explained to his flight instructor, a devout Catholic and superior officer, "why Catholics are going to Hell." We shared a laugh, and I commented on what a stupid career move that had been, to which Chaplain Grams replied, "Fools rush in where wise men fear to tread."

Chaplain Bowmaker's problem with the evangelicals wasn't with other chaplains. He described how he often had to intervene and persuade overzealous enlisted to tone down their religious activities. For example, he had had to have a talk with a young evangelical, acting as an self-appointed and unofficial lay leader, who was discouraging others from attending a ship's scheduled services: "He didn't have much use for the Catholic priest or the other services that were going on," so he would tell everyone to come to his group instead, saying, "'Come hear the real message' and that kind of talk."

Sometimes the enlisted can be persuaded to tread more carefully, and sometimes they can't. Chaplain Grams had intervened after a Wiccan had complained about a sticker on the ship's ATM machine that said "Jesus is the Reason for the Season" at Christmastime. Even after talking to the sailor who put it there about government neutrality, Navy regulations, and how the machine wasn't his to decorate as he pleased, the sticker stuck. In the end it took a direct order from the sailor's supervisor to get it removed.

Whether this incident contributed to the evangelical perception that Chaplain Grams was in league with Lucifer or not is unclear, but it can't have helped. He was sure another encounter had, though. The captain of a ship Chaplain Grams was responsible for had discovered a group of about a dozen sailors conducting a creationist Bible study in secret. The captain generously offered them the use of "this beautiful, VIP stateroom" that was rarely used except to host visiting admirals. After a few weeks, the person responsible for cleaning the stateroom was very upset and complained to Chaplain Grams about the mess they were making. After warnings, the chaplain banned them from the stateroom, "and they said that this was the devil working against them! And I could not undo them seeing it in those terms. That this was persecution. It's like, 'You were thrown this great bone, and you didn't respect the room and now, you know, it's just something that happened. I'm sorry.' It was highly subjective, in terms of their reaction to it. It was very funny" (Presbyterian).

Not everyone is as amused by the evangelical world view. When nonliturgicals proselytize the already devout for example, grave offense can be given. Even if it's done politely, their actions imply that Catholics, Mormons, and liturgical mainliners are lesser Christians. Even in spite of themselves, they easily come across as self-righteous, condescending, and rude.

After asking the chaplains for their definition and examples of *proselytization*, I asked if they thought there was anything they could legitimately do to try to convert others while in the Chaplain Corps. Chaplain Timu thought about it for a long time before simply answering, "No." Chaplain Tzilker, the rabbi, agreed: "Anything that transcends the four walls of the chapel during one of their chapel services or one of their classes, I think is inappropriate. And illegal." Most of the chaplains, however, thought there were things they could do to promote their religion. It's important to understand these things, because it helps explain why many evangelicals manage to stay and thrive in the Chaplain Corps despite the restrictions on proselytizing. As already discussed, chaplains can insert some of their own religious particularity into general worship services and can offer more specialized worship services as well. But even outside "the four walls of the chapel" there are opportunities to influence people.

The big exception to the rule against proselytizing is that chaplains are free to do so if a sailor or marine expresses interest in the chaplain's specific faith. Chaplain Chance, who thought his job was not to "turn anybody into Lutherans" but rather "to meet people's needs rather than my church's needs" had still been able to bring a few people into the Lutheran fold: "If people want to learn more about what I believe, I have the Small Catechism available, I can show it to them and stuff. If they want to become a Lutheran, I've had a couple people, I basically give their names to local pastors and stuff" (ELCA). Chaplain Clement said that he could proselytize if approached by people who told him they didn't feel "spiritually enlightened" or "fed" in their current faith group. If that happened, he would recommend they see a chaplain from their own faith group first, but if they asked about his he was good to go: "See, at that point it's initiated by the service member, or by whomever, and I'm simply giving him answers to what his questions are" (United Methodist).

Chaplains can also have very effective ministries nurturing the faith of people lapsed or only nominally in their own faith group. This is a big part of the Catholic priests' work. Young sailors and marines who loosely identify as Catholic suddenly take an interest in what that actually means. Obviously, this isn't proselytizing by any definition, but at least one of the nonliturgical chaplains, Chaplain Hawthorne (Southern Baptist), was content to focus his ministry on this "pastoral" role over and above the more explicitly evangelical one.

Setting a good example for others is also a way to influence them to a new or deepened faith. "You can win a soul in different ways," said Chaplain Street. "You can win a soul by your lifestyle" (African Methodist Episcopal). Chaplain Szmatula argued there was no such thing as legitimate proselytizing other than "demonstrating your faith in action" through kindness and generosity (Missouri Synod Lutheran). "Anything else is inappropriate," he added. Chaplain Townsend explained why he didn't understand the aggressive proselytization efforts of the evangelicals: "How can I expect somebody to find something attractive about being a Christian if I'm an obnoxious, hard-to-get-along-with person? That's kind of a basic concept. And you'll see that as a thread through many of my answers. If I'm making life hard for you, why are you going to be interested in what I have to say? [. . .] I just don't understand that some people think that the way you convince people is by being ugly. I don't understand that. I can't grasp that" (Reformed Episcopalian). Chaplain Cugrijus also thought it was best to set a good example and be kind to whoever he encountered: "If I love him care for him, there's some chance he might come to Christ." He added, "I've never met anybody who's been Bible-bashed into believing; all that does is create enemies." He rejected what he called "scare tactics," such as telling people they were bound for Hell, because "faith is the antithesis of fear" (LDS). In a similar vein, Chaplain Koch asked himself: "What would Jesus do? How does the Christian respond to someone who comes to them? Graciously! With grace. So I can live out my testimony without having to say, 'Do you know Jesus? Because if you don't you're going to Hell.' OK? So I can do that quite successfully with just living my life as an example. So why can't the rest of the world do that?" (United Methodist).

Of course, the reason "the rest of the world"—that is evangelicals—can't do that is that there isn't enough time. Chaplain Koch was content to "plant seeds" and "trust God and the Holy Spirit to do the work." But for those evangelicals who subscribe to the premillennial view of the end times, where the rapture could happen at any moment,[30] waiting around for sinners to notice and be impressed by good examples or otherwise figure things out for themselves is irresponsible. Trying to save as many individuals as they can while there's still time, evangelicals adopt a strategy called the "personal influence" approach where they try to create warm relationships within which it makes sense to discuss intimate matters such as religion.[31] Once friendship and trust have been established, concern for the other's salvation seems more genuine and is less likely to offend. "It's a relational thing," said Chaplain Street, and that made the military "an excellent place" to win souls (African Methodist Episcopal). Chaplain Metzger had extensive and profound experience with the approach: "I came to Christ when friends began to share their faith with me. And I use the same mode. I believe in this context of friendship we share out faith and do so effectively. For me to walk up to a stranger and start witnessing to them, that's . . . it would be awkward. So in the context of friendship there's always good order and discipline, because what is primary is the friendship" (Chaplaincy of Full Gospel Churches).

Being personal and informal, validating the other's individuality, is central to the personal influence approach and explains why Chaplain Metzger, Chaplain Kanaridis (Conservative Baptist), and Chaplain Irons (Southern Baptist) kept calling me by my first name throughout our interviews. It's an evangelical habit.

Air Force Scandal and the Military Religious Freedom Foundation

In 2004, a Lutheran chaplain at the Air Force Academy (AFA) invited a team from Yale's Divinity School to visit and conduct field observations as new cadets received their basic training. Chaplain Morton wanted this

"Yale Practicum Team" to help chaplains become more effective advocates for victims of sexual harassment in the wake of sex abuse scandals that had rocked the school.[32] The team from Yale praised how available the Air Force chaplains were to the cadets but also discovered that the General Protestant Service had "stridently evangelical themes" and an "overwhelmingly evangelical tone." For example, evangelical cadets were encouraged to witness to those who didn't come to church and warn them that they risked "burning in a lake of fire." According to the memo that Chaplain Morton and the leader of the Yale Practicum Team submitted to the AFA's senior chaplain, Chaplain Whittington, this "encouraged religious divisions rather than fostering spiritual understanding" among cadets.[33] The report was ignored for months and then released to the media. A year later, Chaplain Morton was dismissed from the academy and resigned her commission, telling journalists she had been ordered to transfer to Japan after refusing to renounce the report.[34]

Part of what fueled the tension between evangelicals and others at the AFA is that it is located in Colorado Springs, which is home to so many evangelical organizations and societies that it's been nicknamed "the Protestant Vatican."[35] Demographics on campus played an important part as well. As the cadets were becoming more religiously diverse and more secular, the Air Force's Chaplain Corps had become increasingly evangelical in the ten years before the scandal. Within the Air Force, chaplains from smaller evangelical groups were growing rapidly. For example, among the 600 active-duty Air Force Chaplains in 2005, the Full Gospel Fellowship of Churches and the Church of the Nazarene had increased their combined numbers to 22, from just 6 in 1994. During the same decade, the number of Catholic Air Force chaplains fell from 167 to 94, the number of United Methodists from 64 to 50, the number of chaplains from the Presbyterian Church USA from 30 to 16, and chaplains from the United Church of Christ declined from 11 to 3. Without reporting exact numbers, the Army and Navy said they were experiencing similar trends at the time.[36] Shortfalls of mainline and especially Catholic chaplains have been exacerbated since the AFA scandal, partly due to the wars in Iraq and Afghanistan making the chaplaincy seem a less attractive career option and partly because of denominational clergy shortages.[37] In this context, evangelicals have been able to dramatically increase their representation in the military.

By 2005, the *Los Angeles Times* was reporting that officials at the academy "had received 55 complaints over the last few months" about harassment by evangelical staff and cadets aimed at non-Christians.[38] The civil liberties group Americans United for Separation of Church and State investigated conditions at the AFA and produced a report of their own.

It contained criticism of the academy's football coach, who was alleged to have told his team that he expected to see them in church and to have hung a banner up in the locker room that said "I am a Christian First and Last, I am a member of Team Jesus Christ." The commandant of cadets, General Weida, was described as an unabashed evangelical who sent out a mass email endorsing the National Day of Prayer that appeared to be an order to pray, at least to Americans United. He had also developed a call-and-response routine where he would shout "Airpower" to cadets, and evangelical cadets would shout back "Rock sir!" The purpose of the call was to make those not in the know curious so they would ask what it meant, creating an opening for proselytization, as the evangelicals could explain that Jesus was the rock on which everyone should build their life.

In 2003, a group affiliated with the national organization Campus Crusade for Christ had already published an ad in the academy's newspaper listing the names of several hundred faculty and staff the cadets could approach if they wanted to discuss Jesus. Other than asserting evangelical strength in numbers, this ad may have signaled to cadets that they had best stay in the evangelicals' good graces if they wanted to do well at the Air Force Academy.[39] A history professor was alleged to have required that his class pray before letting them start their exams, and flyers were posted in February of 2004 promoting Mel Gibson's movie "The Passion of the Christ" as an "officially sponsored USAFA event." Images from the film were shown on video screens in the academy's dining hall, where meals are mandatory, and individual flyers placed by each plate at a lunch.[40]

The AFA endorsing a movie accused of being anti-Semitic was far from the only thing making non-Christians uncomfortable on the AFA campus. Religious minorities complained about verbal slurs against their faiths in addition to aggressive proselytization. A Jewish cadet, Casey Weinstein, took his father off campus before telling him how angry he was at being called "filthy Jew" and the like. Whoever harassed Casey had clearly messed with the wrong family. Michael "Mikey" Weinstein, Casey's father and himself a graduate of the Air Force Academy, is today the loudest critic of evangelical influence and religious intolerance in the military.

In 2005, Mikey Weinstein sued the entire Air Force, not just the academy, over Establishment Clause violations by evangelicals. His case was dismissed because the court ruled he didn't have standing.[41] This didn't stop Weinstein, however. In 2006, he published a book about his struggle against an "evangelical coup" in the military.[42] More important than the book is the organization he founded, the Military Religious Freedom Foundation, or MRFF.[43] Its newsletters and website publish accounts of religious excess by chaplains, other officers, and civilian religious groups active in the military. The MRFF facilitates and files lawsuits and provides an outlet for religious minorities and others who believe they have been harassed. Weinstein himself actively tours the country speaking out against the "evangelical coup." I met him briefly and saw him speak to a military audience at the Army War College in Carlisle, Pennsylvania, in 2011. Personally charismatic, his presentation style was compelling and highly combative. Audience members I spoke to in the aftermath, and "aftermath" is the apt way to describe the effect of a Weinstein appearance if this one was typical, agreed that although his forceful personality sometimes overshadowed them, he was raising valid concerns.

CONCLUSION

Despite chaplains' efforts and broad successes in creating and maintaining collegial relationships and effective cooperation, there are undeniable religious fault lines within the Chaplain Corps and military. At the center of the controversy are increasingly powerful evangelicals who refuse to play according to the ecumenical norms of past cohorts. Enough evangelicals believe they are persecuted and oppressed in the military for there to have been numerous appeals to the courts, to Congress, and to the President.[44] At the same time, evangelical excess at the Air Force Academy shows that mainline Protestants, Catholics, and religious minorities have as much to fear from evangelicals as the evangelicals do from them.

How can nonliturgical chaplains feel oppressed while wielding so much power within the military and in the political process? Part of it has to do with their religious world view. Conservative Protestants expect to live in tension with "the world" and typically draw sharp boundaries against it in order to maintain cohesion and solidarity. They may perceive persecution even when it isn't there. That's not to say they're tilting at windmills: the military really does prefer and reward ecumenical chaplains willing to tone down their own particularities for the sake of those they serve. Also, the national religious landscape really is becoming more religiously diverse. Does it still make sense to describe the United States as a "Christian" or "Judeo-Christian" country? Should conservative Protestant norms about sexuality, education, and a host of other issues still prevail or should they be abandoned? If the latter, what is to take their place? On what basis should public morality rest? In Hunter's analysis, the culture war is precisely such a struggle to define America. It is readily apparent that elites such as clergy, lawyers, politicians, and high-ranking military officials have made the Chaplain Corps one more battlefield in the culture war, trying to gain control of that organization within the military. The battle is fierce, as can be seen in the increasing number of lawsuits both for and against the evangelical cause, and in the fact that Mikey Weinstein feels compelled to travel with a bodyguard.

The effect on the chaplains is negative. Resentment and distrust make it harder to work together and especially hard to facilitate the wide range of religious needs that military personnel have. Many of the chaplains I interviewed bemoaned the fact that they couldn't talk to each other freely, because things had gotten so politicized. Many also worried out loud that line officers might conclude the chaplaincy was a net irritant, its conflicts and scandals outweighing the very real good that chaplains do.

So what can be done? It would help if more evangelicals joined the Chaplain Corps in order to promote other people's free exercise rights rather than to assert their own. Endorsing agents have a role to play here, making sure that the chaplains they send to the military understand their role and don't think of the military as a mission field like any other. At their best, evangelicals approach the military as a mission field with unique challenges that require restraint, courage, and sensitivity.

The military might also reform the way chaplaincy is organized. Rank gives chaplains institutional clout and recognition they can use on behalf of religious freedom, but it also gives them a lot to worry about and fight over. Although it may not work in the American context, other nations have chaplains that don't hold a specific rank but assume the rank of whoever they're addressing, all the while wearing a generic officer's uniform. Efforts to reduce the differences in pay and pensions between lower- and higher-ranking chaplains might also be sought in order to take some of the pressure off. Just as the military isn't a mission field like any other, chaplains don't have to be officers like any other.

There are more extreme possibilities, each of which would raise a host of practical, moral, and legal questions. Maybe the ecclesiastical endorsers could rank the chaplains themselves rather than sending them all in as junior officers for the military to control? Maybe the tasks performed by military chaplains can be transferred to others: their counseling to military therapists and social workers, for example, and their religious functions outsourced to civilian contractors? All manner of other military functions have been privatized. What's needed is creative thinking tempered by large doses of caution, because the current arrangement doesn't seem to be working very well.

This is not the chaplains' fault. Anyone who talks to as many chaplains as I have will have come away impressed over and over again by how they find ways to genuinely help people and work together in spite of profound disagreements. The fault, or fault line, that runs through the Chaplain Corps is ultimately an expression of a tension between the Free Exercise Clause and Establishment Clause in the First Amendment.

To the extent the Chaplain Corps prefers general and inclusive ministry, it is vulnerable to attack on Free Exercise grounds by specific faith groups that feel uncomfortable and even punished if they assert their sincere particular commitments. For their chaplains, pluralism itself is an unacceptable compromise. On the other hand, to the extent the Chaplain Corps allows for the free expression of religious particularity, it is vulnerable to attack on Establishment grounds because some groups will use public money, the prestige of their officer's commission, and military resources to advance their specific beliefs. Those who resent the implication that their religious beliefs are false, who don't want their tax dollars spent to promote religious beliefs they disagree with, and who fear that members of their families or faith groups will be targeted by aggressive proselytization have valid and well-grounded concerns—but so do those who fear they have to sacrifice their deeply held religious convictions and sell out to a bland, secularized, state-sponsored spirituality to keep their jobs.

Individual chaplains have their flaws, like everyone else, but as a group they are impressive. Although the Chaplain Corps is full of men and women who work extremely hard with the best possible intentions, recent conflicts reveal that it remains a work in progress. If a Constitutional military chaplaincy is even possible, it will require a balance between the First Amendment's two religion clauses that has not yet been found.

Notes

Chapter 1

1. Roger Williams, "Roger Williams to the Town of Providence," in *The Founders' Constitution*, eds. Philip B. Kurland and Ralph Lerner, http://press-pubs.uchicago.edu/founders/documents/amendI_religions6.html.
2. For a succinct biography, see Edmund S. Morgan's *Roger Williams: The Church and the State* (New York: W. W. Norton, 1967).
3. Staff officers are distinct from line officers even though they are in the same chain of command. Line officers carry out the kinds of missions required to fight a battle, such as shooting and flying, while staff officers serve on the commanding officer's staff as advisors or professional specialists. In general, the shots in a fight would be called by the highest-ranking line officer even if he or she were lower ranking than the senior staff officer on hand; this is to prevent chaplains or other staff officers, such as military dentists or lawyers, from conducting battles.
4. This is how it is described by Navy chaplains.
5. The British military's chaplains wear officer's uniforms, but instead of having a specific rank, they assume the same rank as whoever they're interacting with.
6. Chaplains frequently refer to religious affiliations as "flavors." For example, they may ask newcomers, "What flavor are you?" I was asked several times.
7. See Jose Casanova's influential *Public Religions in the Modern World* (Chicago: University of Chicago Press, 1994).
8. See, for example, James A. Beckford and Sophie Gillat's excellent study of British prison chaplains and religious diversity, *Religion in Prison: Equal Rites in a Multi-Faith Society* (Cambridge: Cambridge University Press, 1998); and Bethany Moreton's study of religion in the business world of Wal-Mart, *To Serve God and Wal-Mart: The Making of Christian Free Enterprise* (Cambridge, MA: Harvard University Press, 2009).

9. D. Michael Lindsay, *Faith in the Halls of Power: How Evangelicals Joined the American Elite* (New York: Oxford University Press, 2008).
10. Diana Eck, *A New Religious America: How a "Christian Country" Has Become the World's Most Religiously Diverse Nation* (San Francisco: Harper Collins, 2001).
11. Jeff Weintraub, "The Theory and Practice of the Public/Private Distinction," in *Public and Private in Thought and Practice*, eds. Jeff Weintraub and Krishnan Kumar (Chicago: University of Chicago Press, 1997).
12. Kim Hays has written an excellent book about the way values are expressed in different institutional settings. See *Practicing Virtues: Moral Traditions at Quaker and Military Boarding Schools* (Berkeley: University of California Press, 1994).
13. Richard Madsen, William M. Sullivan, Ann Swidler, and Steven M. Tipton, *Meaning and Modernity: Religion, Polity, and Self* (Berkeley: University of California Press, 2002).
14. Dale R. Herspring, "Chaplains in the American Military," in *Soldiers, Commissars, and Chaplains: Civil-Military Relations since Cromwell* (Lanham, MD: Rowman and Littlefield, 2001), 17–52.
15. Ibid., 18–26.
16. Ibid., 19.
17. Ibid., 24.
18. Ibid., 26–29.
19. Albert Isaac Slomovitz, *The Fighting Rabbis: Jewish Military Chaplains and American History* (New York: New York University Press, 1999).
20. See Herspring, "Chaplains," 29–32.
21. Tierian (Randy) Cash, "A Short History of the Navy Chaplain Corps." Web resource online, last modified May 4, 2011.
22. Herspring, "Chaplains," 33–38.
23. Ibid., 40. According to Herspring, a quarter of Army personnel sent overseas met with their chaplain at least once in 1942 alone.
24. Ibid., 39–43.
25. Ibid., 45–46.
26. "The Brotherhood of Soldiers at War: The True Story of the Four Chaplains," The Home of Heroes, http://www.homeofheroes.com/brotherhood/chaplains.html, accessed January 15, 2012.
27. Richard G. Hutcheson, *The Churches and the Chaplaincy* (Atlanta: John Knox, 1975). The parenthetical explanations are Hutcheson's.

28. See, for example, *Military Chaplains: From a Religious Military to a Military Religion*, edited by Harvard theologian Harvey Cox (New York: American Report Press, 1972).
29. Herspring, "Chaplains," 43–46.
30. Ibid., 45–46.
31. For additional details about the Wiccan chaplain, see Alan Cooperman's article "A Wiccan Army Chaplain? The Brass Wouldn't Buy It," in the *Seattle Times* of February 24, 2007, http://seattletimes.nwsource.com/html/nationworld/2003586870_wiccan24.html.
32. Pauletta Otis, "An Overview of the U.S. Military Chaplaincy: A Ministry of Presence and Practice," *The Review of Faith and International Affairs* 7, no. 4 (2009): 3–16.
33. *Religious Ministry in the Department of the Navy: Strategic Plan for FY 08–13* (Arlington, VA: RGS Associates Inc., August 31, 2007). Exact numbers of active-duty chaplains are hard to pinpoint because of turnover and chaplains being called up from reserves.
34. Ibid.
35. The concept of greedy institutions is from Mady Wechsler Segal's "The Military and the Family as Greedy Institutions," *Armed Forces and Society* 13, no. 1 (1986): 9–38.
36. In the masculine culture of the military, seeking help of any kind may be viewed as not being "tough." A female chaplain I interviewed as part of a pilot project thought her age and gender might combine to make it easier for young sailors to open up to her and even cry in her presence because she might remind them of their mothers. Her interview is not part of the sample this book relies on, and she was not given a pseudonym.
37. The quote from Washington is well known. See, for example, Hutcheson, *Churches and the Chaplaincy* (1997); and Herspring, "Chaplains."
38. *Religious Ministry in the Department of the Navy: Strategic Plan for FY 08–13* (Arlington, VA: RGS Associates Inc., August 31, 2007).
39. Ibid.
40. This chaplain was interviewed by the author as part of a pilot study focusing on role tensions, and he made the comment when discussing "collateral duties." He is not otherwise included in the sample this book draws on and has not been given a pseudonym.
41. Peter L. Berger and Daniel Pinard, "Military Religion: An Analysis of Education Materials Disseminated by Chaplains," in *Military Chaplains: From a Religious Military to a Military Religion*, ed. Harvey G. Cox (New York: American Report Press, 1972).

42. *Religious Ministry in the Department of the Navy: Strategic Plan for FY 08–13*, Appendix A (Arlington, VA: RGS Associates Inc., August 31, 2007).
43. John D. Carlson, "Cashing in on Religion's Currency?: Ethical Challenges for a Post-Secular Military," *The Review of Faith and International Affairs* 7, no. 4 (2009): 51–62.
44. John W. Brinsfield, "The U.S. Military Chaplaincy: Then and Now," *The Review of Faith and International Affairs* 7, no. 4 (2009): 17–24.
45. Carlson, "Cashing In."
46. Thomas F. Farr, *World of Faith and Freedom: Why International Religious Liberty Is Vital to American National Security* (New York: Oxford University Press, 2008).
47. See the special issue of *The Review of Faith and International Affairs* 7, no. 4 (2009).
48. Paul Wrigley, "The Impact of Religious Belief in the Theater of Operations," *Naval War College Review* 49, no. 2 (1996): 84–101
49. A few details have been altered in this account, but it still includes enough specifics that it's still best not to provide the chaplain's pseudonym.
50. Adams is this Navy chaplain's real name. The incident is described in Carlson, "Cashing In," 56.
51. Carlson, "Cashing In."
52. Douglas M. Johnson, "U.S. Military Chaplains: Redirecting a Critical Asset," *The Review of Faith and International Affairs* 7, no. 4 (2009): 25–32.
53. Hutcheson, *Churches and the Chaplaincy* (1997).
54. The example and quote are from Margaret G. Kibben, "The Role and Mission of Chaplains in Humanitarian Assistance and Peace Operations (HA/Pos)," paper presented by at the Naval War College, Newport, RI. February 12, 1996, and quoted in Hutcheson, *Churches and the* Chaplaincy (1997).
55. Brinsfield, "U.S. Military Chaplaincy"; and Johnson, "U.S. Military Chaplains."
56. Hutcheson, *Churches and the Chaplaincy* (1997).
57. Robert N. Bellah added to his famous 1967 article from *Daedalus* with a full-length book, *The Broken Covenant: American Civil Religion in a Time of Trial* (Chicago: University of Chicago Press, 1975). He again refined his interpretation in "Civil Religion: The American Case," in *Varieties of Civil Religion* with Philip E. Hammond (San Francisco: Harper and Row, 1980).

58. In addition to events and individuals, the American Civil religion contains sacred relics such as the Liberty Bell and sacred places such as Arlington National Cemetery and the Lincoln Memorial. There are also civil religious holidays (Thanksgiving, July 4), rituals (inaugurations, the pledge of allegiance), and texts (the Declaration of Independence and Constitution).
59. Hutcheson, *Churches and the Chaplaincy* (1997).
60. Herspring, "Chaplains."
61. Robert Wuthnow, *The Restructuring of American Religion*. (Princeton, NJ: Princeton University Press, 1988).
62. Hutcheson, *Churches and the Chaplaincy* (1975); Berger and Pinard, "Military Religion."
63. Wuthnow, *Restructuring of American Religion*.
64. Roberta L. Coles, "Manifest Destiny Adapted for 1990s War Discourse: Mission and Destiny Intertwined," *Sociology of Religion* 63, no. 4 (2002): 403–26.
65. For examples, see Christian Smith's edited volume *Disruptive Religion: The Force of Faith in Social Movement Activism* (New York: Routledge, 1996).
66. See Peter L. Berger's *The Sacred Canopy: Elements of a Sociological Theory of Religion* (New York: Anchor Books, 1967) for an excellent and seminal discussion of religious legitimation and delegitimation.
67. The core work on chaplains' relationships to their churches remains Richard G. Hutcheson's two editions of *Churches and the Chaplaincy*.
68. Anne C. Loveland, *American Evangelicals in the U.S. Military 1942–1993* (Baton Rouge: Louisiana State University Press, 1996).
69. Hutcheson, *Churches and the* Chaplaincy (1997).
70. Berger and Pinard, "Military Religion."
71. Arlene Kaplan Daniels, "The Captive Professional: Bureaucratic Limitations in the Practice of Military Psychiatry," *Journal of Health and Social Behavior* 10, no. 4 (1969): 255–65.
72. Waldo W. Burchard, "Role Conflicts of Military Chaplains," *American Sociological Review* 19, no. 5 (1954): 528–35.
73. Quoted in Bryan S. Turner, *Religion and Social Theory* (London: Sage, 1983).
74. Coles, "Manifest Destiny."
75. Hutcheson, *Churches and the Chaplaincy* (1975 and 1997).

CHAPTER 2

1. "Bill of Rights." Charters of Freedom: A New World is at Hand. http://www.archives.gov/exhibits/charters/bill_of_rights_transcript.html.
2. "Accommodation of Religious Practices within the Military Services," Department of Defense Directive 1300.17, February 10, 2009.
3. "Accommodation of Religious Practices," Secretary of the Navy Instruction 1730.8B, October 2, 2008.
4. "Religious Diversity in the U.S. Military," Military Leadership Diversity Commission, Issue Paper #22, June, 2010, http://mldc.whs.mil.
5. Ibid.
6. The DEOMI figure is reached by dividing 65.86 per-cent Christians by 4.78 per-cent religious minorities. The DMDC figure represents 69.25 per-cent divided by 1.78 per-cent, respectively.
7. Ibid.
8. See Alan Wolfe's *One Nation after All* (New York: Penguin, 1998). Robert D. Putnam and David E. Campbell provide ample evidence of American religious toleration in *American Grace: How Religion Divides and Unites Us* (New York: Simon and Schuster, 2010).
9. Richard G. Hutcheson, *The Churches and the Chaplaincy*, rev. ed. (Washington, DC: United States Department of Defense, 1997).
10. The quotes and discussion of this matter are drawn from Israel Drazin and Cecil B. Currey, *For God and Country: The History of a Constitutional Challenge to the Army Chaplaincy* (Hoboken, NJ: KTAV, 1995). Both authors participated in the litigation on the Army's side. Mr. Currey also shared his experience with me at a military chaplains' conference. The case, *Katcoff v. Marsh* [755 F. 2d. 223 (2nd Cir. 1985)], is also described in John T. Noonan and Edward McGlynn Gaffney Jr., *Religious Freedom: History, Cases, and other Materials on the Interaction of Religion and Government* (New York: Foundation Press, 2001).
11. Drazin and Currey, For God and Country
12. *Religious Ministry in the Department of the Navy: Strategic Plan for FY 08–13* (Arlington, VA: RGS Associates Inc., August 31, 2007).
13. Ibid. The examples given of how chaplains care and advise are not exhaustive.
14. Ibid.
15. Mickey R. Dansby, James B. Stewart, and Schuyler C. Webb, eds., *Managing Diversity in the Military: Research Perspectives from the*

Defense Equal Opportunity Management Institute (New Brunswick, NJ: Transaction, 2001).

16. Although both *facilitation* and *good order and discipline* are recurring terms in publications and policies about military chaplaincy, and chaplains use the terms frequently themselves, they are not necessarily paired this way. I do so for analytical purposes. As central terms in discourse about military chaplaincy, the paired commitments to freedom and order frame what Robert Wuthnow calls "an identifiable pattern in the symbolic-expressive dimension of social life." See Wuthnow, *The Restructuring of American Religion* (Princeton, NJ: Princeton University Press, 1988).
17. This is not "Chaplain Hamoud" who is quoted throughout this book.
18. One joke is about a painter who cheats his clients by thinning the paint he uses, and he is told by God to "repaint, and thin no more." Another is about a Baptist pastor who loses money betting on a horse he thinks a Catholic priest has blessed, when in fact the priest was giving the horse last rites.
19. The case was 417 U.S. 733, cited in Carlos C. Huerta and Schuyler C. Webb, "Religious Accommodation in the Military," in *Managing Diversity in the Military: Research Perspectives from the Defense Equal Opportunity Management Institute*, eds. Dansby, Stewart, and Webb (New Brunswick, NJ: Transaction, 2001).
20. "Accommodation of Religious Practices," Secretary of the Navy Instruction 1730.8A, December, 31, 1997.
21. Some Wiccans worship communally in covens; others practice witchcraft alone. See Helen Berger's *A Community of Witches: Contemporary Neo-Paganism and Witchcraft in the United States* (Columbia: University of South Carolina Press, 1999).
22. "The Covenant and the Code of Ethics for Chaplains of the Armed Forces," National Conference on Ministry to the Armed Forces, http://www.ncmaf.org/policies/codeofethics.htm. The older version I refer to was distributed as a handout at an annual meeting of the Military Chaplains Association.
23. Hutcheson, *Churches and the Chaplaincy*.
24. Erving Goffman, *Asylums: Essays on the Social Situation of Mental Patients and Other Inmates* (New York: Anchor Books, 1961).
25. The *Goldman v. Weinberger* case (106 S. Ct 1310, 1986) is discussed in detail in Noonan and Gaffney, *Religious Freedom*.
26. Ibid.
27. Huerta and Webb, "Religious Accommodation."
28. Ibid.

29. "Religious Diversity in the U.S. Military," Military Leadership Diversity Commission, Issue Paper #22, June, 2010, http://mldc.whs.mil.
30. Huerta and Webb, "Religious Accommodation."
31. "Sikhs Regain Right to Wear Turbans in U.S. Army," National Public Radio online, http://www.npr.org/templates/story/story.php?storyId=125142736.
32. Richard Madsen, William M. Sullivan, Ann Swidler, and Steven M. Tipton, *Meaning and Modernity: Religion Polity, and Self* (Berkeley: University of California Press, 2002).
33. Wuthnow, *Restructuring of American Religion.*

CHAPTER 3

1. Samuel P. Huntington, *The Clash of Civilizations and the Remaking of World Order* (New York: Simon and Schuster, 1996).
2. Pau Heelas, *The New Age Movement* (Oxford: Blackwell, 1996).
3. Helen A. Berger, Evan C. Leach, and Leigh S. Shaffer, *Voices from the Pagan Census: A National Survey of Witches and Neo-Pagans in the United States* (Columbia: University of South Carolina Press, 2003).
4. See Robert N. Bellah, Richard Madsen, William M. Sullivan, Ann Swidler, and Steven M. Tipton, *Habits of the Heart: Individualism and Commitment in American Life* (New York: Harper and Row, 1985).
5. "Aunt Susan" and "My pal Al" appear in Robert D. Putnam and David E. Campbell's *American Grace: How Religion Divides and Unites Us* (New York: Simon and Schuster, 2010), where the authors demonstrate that having family members or friends of a different faith increases acceptance of that faith.
6. "Religious Diversity in the U.S. Military," Military Leadership Diversity Commission, Issue Paper #22, June 2010, http://mldc.whs.mil.
7. Dennis Walker, *Islam and the Search for African-American Nationhood: Elijah Muhammad, Louis Farrakhan, and the Nation of Islam* (Atlanta: Clarity Press, 2005).
8. Albert J. Raboteau, *Canaan Land: A Religious History of African Americans* (Oxford: Oxford University Press, 1999).
9. Diana Eck, *A New Religious America: How a "Christian Country" Has Become the World's Most Religiously Diverse Nation* (San Francisco: HarperCollins, 2001).
10. See Peter W. Williams, *America's Religions: From Their Origins to the Twenty-First Century* (Urbana: Illinois University Press, 2001). Also see Walker, *Islam*; and Eck, *A New Religious America.*

11. Eck, *A New Religious America.*
12. Robert Wuthnow, *America and the Challenge of Religious Diversity* (Princeton, NJ: Princeton University Press, 2005).
13. Eck, *A New Religious America*; Wuthnow, *Challenge of Religious Diversity.*
14. Pew Research Center, "Muslim Americans: No Signs of Growth in Alienation or Support for Extremism," report released August 30, 2011, http://www.people-press.org/2011/08/30/section-1-a-demographic-portrait-of-muslim-americans.
15. The Pew Forum on Religion and Public Life, "The Global Muslim Population: Projections for 2010–2030," January 27, 2011, http://www.pewforum.org/future-of-the-global-muslim-population-regional-americas.aspx#1.
16. Heelas, *New Age Movement.*
17. Christopher Partridge, *New Religions: A Guide* (New York: Oxford University Press, 2004). Also Berger et al., *Voices from the Pagan Census.* The quote from George W. Bush is from Alan Cooperman, "For Gods and Country: The Army Chaplain Who Wanted to Switch to Wicca? Transfer Denied," *The Washington Post*, February 19, 2007.
18. Tanya Luhrmann published the results of her participant observation among witches as *Persuasions of the Witch's Craft: Ritual Magic in Contemporary England* (Cambridge, MA: Harvard University Press, 1989).
19. Partridge, *New Religions.*
20. See Helen A. Berger's *A Community of Witches: Contemporary Neo-Paganism and Witchcraft in the United States* (Columbia: University of South Carolina Press, 1999), as well as the follow-up study by Berger et al., *Voices from the Pagan Census.* For the importance of festivals, see Sarah M. Pike, *Earthly Bodies, Magical Selves: Contemporary Pagans and the Search for Community* (Berkeley: University of California Press, 1999).
21. Starhawk is the ritual name of a Californian witch named Miriam Simos, according to Eck (*A New Religious America*). Perhaps the closest thing to a formal creed would be the "Wiccan Rede," which essentially says, "Do what you will, as long as you don't hurt anyone," but there's no authoritative version of it.
22. Helen A. Berger does an excellent job of describing this in *A Community of Witches.*
23. Liam J. Montgomery, "The Devil is in the Details: Policing the Implementation of the Military Chaplaincy." Paper published online in 2008 at http://works.bepress.com/liam_montgomery/2.

24. Berger et al., *Voices from the Pagan Census.*
25. Ibid.
26. Lori Peek, "Becoming Muslim: The Development of a Religious Identity," *Sociology of Religion* 66, no. 3 (2005): 215–42.
27. Wuthnow, *Challenge of Religious Diversity.*
28. See Wuthnow, *Challenge of Religious Diversity*; and Huntington, *Clash of Civilizations.*
29. Eck, *A New Religious America.*
30. Wuthnow, *Challenge of Religious Diversity.*
31. Putnam and Campbell, *American Grace.*
32. See Michelle Sandhoff, "Preliminary Findings on the Experiences of Muslims in the U.S. Military," paper presented to the Defense Equal Opportunity Management Institute Symposium, December 2011. Manuscript made available by Sandhoff.
33. Berger, *A Community of Witches.*
34. Ibid.
35. Berger et al, *Voices from the Pagan Census.*
36. Ibid.
37. These traits of American Protestantism are identified in William R. Hutchison, *Religious Pluralism in America: The Contentious History of a Founding Ideal* (New Haven, CT: Yale University Press, 2003).
38. See Sandhoff, "Preliminary Findings," on the "us vs. them" mentality and the way Islam becomes "other" and "enemy" despite official denials.
39. Flyer downloaded from http://www.amafanvac.org.
40. Presentation at the 2000 National Institute of the Military Chaplains Association in Norfolk, VA.
41. My account summarizes Cooperman, "For Gods and Country."
42. Eck, *A New Religious America.*
43. Sandhoff, "Preliminary Findings."
44. Berger et al, *Voices from the Pagan Census.*
45. There's a joke about a Lutheran rescued after twenty years alone on a deserted island. He shows his rescuers three buildings he's made. One is his house and another is his church. When they ask what the third one, covered in weeds, is for he sneers, "Oh, that's the church I *used* to go to."
46. "Justice Department Clarifies Ashcroft's View of Islam," FoxNews .com, February 12, 2002, accessed February 25, 2012.
47. Wuthnow, *Challenge of Religious Diversity.*

48. Daniel Miller, "'All Muslims Should be Kicked out of the Military,' Claims Leading Tennessee Republican," *The Daily Mail* online, updated November 17, 2011.
49. "U.S. Military Weapons Inscribed with Secret 'Jesus' Bible Codes," ABC News online, January 18, 2010, http://abcnews.go.com/Blotter/us-military-weapons-inscribed-secret-jesus-bible-codes/story?id=9575794&page=2.
50. Jeff Sharlet, "Jesus Killed Mohammed: The Crusade for a Christian Military," *Harper's Magazine* 318, no. 1908 (2009):31–43.
51. "U.S. Soldier Uses Quran for Target Practice; Military Apologizes," CNN World online, May 17, 2008, http://articles.cnn.com/2008-05-17/world/iraq.quran_1_quran-tribal-leaders-military-official?_s=PM:WORLD.
52. Kevin Sieff, "Two NATO Soldiers Killed Inside Afghan Interior Minitsry, Officials Say," *The Washington Post* online, February 24, 2012, http://www.washingtonpost.com/world/seven-dead-in-latest-afghan-violence-over-koran-burning/2012/02/24/gIQAtWLkXR_story.html.
53. Jana Winter, "Exclusive: Former Defense IG Raises Concerns about Military Chaplain Vetting," FoxNews.com, December 1, 2010, http://www.foxnews.com/politics/2010/12/01/exclusive-concerns-military-chaplain-vetting-policy.
54. James Yee, radio interview, *The Mike Malloy Show*, Air America Radio Internet broadcast, streamed November 14, 2005.
55. Ibid. See also James Yee, *For God and Country: Faith and Patriotism under Fire* (New York: Public Affairs, 2005).
56. Yee, *For God and Country*.
57. Ibid.
58. Ibid.
59. Text of the Unclassified Executive Summary of the Evaluation of the Army Investigation of Chaplain (CPT) James J. Yee, Department of Defense Office of Inspector General, Report Number IPO2007E002. See also Neil A. Lewis, "Prosecutors Say It's Unclear Papers Chaplain Carried Were Classified," *The New York Times* online, December 10, 2003, http://www.nytimes.com/2003/12/10/national/10YEE.html.
60. Sandhoff, "Preliminary Findings."
61. The "high church" versus "low church" distinction will be addressed in Chapter 5. For present purposes, the "high church" denominations score high on ceremony and low on enthusiasm, according to

Mark Chaves. See his *Congregations in America* (Cambridge, MA: Harvard University Press, 2004).

62. Darren Sherkat, "Religious Socialization: Sources of Influence and Influences of Agency," in *Handbook of the Sociology of Religion*, ed. Michelle Dillon (Cambridge: Cambridge University Press, 2003).
63. Eck, *A New Religious America*.
64. I refer the reader to Michelle Sandhoff's doctoral research at the University of Maryland and forthcoming presentations.
65. "Veterans Denied Right to Post Religious Symbol on Headstones, ACLU Charges," American Civil Liberties Union online, September 29, 2006, http://www.aclu.org/religion-belief/veterans-denied-right-post-religious-symbol-headstones-aclu-charges. Also see Neela Banerjee, "Use of Wiccan Symbol on Veterans' Headstones Is Approved," *The New York Times* online, April 24, 2007, http://www.nytimes.com/2007/04/24/washington/24wiccan.html.
66. See Wuthnow, *Challenge of Religious Diversity*; and Heelas, *New Age Movement*.
67. Berger et al., *Voices from the Pagan Census*.
68. For a good survey, see Hutchison, *Religious Pluralism in America*. A historically significant benchmark in the debate was Will Herberg's *Protestant, Catholic, Jew: An Essay in American Religious Sociology* (New York: Doubleday, 1955).
69. Richard G. Hutcheson, *The Churches and the Chaplaincy*, rev. ed. (Washington, DC: United States Department of Defense, 1997), emphasis in original.
70. Hutchison, *Religious Pluralism in America*.
71. Partridge, *New Religions*.
72. Peter Beyer, "Social Forms of Religion and Religions in Contemporary Global Society," in *Handbook of the Sociology of Religion*, ed. Michelle Dillon (Cambridge: Cambridge University Press, 2003).
73. Winnifred Fallers Sullivan, *The Impossibility of Religious Freedom* (Princeton, NJ: Princeton University Press, 2005).
74. The anecdotes are told from Chaplain Gunter's point of view in Eck, *A New Religious America*.

CHAPTER 4

1. Anne C. Loveland, *American Evangelicals in the U.S. Military 1942–1993* (Baton Rouge: Louisiana State University Press, 1996).

2. Richard G. Hutcheson, *The Churches and the Chaplaincy*, rev. ed. (Washington, DC: United States Department of Defense, 1997.)
3. "The Covenant and the Code of Ethics for Chaplains of the Armed Forces," published online by the National Conference on Ministry to the Armed Forces at http://www.ncmaf.org/policies/codeofethics.htm.
4. Ibid.
5. See R. Stephen Warner, "Work in Progress toward a New Paradigm for the Sociological Study of Religion in the United States," *American Journal of Sociology* 98, no. 5 (March 1993): 1,044–93.
6. Wade Clark Roof, "Religion and Spirituality: Toward an Integrated Analysis," in *Handbook of the Sociology of Religion*, ed. Michelle Dillon (Cambridge: Cambridge University Press, 2003).
7. Milton J. Coulter, John M. Mulder, and Louis B. Weeks, *Vital Signs: The Promise of Mainstream Protestantism* (Grand Rapids, MI: Eerdmans, 1996).
8. The service was attended by approximately a dozen people, so splitting it in two didn't make sense.
9. On risk factors for domestic violence, see Julie C. Clark and Stephen C. Messer, "Intimate Partner Violence in the U.S. Military: Rates, Risks and Responses," in *Military Life: The Psychology of Serving in Peace and Combat* vol. 3, *The Military Family*, ed. Castro et al. (Westport, CT: Praeger Security International, 2006).
10. Israel Drazin and Cecil B. Currey, *For God and Country: The History of a Constitutional Challenge to the Army Chaplaincy* (Hoboken, NJ: KTAV Publishing House, 1995). For a good overview of relevant legal concepts and principles, including excessive entanglement and the Lemon Test, see Thomas C. Berg, *The State and Religion: In a Nutshell* (St. Paul, MN: Thomson West, 2004).
11. See both editions of Hutcheson, *Churches and the Chaplaincy* (Washington, DC: United States Department of Defense, 1997; and Atlanta: John Knox, 1975).
12. Hutcheson, *Churches and the Chaplaincy* (1997).
13. Ibid.
14. "Religious Ministry within the Department of the Navy," Secretary of the Navy Instruction 1730.7D, August 8, 2008.
15. Ibid.
16. For reporting on the Klingenschmitt case, see Alan Cooperman, "Navy Chaplain Guilty of Disobeying an Order," *Washington Post* online, September 15, 2006, http://www.washingtonpost.com/wp-dyn/content/article/2006/09/14/AR2006091401544.html. Also

see Bryant Jordan, "Ex-Chaplain Sues for Reinstatement or Retirement," Military.com, November 10, 2011. http://www.military.com/news/article/ex-chaplain-sues-for-reinstatement-or-retirement.html.

17. Will Herberg, *Protestant, Catholic, Jew: An Essay on American Religious Sociology* (New York: Doubleday, 1955).
18. In the interview, the chaplain said "Muslim" here but clearly meant Mormon.
19. Nancy Tatom Ammerman, *Bible Believers: Fundamentalists in the Modern World* (New Brunswick, NJ: Rutgers University Press, 1987).
20. Chapter 5 looks more closely at different ways of categorizing chaplains.

CHAPTER 5

1. See Table 4 in "Religious Diversity in the U.S. Military," Military Leadership Diversity Commission, Issue Paper #22, June, 2010, http://mldc.whs.mil.
2. See Table 14.1 in Robert D. Putnam and David E. Campbell, *American Grace: How Religion Divides and Unites Us* (New York: Simon and Schuster, 2010).
3. Jeffrey P. Moran, *The Scopes Trial: A Brief History with Documents* (New York: Palgrave Macmillan, 2002).
4. Christian Smith, *American Evangelicalism: Embattled and Thriving* (Chicago: University of Chicago Press, 1998).
5. See Robert Wuthnow and John Evans's edited book, *The Quiet hand of God: Faith-Based Activism and the Public Role of Mainline Protestantism* (Berkeley: University of California Press, 2002).
6. Peter Berger, *The Desecularization of the World: Resurgent Religion and World Politics* (Grand Rapids, MI: Eerdmans, 1999).
7. Putnam and Campbell, *American Grace.* See also Christian Smith, *Christian America? What Evangelicals Really Want* (Berkeley: University of California Press, 2002). For a sensitive and well-grounded analysis of the conservative Protestant world view, see Nancy Tatom Ammerman's *Bible Believers: Fundamentalists in the Modern World* (New Brunswick, NJ: Rutgers University Press, 1987).
8. Putnam and Campbell, *American Grace.*
9. James Davidson Hunter, Culture Wars: the Struggle to Control the Family, Art, Education, Law, and Politics in America. (New York: Basic Books, 1991)
10. "Santorum: Satan Is Systematically Destroying America," Right Wing Watch blog, February 16, 2012, http://www.rightwingwatch.org/content/santorum-satan-systematically-destroying-america.

11. Alan Wolfe, *One Nation after All* (New York: Penguin, 1998). Also see Putnam and Campbell, *American Grace*.
12. James Davidson Hunter, "Culture Wars Revisited," *INSight* newsletter, University of Virginia Institute for Advanced Studies in Culture, Spring 2004.
13. See Anne C. Loveland, *American Evangelicals in the U.S. Military 1942–1993* (Baton Rouge: Louisiana State University Press, 1996). See also Israel Drazin and Cecil B. Currey, *For God and Country: The History of a Constitutional Challenge to the Army Chaplaincy* (Hoboken, NJ: KTAV, 1995).
14. Putnam and Campbell, *American Grace*.
15. Loveland, *American Evangelicals*.
16. This was explained to me by Chaplain Clement.
17. Nathan O. Hatch, *The Democratization of American Christianity* (New Haven, CT: Yale University Press, 1989).
18. William A. Wildhack III, "Navy Chaplains at the Crossroads: Navigating the Intersection of Free Speech, Free Exercise, Establishment, and Equal Protection," *Naval Law Review* 51 (2005): 217–51.
19. Mark Chaves, *Congregations in America* (Cambridge, MA: Harvard University Press, 2004).
20. National Conference on Ministry to the Armed Forces, "The Covenant and The Code of Ethics for Chaplains of the Armed Forces," http://www.ncmaf.org/policies/codeofethics.htm.
21. Navy Chaplain Corps Reform Information Site, http://chaplainreform.com.
22. "Evidence in Support of Our Claims," http://chaplainreform.com/Evidence.htm. Also refer to "A Summary of Facts About the Class Action Lawsuit," http://chaplainreform.com/ClassAction.htm.
23. Keep in mind that my sample is not representative of the chaplain corps.
24. Loveland, *American Evangelicals*.
25. The table is posted online at http://chaplainreform.com/Mar2011/Ex%2063.pdf.
26. A water-walker is someone with miraculous powers. The reference is to Jesus walking on water.
27. Harold R. Leuba, "Analysis of Promotion Board Composition and Promotion Board Decisions," statistical analysis, http://chaplainreform.com/PDF%20Files/Appendix%20M%20Board%20Impact.pdf.
28. One reason to be cautious about the statistical evidence provided by the plaintiffs is that outcomes can be manipulated by strategically choosing which denominations and individuals should count as liturgicals and nonliturgicals (Catholic being much easier to

assign to their group). This kind of manipulation is especially likely in adversarial proceedings. Another reason is that it's not necessarily warranted to assume an individual chaplain is evangelical just because his or her denomination is. The military chaplaincy would be a good career path for clergy who are more theologically liberal than their denominations. Chaplain Dyren comes to mind, as does Chaplain Larsen, who wanted to switch affiliation to Wicca.

29. See Christian Smith, *American Evangelicalism*; and Ammerman, *Bible Believers*.
30. Paul Boyer, *When Time Shall Be No More: Prophecy Belief in Modern American Culture* (Cambridge: Belknap Press, 1994).
31. Smith, *Christian America?*
32. Heather Cook, "Service before Self? Evangelicals Flying High at the U.S. Air Force Academy," *Journal of Law and Education* 36, no. 1 (2007).
33. Cook, "Service before Self?" See also Melinda S. Morton and Kristen J. Leslie, "Memorandum for CH COL Michael Whittington," July 30, 2004. The memo describes the Yale Practicum Team's findings. Available online at http://www.yale.edu/divinity/notes/050516/AFA_Report.7.04.pdf.
34. See two articles by Laura Goodstein in *The New York Times*: "Air Force Chaplain Tells of Academy Proselytizing" (May 12, 2005) and "Air Force Chaplain Says She Was Removed for Being Critical" (May 15, 2005).
35. Cook, "Service before Self?"
36. Laura Goodstein, "Evangelicals Are Growing Force in the Military Chaplain Corps," *The New York Times*, July 12, 2005.
37. See "Chaplains Fading Away," November 24, 2010, http://www.strategypage.com/htmw/htmoral/articles/20101124.aspx; and "Looking for a Few Good Chaplains," Evangelical Lutheran Church in America website, July 2007, http://www.thelutheran.org/article/article.cfm?article_id=6542.
38. David Kelly, "Non-Christian Air Force Cadets Cite Harassment," *The Los Angeles Times*, April 20, 2005.
39. "Report of Americans United for Separation of Church and State on Religious Coercion and Endorsement of Religion at the United States Air Force Academy," report created by the Legal Department of Americans United for Separation of Church and State, April 28, 2005, http://members.au.org/pdf/050428AirForceReport.pdf. See also Cook, "Service before Self?"

40. "Report of Americans United"; and Cook, "Service before Self?" Also see Michael L. Weinstein and Davin Seay, *With God on Our Side: One Man's War against an Evangelical Coup in America's Military* (New York: St. Martin's, 2006).
41. Cook, "Service before Self?"
42. Weinstein and Seay, *With God on Our Side.*
43. Michael L. Weinstein and Davin Seay, *No Snowflake in an Avalanche: The Military Religious Freedom Foundation, Its Battle to Defend the Constitution, and One Family's Courageous War against Religious Extremism in High Places* (Los Angeles: Rare Bird Books, 2012).
44. See Neela Banerjee, "Proposal on Military Chaplains and Prayer Holds Up Bill," *The New York Times* online, September 19, 2006.

Bibliography

"Accommodation of Religious Practices." Secretary of the Navy Instruction 1730.8A, December 31, 2008. http://www.cnic.navy.mil/navycni/groups/public/@pub/@hq/document/cnicc_068591.pdf.

"Accommodation of Religious Practices." Secretary of the Navy Instruction 1730.8B, October 2, 2008.

"Accommodation of Religious Practices within the Military Services." Department of Defense Directive 1300.17, February 10, 2009.

Ammerman, Nancy Tatom. *Bible Believers: Fundamentalists in the Modern World.* New Brunswick, NJ: Rutgers University Press, 1987.

Banerjee, Neela. "Proposal on Military Chaplains and Prayer Holds Up Bill." *The New York Times* online, September 19, 2006.

———. "Use of Wiccan Symbol on Veterans' Headstones Is Approved." *The New York Times* online, April 24, 2007.

Beckford, James A., and Sophie Gillat. *Religion in Prison: Equal Rites in a Multi-Faith Society*. Cambridge: Cambridge University Press, 1998.

Bellah, Robert N. *The Broken Covenant: American Civil Religion in a Time of Trial.* Chicago: University of Chicago Press, 1975.

———. "Civil Religion in America." *Daedalus* 96, no. 1 (1967): 1–21.

Bellah, Robert N., and Philip E. Hammond. *Varieties of Civil Religion.* San Francisco: Harper and Row, 1980.

Bellah, Robert N., Richard Madsen, William M. Sullivan, Ann Swidler, and Steven M. Tipton. *Habits of the Heart: Individualism and Commitment in American Life*. New York: Harper and Row, 1985.

Berg, Thomas C. *The State and Religion: In a Nutshell.* St. Paul, MN: Thomson West, 2004.

Berger, Helen A. *A Community of Witches: Contemporary Neo-Paganism and Witchcraft in the United States*. Columbia: University of South Carolina Press, 1999.

Berger, Helen A., Evan C. Leach, and Leigh S. Shaffer. *Voices from the Pagan Census: A National Survey of Witches and Neo-Pagans in the United States*. Columbia: University of South Carolina Press, 2003.

Berger, Peter L., ed. *The Desecularization of the World: Resurgent Religion and World Politics*. Grand Rapids, MI: Eerdmans, 1999.

———. *The Sacred Canopy: Elements of a Sociological Theory of Religion.* New York: Anchor Books, 1967.

Berger, Peter L., and Daniel Pinard. "Military Religion: An Analysis of Education Materials Disseminated by Chaplains." In *Military Chaplains: From a Religious Military to a Military Religion*, edited by Harvey G. Cox, 87–108. New York: American Report Press, 1972.

Beyer, Peter. "Social Forms of Religion and Religions in Contemporary Global Society." In *Handbook of the Sociology of Religion*, edited by Michelle Dillon, 45–60. Cambridge: Cambridge University Press, 2003.

Boyer, Paul. *When Time Shall Be No More: Prophecy Belief in Modern American Culture*. Cambridge, MA: Belknap Press, 1994.

Brinsfield, John W. "The U.S. Military Chaplaincy: Then and Now." *The Review of Faith and International Affairs* 7, no. 4 (2009): 17–24.

Burchard, Waldo W. "Role Conflicts of Military Chaplains." *American Sociological Review* 19, no. 5 (1954): 528–35.

Carlson, John D. "Cashing in on Religion's Currency? Ethical Challenges for a Post-Secular Military." *The Review of Faith and International Affairs* 7, no. 4 (2009): 51–62.

Casanova, Jose. *Public Religions in the Modern World*. Chicago: University of Chicago Press, 1994.

Cash, Tierian (Randy). "A Short History of the Navy Chaplain Corps." Online. Last modified May 4, 2011.

"Chaplains Fading Away." Strategy Page. November 24, 2010. http://www.strategypage.com/htmw/htmoral/articles/20101124.aspx.

Chaves, Mark. *Congregations in America*. Cambridge, MA: Harvard University Press, 2004.

Clark, Julie C., and Stephen C. Messer. "Intimate Partner Violence in the U.S. Military: Rates, Risks and Responses." In *Military Life: The Psychology of Serving in Peace and Combat*. Vol. 3, *The Military Family*, edited by Carl Andrew Castro, Amy B. Adler, and Thomas W. Britt. Westport, CT: Praeger Security International, 2006.

Coles, Roberta L. "Manifest Destiny Adapted for 1990s War Discourse: Mission and Destiny Intertwined." *Sociology of Religion* 63, no. 4 (2002): 403–26.

Cook, Heather. "Service before Self? Evangelicals Flying High at the U.S. Air Force Academy." *Journal of Law and Education* 36, no. 1 (2007).

Cooperman, Alan. "For Gods and Country: The Army Chaplain Who Wanted to Switch to Wicca? Transfer Denied." *The Washington Post*, February 19, 2007.

———. "Navy Chaplain Guilty of Disobeying an Order." *The Washington Post* online, September 15, 2006, http://www.washingtonpost.com/wp-dyn/content/article/2006/09/14/AR2006091401544.html.

———. "A Wiccan Army Chaplain? The Brass Wouldn't Buy It." *Seattle Times*, February 24, 2007, http://seattletimes.nwsource.com/html/nationworld/2003586870_wiccan24.html.

Coulter, Milton J., John M. Mulder, and Louis B. Weeks. *Vital Signs: The Promise of Mainstream Protestantism*. Grand Rapids, MI: Eerdmans, 1996.

Cox, Harvey G., ed. *Military Chaplains: From a Religious Military to a Military Religion*. New York: American Report Press, 1972.

Daniels, Arlene Kaplan. "The Captive Professional: Bureaucratic Limitations in the Practice of Military Psychiatry." *Journal of Health and Social Behavior* 10, no. 4 (1969): 255–65.

Dansby, Mickey R., James B. Stewart, and Schuyler C. Webb, eds. *Managing Diversity in the Military: Research Perspectives from the Defense Equal Opportunity Management Institute*. New Brunswick, NJ: Transaction, 2001.

Drazin, Israel, and Cecil B. Currey. *For God and Country: The History of a Constitutional Challenge to the Army Chaplaincy*. Hoboken, NJ: KTAV, 1995.

Eck, Diana. *A New Religious America: How a "Christian Country" Has Become the World's Most Religiously Diverse Nation*. San Francisco: Harper Collins, 2001.

"Evidence in Support of Our Claims." Navy Chaplain Corps Reform Information Site. Last updated March 2011. http://chaplainreform.com/Evidence.htm.

Farr, Thomas F. *World of Faith and Freedom: Why International Religious Liberty Is Vital to American National Security*. New York: Oxford University Press, 2008.

Goffman, Erving. *Asylums: Essays on the Social Situation of Mental Patients and Other Inmates*. New York: Anchor Books, 1961.

Goodstein, Laura. "Air Force Chaplain Says She Was Removed for Being Critical." *The New York Times*, May 15, 2005.

———. "Air Force Chaplain Tells of Academy Proselytizing." *The New York Times*, May 12, 2005.

———. "Evangelicals Are Growing Force in the Military Chaplain Corps." *The New York Times*, July 12, 2005.

Hatch, Nathan O. *The Democratization of American Christianity*. New Haven, CT: Yale University Press, 1989.

Hays, Kim. *Practicing Virtues: Moral Traditions at Quaker and Military Boarding Schools*. Berkeley: University of California Press, 1994.

Heelas, Paul. *The New Age Movement*. Oxford: Blackwell, 1996.

Herberg, Will. *Protestant, Catholic, Jew: An Essay in American Religious Sociology*. New York: Doubleday, 1955.

Herspring, Dale R. *Soldiers, Commissars, and Chaplains: Civil-Military Relations since Cromwell*. Lanham, MD: Rowman and Littlefield, 2001.

Huerta, Carlos C., and Schuyler C. Webb. "Religious Accommodation in the Military." In *Managing Diversity in the Military: Research Perspectives from the Defense Equal Opportunity Management Institute*, edited by Mickey R. Dansby, James B. Stewart, and Schuyler C. Webb, 77–96. New Brunswick, NJ: Transaction, 2001.

Hunter, James Davidson. *Culture Wars: The Struggle to Define America*. New York, Basic Books, 1991.

———. "Culture Wars Revisited." *INSight* newsletter. University of Virginia Institute for Advanced Studies in Culture. Spring 2004.

Huntington, Samuel P. *The Clash of Civilizations and the Remaking of World Order*. New York: Simon and Schuster, 1996.

Hutcheson, Richard G. *The Churches and the Chaplaincy*. Atlanta: John Knox, 1975.

———. *The Churches and the Chaplaincy*. Rev. ed. Washington, DC: United States Department of Defense, 1997.

Hutchison, William R. *Religious Pluralism in America: The Contentious History of a Founding Ideal*. New Haven, CT: Yale University Press, 2003.

Johnson, Douglas M. "U.S. Military Chaplains: Redirecting a Critical Asset." *The Review of Faith and International Affairs* 7, no. 4 (2009): 25–32.

Jordan, Bryant. "Ex-Chaplain Sues for Reinstatement or Retirement." Military.com. November 10, 2011. http://www.military.com/news/article/ex-chaplain-sues-for-reinstatement-or-retirement.html.

"Justice Department Clarifies Ashcroft's View of Islam." FoxNews.com. February 12, 2002. http://www.foxnews.com/story/0,2933,45410,00.html.

Kelly, David. "Non-Christian Air Force Cadets Cite Harassment." *The Los Angeles Times*, April 20, 2005.

Kibben, Margaret G. "The Role and Mission of Chaplains in Humanitarian Assistance and Peace Operations (HA/Pos)." Paper presented at the Naval War College, Newport, RI. February 12, 1996.

Leuba, Harold R. "Analysis of Promotion Board Composition and Promotion Board Decisions." Statistical analysis. http://chaplainreform.com/PDF%20Files/Appendix%20M%20Board%20Impact.pdf.

Lewis, Neil A. "Prosecutors Say It's Unclear Paper Chaplain Carried Were Classified." *The New York Times* online, December 10, 2003. http://www.nytimes.com/2003/12/10/national/10YEE.html.

Lindsay, D. Michael. *Faith in the Halls of Power: How Evangelicals Joined the American Elite*. New York: Oxford University Press, 2008.

"Looking for a Few Good Chaplains." Evangelical Lutheran Church in America website. July 2007. http://www.thelutheran.org/article/article.cfm?article_id=6542.

Loveland, Anne C. *American Evangelicals in the U.S. Military 1942–1993*. Baton Rouge: Louisiana State University Press, 1996.

Madsen, Richard, William M. Sullivan, Ann Swidler, and Steven M. Tipton. *Meaning and Modernity: Religion Polity, and Self.* Berkeley: University of California Press, 2002.

Miller, Daniel. "'All Muslims Should Be Kicked Out of the Military,' Claims Leading Tennessee Republican." *The Daily Mail* online, November 17, 2011.

Montgomery, Liam J. "The Devil Is in the Details: Policing the Implementation of the Military Chaplaincy." Unpublished paper. 2008. https://works.bepress.com/liam_montgomery/2.

Moran, Jeffrey P. *The Scopes Trial: A Brief History with Documents*. New York: Palgrave Macmillan, 2002.

Moreton, Bethany. *To Serve God and Wal-Mart: The Making of Christian Free Enterprise*. Cambridge, MA: Harvard University Press, 2009.

Morgan, Edmund S. *Roger Williams: The Church and the State*. New York: W. W. Norton, 1967.

Morton, Melinda S., and Kristen J. Leslie. "Memorandum for CH COL Michael Whittington." July 30, 2004. Online. http://www.yale.edu/divinity/notes/050516/AFA_Report.7.04.pdf.

National Conference on Ministry to the Armed Forces. "The Covenant and the Code of Ethics for Chaplains of the Armed Forces." November 2, 2011. http://www.ncmaf.org/policies/codeofethics.htm.

Noonan, John T., and Edward McGlynn Gaffney Jr. *Religious Freedom: History, Cases, and Other Materials on the Interaction of Religion and Government*. New York: Foundation Press, 2001.

Otis, Pauletta. "An Overview of the U.S. Military Chaplaincy: A Ministry of Presence and Practice." *The Review of Faith and International Affairs* 7, no. 4 (2009): 3–16.

Partridge, Christopher. *New Religions: A Guide*. New York: Oxford University Press, 2004.

Peek, Lori. "Becoming Muslim: The Development of a Religious Identity." *Sociology of Religion* 66, no. 3 (2005): 215–42.

Pew Forum on Religion and Public Life, "The Global Muslim Population: Projections for 2010–30." January 27, 2011. http://www.pewforum.org/future-of-the-global-muslim-population-regional-americas.aspx#1.

Pew Research Center, "Muslim Americans: No Signs of Growth in Alienation or Support for Extremism." August 31, 2011. http://www.people-press.org/2011/08/30/section-1-a-demographic-portrait-of-muslim-americans.

Pike, Sarah M. *Earthly Bodies, Magical Selves: Contemporary Pagans and the Search for Community*. Berkeley: University of California Press, 1999.

Putnam, Robert D., and David E. Campbell. *American Grace: How Religion Divides and Unites Us*. New York: Simon and Schuster, 2010.

Raboteau, Albert J. *Canaan Land: A Religious History of African Americans*. Oxford: Oxford University Press, 1999.

"Religious Diversity in the U.S. Military." Military Leadership Diversity Commission. Issue Paper #22. June 2010. *http://mldc.whs.mil/download/documents/Issue*%20Papers/22_Religious_Diversity.pdf.

Religious Ministry in the Department of the Navy: Strategic Plan for FY 08–13. Arlington, VA: RGS Associates Inc., August 31, 2007.

"Religious Ministry within the Department of the Navy." Secretary of the Navy Instruction 1730.7D, August 8, 2008.

"Report of Americans United for Separation of Church and State on Religious Coercion and Endorsement of Religion at the United States Air Force Academy." Report by the Legal Department of Americans United for Separation of Church and State. Online. April 28, 2005. http://members.au.org/pdf/050428AirForceReport.pdf.

Roof, Wade Clark. "Religion and Spirituality: Toward an Integrated Analysis." In *Handbook of the Sociology of Religion*, edited by Michelle Dillon, 137–48. Cambridge: Cambridge University Press, 2003.

Sandhoff, Michelle. "Preliminary Findings on the Experiences of Muslims in the U.S. Military." Paper presented to the Defense Equal Opportunity Management Institute Symposium, Patrick Air Force Base, FL. December 6–8, 2011.

"Santorum: Satan Is Systematically Destroying America." Right Wing Watch blog. Posted February 16, 2012. http://www.rightwingwatch.org/content/santorum-satan-systematically-destroying-america.

Segal, Mady Wechsler. "The Military and the Family as Greedy Institutions." *Armed Forces And Society* 13, no. 1 (1986): 9–38.

Sharlet, Jeff. "Jesus Killed Mohammed: The Crusade for a Christian Military." *Harper's Magazine* 318, no. 1908 (2009): 31–43.

Sherkat, Darren. "Religious Socialization: Sources of Influence and Influences of Agency." In *Handbook of the Sociology of Religion*, edited by Michelle Dillon, 151–63. Cambridge: Cambridge University Press, 2003.

Sieff, Kevin. "Two NATO Soldiers Killed Inside Afghan Interior Ministry, Officials Say." *The Washington Post* online, February 24, 2012. http://www.washingtonpost.com/world/seven-dead-in-latest-afghan-violence-over-koran-burning/2012/02/24/gIQAtWLkXR_story.html.

"Sikhs Regain Right to Wear Turbans in U.S. Army." National Public Radio online. March 24, 2010 http://www.npr.org/templates/story/story.php?storyId=125142736.

Slomovitz, Albert Isaac. *The Fighting Rabbis: Jewish Military Chaplains and American History*. New York: New York University Press, 1999.

Smith, Christian. *American Evangelicalism: Embattled and Thriving*. Chicago: University of Chicago Press, 1998.

———. *Christian America? What Evangelical Really Want*. Berkeley: University of California Press, 2002.

———, ed. *Disruptive Religion: The Force of Faith in Social Movement Activism*. New York: Routledge, 1996.

Sterner, C. Douglas. "The Brotherhood of Soldiers at War: The True Story of the Four Chaplains." *Home of Heroes*. http://www.homeofheroes.com/brotherhood/chaplains.html.

Sullivan, Winnifred Faller. *The Impossibility of Religious Freedom*. Princeton, NJ: Princeton University Press, 2005.

"A Summary of Facts about the Class Action Lawsuit." Navy Chaplain Corps Reform Information Site. Last updated March, 2011. http://chaplainreform.com/ClassAction.htm.

"Text of the Unclassified Executive Summary of the Evaluation of the Army Investigation of Chaplain (CPT) James J. Yee." Department of Defense Office of Inspector General, Report Number IPO2007E002.

Turner, Bryan S. *Religion and Social Theory*. London: Sage, 1983.

"U.S. Military Weapons Inscribed with Secret 'Jesus' Bible Codes." ABC News online. January 18, 2010. http://abcnews.go.com/Blotter/us-military-weapons-inscribed-secret-jesus-bible-codes/story?id=9575794&page=2.

"U.S. Soldier Uses Quran for Target Practice; Military Apologizes." CNN World online. May 17, 2008. http://articles.cnn.com/2008-05-17/world/iraq.quran_1_quran-tribal-leaders-military-official?_s=PM:WORLD.

"Veterans Denied Right to Post Religious Symbol on Headstones, ACLU Charges." American Civil Liberties Union online. September 29, 2006. http://www.aclu.org/religion-belief/veterans-denied-right-post-religious-symbol-headstones-aclu-charges

Walker, Dennis. *Islam and the Search for African-American Nationhood: Elijah Muhammad, Louis Farrakhan and the Nation of Islam*. Atlanta: Clarity Press, 2005.

Warner, R. Stephen. "Work in Progress toward a New Paradigm for the Sociological Study of Religion in the United States." *American Journal of Sociology* 98, no. 5 (March 1993): 1044–93.

Weinstein, Michael L., and Davin Seay. *No Snowflake in an Avalanche: The Military Religious Freedom Foundation, Its Battle to Defend the Constitution, and One Family's Courageous War against Religious Extremism in High Places*. Los Angeles: Rare Bird Books, 2012.

———. *With God on Our Side: One Man's War against an Evangelical Coup in America's Military*. New York: St. Martin's, 2006.

Weintraub, Jeff. "The Theory and Politics of the Public/Private Distinction." In *Public and Private in Thought and Practice*, edited by Jeff Weintraub and Krishnan Kumar, 1–42. Chicago: University of Chicago Press, 1997.

Wildhack, William A., III. "Navy Chaplains at the Crossroads: Navigating the Intersection of Free Speech, Free Exercise, Establishment and Equal Protection." *Naval Law Review* 51 (2005): 217–51.

Williams, Peter W. *America's Religions: From Their Origins to the Twenty-First Century*. Urbana: Illinois University Press, 2001.

Williams, Roger. "Roger Williams to the Town of Providence." In *The Founders' Constitution*, edited by Philip B. Kurland and Ralph Lerner. http://press-pubs.uchicago.edu/founders/documents/amendI_religions6.html.

Winter, Jana. "Exclusive: Former Defense IG Raises Concerns about Military Chaplain Vetting." FoxNews.com. December 1, 2010. http://www.foxnews.com/politics/2010/12/01/exclusive-concerns-military-chaplain-vetting-policy.

Wolfe, Alan. *One Nation after All*. New York: Penguin, 1998.

Wrigley, Paul. "The Impact of Religious Belief in the Theater of Operations." *Naval War College Review* 49, no. 2 (1996): 84–101.

Wuthnow, Robert. *America and the Challenge of Religious Diversity*. Princeton, NJ: Princeton University Press, 2005.

———. *The Restructuring of American Religion*. Princeton, NJ: Princeton University Press, 1988.

Wuthnow, Robert, and John H. Evans, ed. *The Quiet Hand of God: Faith-Based Activism and the Public Role of Mainline Protestantism*. Berkeley: University of California Press, 2002.

Yee, James. *For God and Country: Faith and Patriotism under Fire*. New York: Public Affairs, 2005.

———. Radio interview. *The Mike Malloy Show*. Air America Radio Internet broadcast. Streamed November 14, 2005.

Index